Washington, Westminster and Whitehall

WASHINGTON, WESTMINSTER AND WHITEHALL

Walter Williams

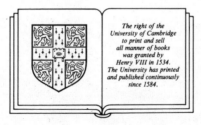

The right of the
University of Cambridge
to print and sell
all manner of books
was granted by
Henry VIII in 1534.
The University has printed
and published continuously
since 1584.

CAMBRIDGE UNIVERSITY PRESS
Cambridge
New York   New Rochelle
Melbourne   Sydney

Published by the Press Syndicate of the University of Cambridge
The Pitt Building, Trumpington Street, Cambridge CB2 1RP
32 East 57th Street, New York, NY 10022, USA
10 Stamford Road, Oakleigh, Melbourne 3166, Australia

Cambridge University Press 1988

First published 1988

Printed in Great Britain at the University Press, Cambridge

British Library cataloguing in publication data
Williams, Walter
Washington, Westminster and Whitehall.
1. Great Britain. Government
I. Title
354.41

Library of Congress cataloguing in publication data
Bibliography: p.
Includes index.
1. Administrative agencies–Great Britain–Management.
2. Administrative agencies–Great Britain–Reorganization. 3. Great Britain–
Executive department–Management. 4. Great Britain–Executive
departments–Reorganization. 5. Great Britain. Parliament–Reform.
6. Great Britain–Politics and government–1979–
I. Title.
JN318.W58   1988   320.441   88–11852

ISBN 0 521 35185 5

To Robert Levine and George Jones

CONTENTS

PREFACE

Mine is not the first, and almost certainly not the last book by an American on Westminster and Whitehall. It is, however, one of the most critical. And it treats British central government from the unusual perspective of analytic and managerial capability, not from the more traditional political science or constitutional frameworks. Moreover, the perspective is that of one who was involved in policy analysis and management efforts in Washington (D.C.) two decades ago and since has written about these central government functions.

The Washington perspective is central. Indeed, the two Cambridge University Press reviewers proffered diametrically opposite advice. One warned of British distaste for American views and bade me hide my Washington perspective until I had laid out my ideas and perhaps convinced readers I was not another crazy American. The other reader added Washington to the then working title of *Westminster and Whitehall*. We Americans make much over truth in packaging and I have followed the latter course down to the book title itself.

The book is dedicated to Robert A. Levine and George Jones – the two persons to whom I am most indebted for providing intellectual direction for my effort. To Levine my debt is older and broader and includes bringing me to Washington to work at the Office of Economic Opportunity in the first domestic policy analysis office in the U.S. government. My nearly four years in that office from July 1965 to Spring 1969, during one of the most dramatic and traumatic periods of American history, put me in a ringside seat to watch domestic policy analysis and management efforts at the top of the American government. During all but the last few months of that period, I served under Levine first as a staff member of the policy analysis division he headed and then as the head of that division when Levine became the director of the entire OEO policy operation and the principal adviser to the OEO director.

Finally, a decade after our OEO experience, Levine started me on study of British central government. He had a grant to consider evaluation and analysis in the United States, Canada, and several European countries including Britain. One of Levine's summary findings was that the Central Policy Review Staff was an interesting example of such efforts and merited more study than he had given it in his quick look at several nations. Levine, who had other commitments that precluded his own extensive involvement, asked John Ellwood, an American political scientist now at Dartmouth, and me to look at CPRS.

I met George Jones at the end of the first of my four trips to Britain during this project. He was instrumental in my spending a sabbatical six months in the Department of Government at the London School of Economics and Political Science. Particularly during that stay, but before and after, Jones gave unstintingly of his time both in extended discussions and in critiques of several pieces I wrote and finally of my manuscript. In particular, his comments on the first full draft of the manuscript were instrumental in helping me reshape it. I think it fair to say I may not have finished the book without Jones' substantive contributions.

Two other persons made particularly important contributions. Levine had given me William Plowden's name, and Plowden, despite his busy schedule, not only helped me understand some of the intricacies of British government but made invaluable contacts for me with key former CPRS staff members and later with a number of top policy advisers in the Thatcher government. My colleague at the University of Washington political scientist John Keeler, a specialist on Western Europe, made significant contributions both in a seminar on comparative politics we jointly taught and in verbal and written comments.

In addition, a number of other people read part or all of the manuscript or gave freely of their time in discussing various aspects of British central governance: Douglas Ashford, John Ashworth, Tessa Blackstone, Meghnad Desai, Rt. Hon. Edmund Dell, Lord Bernard Donoughue, Sir Gordon Downey, John Garrett, Howard Glennerster, Andrew Gray, Fred Greenstein, Kenneth Harris, Victor Hausner, Peter Hennessy, Sir John Hoskyns, W. I. Jenkins, Peter Kellner, David Lipsey, Peter May, John Mayne, Kenneth Morgan, Peter Mountfield, David Piachaud, Adam Ridley, and Richard Rose. Several typists went through a number of false starts and endless chapter revisions. I am particularly indebted to Karen McLaughlin and Dorothy Moritz who finished the task. The study was in part supported by a grant from the German Marshall Fund. Neither that institution nor any of the individuals named bear any responsibilities for what appears in the book.

One other OEO experience needs relating. Although neither he nor I appreciated it at the outset, Levine cast me in a role that was most unusual for a policy analyst and was to have great weight on how I came to understand governance. I moved willy-nilly from being the analyst of OEO manpower training policy to being both the chief agency negotiator for a new combined OEO/Department of Labor manpower training program and (briefly) an implementor of that program. That experience was to focus me on emerging implementation issues and lead me to argue that "implementation was the Achilles' heel of the Johnson administration's social policy."[1] Over time the study of implementation in the U.S. became a primary vehicle for looking at the broad question of public management.

Last but not least in deserving thanks are a large number of individuals not cited by name – then current and ex-civil servants, ministers, and MPs; media persons (mainly print), and members of universities and research organizations – who often granted more than one interview. The decision to do the interviews off-the-record was mine, a practice I have followed for a number of years. The advantage is candor, or at the extreme, the willingness to be interviewed. The obvious drawback is that the reader does not know the source and further that the author may shape the interview information to his purposes (or simply misquote it inadvertently) without the checks of the interviewee to call the evidence into question. I do try to provide the reader with a description of the quoted person without being so specific as to allow exact identification (e.g., I may describe a member of CPRS as a member of the Cabinet Office).

I need to record two groups that I did not interview. First are the top ministers including the prime minister. I did not try for two reasons. First, such interviews are difficult to obtain, often postponed or cancelled, and almost always unsatisfactory since a good politician, even off-the-record, will carefully control what he or she says. Second, there are better sources, for example, journalists who follow the prime minister are much better able to elicit useful information and off-the-record will share it. The same is true of top level staff when the interviewer has had time to build trust.

The second group I never interviewed, try as I might, were *sitting* permanent secretaries. I interviewed at length former permanent secretaries including many of the super stars of past administrations. Mainly they were generous with their time and quite forthcoming. But current permanent secretaries were "too busy." As will be clear from later analysis, this is not a healthy state of affairs.

One final point: I am highly critical of British central government in general and of Prime Minister Margaret Thatcher in particular. I have been just as critical or more so of American government and particularly of Presidents Jimmy Carter and Ronald Reagan, whom I consider the worst president of the postwar era. I am critical in both the U.S. and British cases because I believe my extensive background in public policy analysis and management offer a useful base for constructive critiques. I would be the first to admit I may be wrong. What I do stress is that the criticism is well-intended and is offered by one who fears for the welfare of both countries.

INTRODUCTION

British central government is both pre-modern and anti-modern. It is a closed system shrouded in secrecy, poorly managed, and has limited analytic and strategic capability at the top. It is increasingly out-of-date – an antique vehicle suited to the nineteenth century. If the British central government does not break its present pattern, the nation again may suffer severe and continuing economic decline and fall into a political instability that menaces Britain's most cherished values and institutions.

The Britain Is Dying theme and the portentous call for immediate action have become a cottage industry offering curatives for the "British Disease."[1] My message is different in that its emphasis is on modernizing the machinery of government.[2] Government is treated as both part of the problem and of the solution. It is pivotal – the first crucial element in turning the economy around. Present British central government institutions cannot cope with the complexity of the modern welfare state and the managed economy and must be changed dramatically.[3] Pre-modern, anti-modern British central government and the British Disease are linked inextricably.[4]

In the face of this threat, ministers and mandarins alike are often complacent and unwilling to face up to the fundamental changes required in Cabinet, in Parliament, in the Whitehall departments, and in the higher civil service. A former high level analyst who served at the center of the British government said of the mandarins in one of my off-the-record interviews to be discussed shortly: "They combine arrogance and ignorance. They're so sure of their methods. They're engaged in a terrible fight to block out the twentieth century, trying to

1

keep the experts at bay. They haven't the slightest idea what they don't understand. They don't really think in modern terms." Substitute "minister" for "mandarin," and the quote applies with even greater force.

The call is for dramatic change. I have labeled such critical, transforming periods that set bold new directions in either government policy or structure "great leaps."[5] Great leaps are characterized by large (nonincremental) policy impacts, both intended and unintended. For example, Ronald Reagan's 1981 tax cuts were by far the largest in American history. The cuts were not expected to be associated with large, deleterious budget and trade deficits. The last point underscores that great leaps or elements of great leaps (larger defense outlays and smaller grants to states and localities were other elements of the "Reagan Revolution") can be negative. The "great" connotes distance with period A being very different from period B because of a policy change(s); it does not imply a positive impact, only a large one.

Classic examples of great leaps are the American New Deal and Britain's immediate postwar Labour government years. That administration and the organizational leadership of Clement Attlee are an exemplary effort in guiding needed changes. But Labour's great leap involved policies and programs, not the main central government institutions. If there is a British model it is the Grey government's passing of the Great Reform Act in 1831–2. Even more relevant is the deGaulle regime's efforts that brought France in two stages from splintered parliamentary rule to a strong executive. What marks the 1831–2 British case and the 1958–62 French case as distinctly different from the 1945–51 British experience is that the basic rules of the institutional game were altered significantly. Individual members of the ruling elite itself had to surrender power, position and status. Such basic changes in structure and ultimately in institutional behavior demand the highest level of political leadership. I shall discuss the Great Reform Act shortly and the French case in the final chapter because of their direct relevance.

Britain's first pressing need is an institutional great leap unparalleled in this century by a British government. Then, a second great leap that treats the grave economic problems is demanded if the nation is to avoid political and social instability. As Wilks has argued: "[A]n upheaval in the institutions of economic life [is needed] ... The need is

2

for basic reform of the institutions, policymaking processes and some of the traditional features of economic structure ... The failure of the state has been a failure to recognize this urgent reality and to reform."[6] The two great leaps are linked. Fundamental institutional changes, however, must come first. *A modernized British central government is needed to provide the institutional capacity to cope with the policy demands of the British Disease.* David Steel set out the measure of the problem most succinctly: "Neither the people nor the organization of Westminster and Whitehall are up to the job of reviving Britain's economic fortunes."[7]

An ailing machinery of government is not the primary cause of Britain's problems. It almost certainly ranks well behind two other sets of factors. Most important are exogenous variables that are beyond the capacity of government to influence. Global economic factors are a good example. OPEC price changes have had a major impact with higher prices in the 1970s resulting in double digit inflation and with lower prices in the 1980s bringing prices down. One group of world leaders from that earlier decade were blamed for inflation while their 1980s counterparts were praised for deflating prices. These exogenous variables likely dominate and restrict greatly drawing conclusions about the results of policy. Pure luck – bad or good – may be the driving force. The variables over which leaders and governments can have a policy impact (the policy variables) may be small as compared to the exogenous forces. Moreover, our research tools do not allow us to determine leader and government contribution to impact – a sobering thought to keep in mind as we proceed (a point returned to shortly).

Among the policy variables, underlying failures of industrial spirit and lack of political will, energy, and foresight are deeper and more important factors than government structure.[8] Nor does the modernization of the central government machinery guarantee the curing of the British Disease. Even if the first (institutional) great leap is successful (and what this means needs spelling out), the difficult task of major policy changes remains. My claim is that a modernized central government can provide analytic and strategic thinking and the positive management that can contribute to effective *policy* change.

The major theme is that central government is pivotal for Britain, much more so than, say, for the United States, because other British

3

institutions – particularly business – are so weak. The hard choice is between standing pat and very likely suffering dire political, social and economic consequences or making dramatic changes that raise the odds of a better outcome but do not guarantee it. Without extreme good luck, a policy of only limited changes can threaten Britain's underlying social and political stability. The great danger is not revolution but *apathy* if Britain's economic decline continues.

Even those who see the British Disease as life-threatening can still believe as Ralf Dahrendorf does: "Britain is so strong at its social core – surely it must be possible to apply this strength to its economic, political, and more general social problems."[9] But to see a reasonable chance for improvement must not be a siren call to believe matters will work themselves out without major, wrenching changes. C. P. Snow's warning a quarter of a century ago is even more compelling today:

More often than I like, I am saddened by a historical myth. Whether the myth is good history or not, doesn't matter; it is pressing enough for me. I can't help thinking of the Venetian Republic in their last half-century. Like us, they had once been fabulously lucky. They had become rich, as we did, by accident. They had acquired immense political skill, just as we have. A good many of them were tough-minded, realistic, patriotic men. They knew, just as clearly as we know, that the current of history had begun to flow against them. Many of them gave their minds to working out ways to keep going. It would have meant breaking the pattern into which they had crystalized. They were fond of the pattern, just as we are fond of ours. *They never found the will to break it.*[10]

Time may be running out on Britain, just as it did for Venice. British government needs a new path "to break the pattern."

METHOD AND APPROACH

This book is about Westminster and Whitehall as seen from a Washington (American) perspective, hence the title. It differs from the typical comparative study where two (or more) nations are treated similarly as to criticism and prescription. Instead I focus on British central government through a Washington lens using the American experience to develop a framework for analyzing how British central government may be modernized. The main concern of the book is with structural and staffing options for changing the institutional behavior of the key actors in British central government policymaking – the prime minister, the Cabinet, Parliament – and high level staff serving the key actors. A basic issue is how Britain can build the foundation for a central government institutional capacity sufficient to support a second great leap involving economic and domestic policy changes.

The critique of policymaking at the top with a goal of prescription is a hazardous undertaking with two immediate concerns – generality and causality. How is it to be determined that a policy or policies were poor? Is a sample to be drawn of policies and if so what is the sample frame? Are policies to be rated on a scale as to quality and if so by whom? How is cause to be determined in such a complex, interactive, interdependent process as that at the top of the government? Two alternatives merit consideration even though neither offers a totally satisfying solution. The first, more frequently used, option is to determine a bad policy (or policies) and try to say why it went awry. For example, President Reagan appointed a Special Review Board chaired by former Senator John Tower to consider the Iran-Contra affair.[11] The Board concluded that the culprit was not the prescribed national security process but the failure of the Reagan administration to use it and noted, as politely as possible, that the president himself was much too detached and did not manage the process properly in this case. The February 27, 1987 issue of *The New York Times* reported that Tower at a news conference in response to the question "do you think [Reagan has] had a weak style of management?" replied that the Iran-Contra affair was "an aberration," hardly an unchallenged view. But the fact remains, a single case study often leaves more unanswered questions than one started with. And more generally, determining cause – e.g., that Treasury actions are the culprits in a specific policy failure – is almost always difficult and usually impossible.[12]

A second option is to look at institutional structure, process and staff to ask if they are likely to support sound policymaking and by inference sound policies. I selected this second approach in part because British government secrecy keeps one from knowing a great deal about how policies of recent governments were made and in part because much more is known about the overall policymaking process, which in its main dimensions does not change drastically from government to government (recent changes are a key focus). A key element of my strategy is to draw lessons from America's policymaking process experience in the last quarter century that could help guide British central government in a major modernization effort. American offers a rich, varied body of experience in policy analysis and management. The United States government has tried almost everything in its efforts to modernize government. Although many attempts have failed, some have succeeded. There is much to gain from such experience. Failures often are even more illuminating than successes. For example, the White House gives up much accumulated knowledge and experience by keeping career civil servants several levels down in the decisionmaking process. Or, the Iran-Contra affair shows the dangers both of secrecy and of trying to circumvent the cabinet agencies. *My argument is not that America is doing it right but that this rich experience is well worth mining for the handful of nuggets of real gold and for the warnings given by the more frequently found false gold.*

The American experience in public management and policy analysis must be interpreted carefully. The American tools of modern government have been forged in a setting of maximum stress flowing from the difficulties of governing America's unique blend of federalism. The United States is by far the most difficult of the advanced Western nations to govern from the center with fifty separate state governments in a nation made up of large proportions of racial and ethnic groups, where high population mobility and geographic diversity compound problems, where violence is a critical element, and where the Constitution, in response to George III, established checks and balances that at times seem to have as a main intent the blocking of effective central governance.

Nor is the basic constitutional structure likely to be changed significantly because of the complexity of the constitutional change process and the impediments to change embedded in the Constitution itself.[13] The key point in terms of Britain is that the U.S. Constitution has forced presidents and Congress to seek the most advanced analytic and management approaches to try to cope with increasingly complex central governance. The British center in constitutional terms can be reshaped by Parliament alone.

Part of my optimism for Britain flows from the fact that problems of central governance in a unitary state with a relatively homogeneous, stable population such as Britain generally are not as difficult technically as those of the United States. If managerial and analytic

6

approaches work at all in the United States they ought to work better in Britain. At the same time, Britain's economic problems mean its central government has less room than the U.S. central government for domestic and economic policy error. Moreover, there is a limited time for correction, hence the stress on the urgent need for dramatic action.

A PRE-MODERN, ANTI-MODERN GOVERNMENT

Parliament is the most vexing of British public institutions, at one and the same time both all-powerful and relatively powerless. Except for a few ministers from the House of Lords, the House of Commons supplies the government's leaders and opposition and centers these people and the top mandarins on endless chamber debate that emphasizes political theatre, not policy performance. Great power is exercised in the intense pressure put on ministers and mandarins to protect careers and prove toughness and quickness in action on the floor of the House of Commons. And yet Parliament is also relatively powerless, having limited impact on policy. It remains a nineteenth-century institution where "the perennial difficulty has been that the parties and the ministers drawn from them are unprepared to play their role in governing."[14] The talent pool is much too small – a tight club closed to outsiders who may have the skills and experience to provide effective organizational leadership in the departments of state.[15] Further, more specialist staff is desperately needed, especially to do analyses in support of a new committee system. The current select committees may be a base for real reform, but we need to be clear that thus far "the effect of these committees on ministerial and departmental policymaking has been indirect, and marginal."[16] If Parliament continues as it is or else makes only cosmetic changes, modernizing British central government will be difficult, if not impossible.

Only a little of tongue in cheek, William Plowden has written that "since the 1950s, the most obvious changes [for civil servants] have been the coming of the photocopier, the end of regular Saturday working, and the virtual disappearance of the bowler hat."[17] Still dominant are the Oxbridge types going through high flyer positions that have kept them from acquiring managerial or analytic skills. The day of the "generalist generalist," however, is past. Yet, it cannot be

7

emphasized too strongly that the modernized British government will still need generalists. The demands of the modern welfare state are such that the competent generalist also needs a strong specialized and/or substantive background. Mandarins, to be competent policy generalists and managers, need different training and experience than that of the current menu. That does not rule out the Oxbridge types. But it argues strongly against the current practice of policy (really politics) mongering jobs where the high flyer seldom is put in a responsible operational position and further receives little or no training.

Central to effective British governance is *individual* responsibility – a prime minister and each minister accountable for his or her actions, formulating and implementing policies for each individual steward-ship. Instead, ministers flee from individual responsibility. They hide behind obsolete notions of ministerial responsibility (accountability for every ministerial action which is an absurdity) and collective responsibility (group accountability which is a smokescreen). No one has put it better than Edmund Dell: "The principal administrative objection to collective responsibility is that it confuses responsibility. To make everyone responsible means in the end that no one feels responsible."[18]

A competent government should think through where it wants to go and how to get there. That requires analysis and strategy. Strong policy analysis units are needed at the top, both at the center and in the departments. The call is for openness and competition. As I have observed elsewhere: "The lack of ... policy analysis is a symptom of a pre-modern central government that has not faced up to the informa-tion and analytic demands of running a complex welfare state. British policymaking exclusiveness and the related aura of secrecy have stopped the development of a process of scrutiny and challenge which is needed in order to put information and analysis to the test of competition."[19]

The case that British central government is pre-modern is over-whelming. But what about anti-modern? In the aforementioned off-the-record interviews, a former minister told me: "Despite all of Britain's woes there is still found in Parliament an intense satisfaction with the system. *The most destructive thing in the British system is complacency.*" Mandarins worried both about attacks made on them as obstructionist and their declining image often still believe that

8

criticism is misguided, coming from those who do *not* understand their problems.[20] Even more generally, the London Business School's John Stopford has observed that "complacency is enemy number one in this country; that old willingness to make do."[21]

Toward the end of my interviews in May 1985, one of the most insightful interviewees (a former civil servant) took exception to use of the term "complacent" and said: "Rather than complacent, ministers and higher civil servants are concerned, but cannot break out of their current mental set. They are like a man clinging to a rock in a storm, afraid to let go and jump to a safer rock." Over my years of interviewing (1980-5), I have seen a greater willingness to recognize fundamental problems and consider basic changes. However, even if the notion of complacency no longer fully captures the mood, far too few are willing to break the pattern that has crystallized. Too many, even if less comfortable, remain comfortable enough not to want to risk change.

THE THATCHER FACTOR

The 1987 Conservative election victory underscored both Thatcherism as the major British socioeconomic and political change of the last half of the twentieth century and Mrs Thatcher herself as extraordinary, one of a handful of dominant or great (not the same thing) prime ministers of British history. S. E. Finer summed her up admirably for her first two governments in observing that Prime Minister Thatcher "has towered over her contemporaries ... She is 'big'. She has impressed herself on government as nobody has since the war years of Churchill. She falls short of greatness, but she radiates dominance. I do not believe that in our lifetime we shall ever look upon her like again."[22] John Cole writing shortly before the 1987 election argued that her third victory "would turn her into a Conservative figure to be compared only with Churchill in this century."[23]

The critical point to make is that extraordinary prime ministers and presidents – extraordinary, it should be underscored, compared to other heads of state, not simply to citizens – can to some extent defy the rules of the game and operate in ways not open to ordinary leaders. Mrs Thatcher is a brute force who can override the political and bureaucratic blockages that would defeat an ordinary prime minister.

9

Later the Attlee government leadership will be discussed. This extraordinary government (mainly the so-called "Big Five") was able to bring critical policy changes without significant modification of the obsolete central government structure. What this earlier government did with bureaucratic manipulation based on institutional knowledge, Prime Minister Thatcher has done with direct force. *Prime ministers who follow are unlikely to have her dominant character and so must play by the rules of Britain's pre-modern government.*

The 1987 election forces a harder look at the Thatcher years – both those that have passed, in which period she has made the "Britain Is Dying" theme legitimately debatable, and those years ahead, during which she well might lead two more governments and fundamentally turn Britain around, bringing it for the foreseeable future toward the upper end of the Western European economic growth rates. When this study began in 1980, Britain clearly was the economic sick man of Western Europe. The British Disease was the starting point of any serious analysis of that nation's problems. Britain then was suffering what came to be the worst recession of the postwar era. Prime Minister Margaret Thatcher, rhetoric aside, looked to be just another *ordinary* leader floundering about and mired down less by a weak Labour opposition than the "wets" in her own party. But that changed dramatically after Falklands and the economic recovery. Prime Minister Thatcher in her first two governments sought both economic and institutional great leaps. By the end of that period, she had failed to make major structural changes in British central government. On the economics side, Thatcher had not clearly succeeded or failed.

Britain, once the recession ended, has led Western Europe in economic growth, albeit amid the slowest EEC growth in the postwar years. The "Thatcher Economic Miracle," however, is still far from a *fait accompli.* Just a few examples at this point will do. First, Thatcher's overall economic growth record, which includes the deep recession, is the worst postwar performance, trailing even the most recent Labour government record that was considered a disaster. Second, what has marked the 1980s so far generally in the advanced West and particularly in Western Europe is extremely slow growth. The anomaly is that British economic growth in the Thatcher years, even if only the post recession years are considered, is not outstanding compared to a number of earlier postwar years in Britain and certainly the rest of Western Europe, but looks good in relative terms as Western Europe fell on hard times. Third, Prime Minister Thatcher's macroeconomic policies generally have not invested scarce government resources wisely and have favored the advantaged over the disadvantaged. C. F. Pratten argues quite correctly:

The critical failures of Mrs Thatcher's [first two] governments have been failures to use North Sea oil to expand demand, failure to use the resources which she has allowed to be wasted in mass unemployment, and failure to provide sound training and higher education for youth. Very late in the day attempts [during her second government] have been made to correct these failures. Her economic legacy is to leave a shrunken manufacturing sector and a labor force whose training has not kept pace with that of our competitors. Finally, her policies have worked to the advantage of the "top cats" in society and against those of the underdogs.[24]

At the end of her second government, conflicting data do not permit a definitive claim that Mrs Thatcher's economic performance is either a miracle or an abject failure. However, the weight of the evidence of the two Thatcher governments is more failure than success. *The British Disease lives on.* With her third term underway and a fourth a stated goal, she may yet have her desired impact of a permanent upward shift of Britain's economic performance level. I think not, but that is at best an educated guess.

The Thatcher government stands as the latest attempt to restructure British central government. Thatcher has brought the management issue to center stage, and more importantly, held it there. Management has become a "hooray" word in Thatcherism. From the appointment of Derek (Lord) Rayner as her special adviser on efficiency, to the Financial Management Initiative, to her search for permanent secretaries who are "doers rather than thinkers," Mrs Thatcher has sought the holy grail of management.

The Thatcher government rates an A for continuing effort but merits a lower grade on performance. "[The British] government is struggling with an impoverished concept of [public] management."[25] Two critical errors have weighed down the Thatcher management approach. First, the Thatcher "management revolution" in action mainly boiled down to cost-cutting – an accountant's view of management, not a manager's. The positive people and performance-oriented elements were missing. Modern management is about getting things done efficiently, not just cutting costs. Thatcher management strategy so often was negative where modern management strategies are positive.

Second, management under Thatcher is discussed almost entirely in terms of the civil service "mandarins" – the allegedly smooth, bloodless, cautious careerists who do battle for the status quo. Blameless, the mandarins are not. But if culpability is the issue, the politicians – the mandarins' masters – win hands down over Whitehall. Focusing on Westminster versus Whitehall, however, is misleading. What is critical is that the two together dominate and preserve the pre-modern, anti-modern British central government.

The modernization of British government must be far broader than that envisioned by the Thatcher government. At the same time the Thatcher government's continuing emphasis on management has forced a rethinking both of its importance and of the need to incorporate modern managerial approaches. A mandarin told me: "Some of us are beginning to prevail in arguing that the so far mechanistic Financial Management Initiative must be transformed by the notion that the machinery is inhabited by people who need to be led, motivated and treated as human beings by line managers, and that the budgetary systems we are setting up must lay the responsibility for people management firmly on the shoulders of line managers." Prime Minister Thatcher using her tenacity, longevity and dominance has pushed the governmental system with brute force to a degree not seen in the postwar era, if at all in British history except in major wars. She has shown how a strong prime minister intent on dominating the central government can do so. Thatcher, however, did not seek fundamental structural changes to modernize British central government.

AN AMERICAN'S VIEW

Since 1980, I have been concerned with developing options both for increasing the amount of sound information and policy analysis in support of policymaking and for improving leadership and management at the top of the British and U.S. governments. Critical to this effort have been a large number of in-depth, off-the-record interviews. Such interviews escape the often guarded mandarin-crafted language that comes forth when those at the top speak or write about the machinery of government for public consumption. Except in confidence, when would an ex-mandarin say, accurately I would note, that the mandarins as a class are "cripples in an analytic sense"?

In the British case, interviews are with politicians and ex-politicians, mandarins and former mandarins, "media" people (mainly newspaper journalists but also individuals in television, radio and magazine writing), and people in research organizations and universities. Much of the biting criticism found in the book is from Britishers either speaking off-the-record or going public in speeches and publications. My comparative advantage is synthesis and perspective. I make the links among the center, Parliament, the government departments, and the mandarins. What I also can do is translate American experience into terms relevant for Britain – not an easy task in that Britain and the United States are often at opposite poles. Finally, and this is almost always a foreigner's advantage, I am, generally speaking, more able to step back further than the indigenous critic. No matter how perceptive he or she is, the internal critic often pulls back from the harsh conclusions to which evidence and logic point.

Given the caustic comments about British government so far, it may strike the reader as disingenuous to claim to be an Anglophile. After several stays in Britain, I find much that is extremely appealing, often in direct contrast to my own country. Moreover, I have come to admire the brilliance of a number of individuals both inside and outside the government. Yet it would be false friendship to cast aside whatever tools I have for doing hard-edged, pragmatic policy analysis. It would be a disservice to praise British government rather than to criticize it in a search for ways to improve it or, when necessary, fail to criticize the elite groups which contain people I like and admire.

My Washington perspective that leads to the call for dramatic changes to modernize British government can lead to three misunderstandings. The first that I want Britain to adopt U.S. institutions and to be like the United States. Not so. At the same time I underscore the value of the lessons to be learned from the American experience. A country with Britain's problems should not throw away useful information even if it comes from countries it does not care to emulate. The problem is to put such information in its proper context. I can illustrate this point by considering a frequent British comment when I have discussed modernizing Parliament by adding analytic staff: "But we don't want Parliament to be like your Congress with thousands of staff running all over each other." I agree. Congress is overstaffed. But my answer is that Britain lacks the qualified people, the money, and the ethos to overstaff. It is much more likely to err on the side of too few staff than too many. There is something between anorexia and obesity. Britain can do much better than the United States if it gets over its "either/or" hangup because it is most unlikely to overstaff grossly as has been the American case. The basic point is the need for the careful mining of the American experience.

Second is that the argument boils down to a larger, more centralized British government. Stronger central government is not to be equated with either greater centralization or more public as opposed to private effort. As to the former, Jones and Stewart make the key point with which I agree, that "the unnecessary handling of [local] problems by national government may prevent it from dealing adequately with those problems which can be dealt with only at the centre."[26] Much the same case can be made in terms of governments in general carrying out activities that are not required and can be performed by the private sector. My argument is that strong central government is needed, given the current setting, if it is to execute successfully, whether the policy be more or less centralization or more or less privatization, because the formulation and implementation of such new strategies takes great competence.

The final possible misunderstanding is that I gloss over the real dangers in a major institutional reform of British central government. It is an issue of great concern, and many of my earlier writings caution against a rapid change in institutions.[27] But in Britain, the fundamental question is how one evaluates *two* dangers, one of standing pat and the other of making dramatic changes. Is the British Disease a life-threatening malady where powerful, but dangerous drugs or major surgery are the only feasible options? Is the current structure so obsolete that it no longer provides the institutional base for coping with Britain's social and economic crisis? I answer a strong yes to both questions. My fear is that Britain will cease to be Britain as we know it if it does not act.

Two more personal points need making. First, the reader may feel that my portrait of British central government is too grim, too one-sided, pouncing on weaknesses, ignoring strengths. Admittedly, a study of this type stresses the warts to emphasize needed improvement. A bottle may be viewed as half empty or half full. But in the

British case, the bottle appears no more than one-third full. Second, although I am only a late comer to the growing chorus crying "Britain Is Dying?" the question remains as to whether we are unnecessarily alarmists or potential Cassandras who hope the dangers will be perceived and acted on. Prophecy is risky business under the best of circumstances. Moreover, nations seldom die in the sense of disappearing from the map. But Britain can drop further on the economic scale. Edward Heath's 1973 warning still holds: "The alternative to expansion is not, as some occasionally seem to suppose an England of quiet market towns linked only by trains puffing slowly and peacefully through green meadows. The alternative is slums, dangerous roads, old factories, cramped schools, stunted lives."[28]

Finally, I am all too painfully aware of the problem of accepting criticism from an American. The British liked it much better when we praised British central government institutions as the vehicle for sensible, sound governance – the model for a backward America. For an American to level harsh criticism against British government structure surely smacks a bit of Don Quixote battling the windmill. My response is that I would be a false friend not to try to convince the British of what I truly believe. Better being Don Quixote than a flatterer saying what is desired by the listener (reader).

THE PATH AHEAD

Several points will be considered in looking ahead. First, the kinds of institutional changes needed and the rationale underlying them are spelled out. Second, the case is made that the structural changes proposed are conservative in the best sense. Third, I argue that the ultimate demand, if British central government is to be effective, is for political leadership combined with organizational mastery; however, the former must come first.

Toward a more efficient, effective central government

Call it "modernization," call it "reform," call it what you will, the search is for *more efficient and effective central government institutional performance*. It is a goal hard to quarrel with. As Sir Gordon Downey, the Comptroller and Auditor General, was quoted as saying: "Where everyone can agree is that, if the [government of the day's] policy is that privatization should take place, it is better that privatization take place efficiently and effectively and with proper regard to the interests of the taxpayer."[29]

Table 1 indicates fifteen institutional changes aimed at improving central government performance. A few comments are needed. First, the specific institutional changes are not a proposal for all seasons. It would be ridiculous to argue that each of the fifteen changes is absolutely necessary or should emerge precisely as proposed. What these options do indicate is how significant may be the level of change required to modernize British central government. I am much more confident of the sweeping nature of the needed structural changes than of the specifics of the particular policy options. The demand is for an institutional great leap that transforms British central government. The call ultimately is for a political leader who can see the needed institutional change, sell this vision, and provide directional guidance in implementing the basic central government reform. The policy analysis in the remainder of the book is aimed at providing a strong base for considering the dimensions of such reform.

Table 1. *Institutional changes to improve British central government performance*

House of Commons

An elimination of question time and other procedures that center the House of Commons on chamber debate

A significant increase in policy analysts serving the parliamentary committees and individual MPs

A structure that casts committees as the primary vehicle for executing Parliament's main functions

Prime minister and Cabinet

Prime ministers charged explicitly with the responsibility for overall strategic leadership

A prime minister's policy analysis unit

The Cabinet Office expanded to include new analytic and strategic units

Whitehall departments

Ministers having direct control over all high level department appointments with such appointments chosen from MPs, higher civil servants and outsiders

Ministers and junior ministers, if not members of Parliament, to have full access to the House of Commons including serving on the front benches and answering for their departments

Each minister to have a strategic and analytic unit

A management strategy aimed at increasing the commitment and capacity of local authorities to deliver services

The abolition of the single permanent secretary responsible for all departmental civil servants to be replaced by a layer of top departmental executives through which all subordinates report

A promotion structure for "high flyers" and higher civil servants that combines in service training and on-the-job policy, analytic and managerial experiences

An elite college or colleges having as its main task the preparing of persons for high level government management and analytic roles

Public information

Increased central government funding of nongovernmental research and analytic organizations to develop and execute policy relevant research and analyses

A strong freedom of information act based on the presumption of information being available to the public and its representatives, except in narrowly specified cases such as national security, combined with abolishing the parliamentary press Lobby and replacing it with open news conferences and briefings

Second, the institutional changes proposed are aimed at providing British central government with the *generalized capacity* to cope with the British Disease; however, no plan will be set out for the second (programatic) great leap needed to ameliorate Britain's economic woes. That would be premature since such an economic game plan demands a modernized central government capable both of formulating the needed economic policy strategy and of implementing, and if necessary of recasting, that strategy over time. Task one is the development of generalized capacity and structural processes to provide sound, timely information, analysis and advice and to establish clean lines of responsibility.

Third, the structural and staffing changes sought have an unfortunate asymmetry. A successful institutional great leap does not guarantee an economic policy strategy that will turn Britain around. But no structural great leap – continuing pre-modern, anti-modern British central government – could doom the nation to economic decline and political instability unless good fortune far in excess of North Sea oil intervenes – *deus ex machina.*

A prudent act of daring

A truly conservative political act balances environmental forces by both preserving the most essential elements of the political and social institutions at risk *and* meeting the demands of the changing environment. This concept of conservatism takes on real meaning only in dynamic terms. *The point of conservative balance is not fixed – indeed not knowable – at the start of the political search process but rather emerges through a groping within that process.* Bernard Asbell, in describing a two year legislative effort led by (then) Senator Edmund Muskie that ended in the enactment of a new Clean Air Act, reports that "Muskie himself is satisfied that the law has located itself at that magical point of political balance: the boldest feasible act in the public interest that takes into account the relative political strengths and conflicting demands for justice of all contenders."[30]

Where will the point be located that balances preservation of essential social and political factors and environmental pressures? In some cases the new conservative equilibrium will come from incremental change that might go a bit forward or a bit backward toward reviving practices that once worked well but had (perhaps foolishly) fallen into disuse. But with enough environmental pressure, the changes needed to reach the conservative balance must be dramatic, moving far from current structures and practices with concomitant charges of radicalism and unconstitutionality.

With powerful forces at work the truly conservative balance point does not arise from sheer political expedience – the kind of least-common-denominator compromise that may do the job when the needed movement is small (incremental). Where mighty political and social forces swirl about, guiding the groping process toward a conservative balance demands the highest order of artful political leadership (steering) to hit the mark rather than undershoot or overshoot. The Great Reform Act, so bold in its day, is a classic case. The opposition had expected a mild measure, perhaps doing away with a handful of the worst of the rotten boroughs to give representation to the cities of the North. The expectation was not fulfilled. As Brock has observed; "Although the expectations of a moderate Bill were foolish, it would have taken a very wise man to predict a scheme as sweeping as the one published on 1 March [1831]. Historians have been nearly as puzzled by its boldness as were contemporaries."[31]

Why the boldness at the outset? Was revolution really in the air? Brock finds as the key explanation, the one that is simplest and most straight forward: "[The Whigs] brought in a sweeping Bill because the events of 1830 had told them that it was now an urgent task to sweep away the electoral system."[32] Bold as the original bill was, it was an act of aristocrats to keep aristocrats in power by enfranchising more of the middle class – not an enormous jump to democracy as we know it today with secret ballot and universal suffrage.[33]

We need to cast ourselves back to that time when memories of the 1789 French Revolution and the much more mild French uprising of 1830 helped shape British thinking. The former kept vivid the fear of the mob; the latter indicated the dangers of standing pat. Earl Grey's government over fifteen months of growing discontent groped for a solution yet never retreated very far from the original bold bill of March 1831. Did the final result come to rest at a balancing point that was truly conservative? Trevelyan said of the bill's most critical provision – attacking the rotten boroughs – that it was "one of the *most prudent acts of daring* in history," and added that "a more *perfect* Bill [judged by twentieth century standards] ... would have failed to pass in 1832, and its rejection would sooner or later have been followed by a civil war."[34]

A prudent act of daring – what a wonderfully apt description for a conservative outcome forged where there was great pressure for change. The act would have passed much earlier if only Grey and the other Whig leaders had been willing to retreat to incrementalism. But they did not. They carried the country close to rebellion to prevent revolution. As Brock argued: "To enact the Reform Act by peaceful means was a great and beneficent feat of statesmanship."[35] Powell has captured the conservatism of the Act: "The great reform crisis has been viewed as the classic case of environmental pressure and democratic response ... Grey managed to build an unlikely coalition, which eventually included an overwhelming majority of mobilized political resources, to carry a measure of significant change without severely damaging or alienating any single institution or class group."[36] This bold leadership that stayed on course during a stormy fifteen months is conservatism in its best sense. Grey exemplifies the kind of political leadership that Britain now needs.

Even more broadly, Robert Blake in his biography of Disraeli saw the fundamental conservatism of both the Great Reform Act and the repeal of the Corn Laws where the Tories in trying to stop needed changes were the reactionary party:

The classes which governed England both before and after 1832 were basically conservative with a small "c." They wished to preserve the Crown and Parliament, to retain the Church of England ... the rights of property and inheritance, with no more concession than was necessary to the forces which were transforming society. Politics largely turned on just how much concession was necessary. For the second time in sixteen years the Tory party ... seemed to have misjudged the amount needed. The first occasion was over parliamentary reform. On that issue and on the Corn Law crisis the governing class in effect decided that the high Tory policy would provoke into reality that perennial nightmare of early nineteenth-century England, violent revolution. In other words conservatism was not best maintained by supporting the Conservative party.[37]

Only bold action by a leader, only a great leap would make the necessary concessions.

Political and organizational demands

As the book moves from this broad introduction to more detailed discussion that delves into issues of modern organizational structure and management, we must keep before us the need for political leadership. There is no unique institutional structure, no abstract equations that show the precise balancing point. What must be sought is a politically viable solution, not an organization chart with its boxes and arrows.

Today just as a century and a half ago, Britain needs political leaders who have both the vision to see the required structural reform and the capacity to guide it toward fruition. These leaders must confront portentous claims that the proposed changes are unconstitutional, and that the system at most needs a spot of tinkering. Such political barriers are the initial great hurdle. They will not be leaped with a grand technical fix. Hence, to lose sight of the first fundamental need of political leadership is fatal.

Here Thatcher's political leadership offers a critical example. She saw the political power of her office. As King has observed: "It is open to a determined prime minister to take more and more decisions and to defy other members of the Cabinet to say that he or she has no right to take these decisions ... Margaret Thatcher's example will be important in future not least because it will make clear to her successors that the job of prime minister can be an even bigger one than had previously been supposed."[38] Mrs Thatcher had both a vision of the new Britain and the political leadership skills to pursue it. What she did not understand was governmental structure. After discussing two categories of leaders who either think instinctively in organizational terms or people terms, but not both, King argues: "The third category, considerably rarer than either of the others, consists of people capable of thinking both organizationally and in human terms at the same time ... Hers is an almost exclusively people-centered style of government. Her interest in the structure of government is minimal."[39]

Political leaders need to understand the organizational aspects of the institutional changes required to modernize British central government. This requirement leads to a call for a leader who is an "organization-man" in the good sense of Clement Attlee and Dwight Eisenhower. The demand is for an extremely high order of political *and* organizational mastery. The primary task of the book is to illuminate the latter and to show its relationship to political mastery. Such emphasis is warranted because the deep organizational understanding at the top that marked the Attlee governments, is today a missing and often unrecognized element. We must not forget that political leadership is the driving factor. At the same time the understanding at the top of how organizations and institutional processes work and the ability to use such knowledge are the critical missing links needed to guide that political power in the desired direction.

1

THE GOVERNANCE PROBLEM IN BROAD PERSPECTIVE

The postwar period ushered in the modern welfare state throughout the entire industrialized West. Powerful central government moved to center stage. What so distinguishes this forty year period after World War II is the rapidity of change and concomitantly the increase in three related factors: policy *complexity*, public *expectations*, and the *competence* of government to cope with the first two. The first quarter century of the postwar era was mainly a time of confidence; since then the mood has been marked by growing discontent. The OPEC price increases that started in 1973 are a good dividing line worldwide between the two periods. At the heart of the discontent is the unequal footrace among the three earlier mentioned factors: *Complexity and expectations have far outdistanced governments' competence to cope with a vast array of problems.*

Before turning directly to Westminster and Whitehall, the governance issue needs to be cast in broad perspective. How do complexity, expectations, and competence (or lack thereof) interact to make the modern welfare state so hard to manage? Why are we so displeased both with government leaders and the experts who have become increasingly prominent in government? What skills and experience are needed for effective policy leadership in the modern welfare state? What are the components of political power? How critical are a modernized central government and a basic governmental strategy to effective treatment of the British Disease? This diverse set of larger issues shapes our search for means of modernizing British central government.

22

THE COMPLEXITY–EXPECTATIONS–COMPETENCE CONUNDRUM

The most threatening, vexing conundrum facing world government leaders today can be set out succinctly. An expanding imbalance between complexity and competence brings both a growing incapacity to govern and a mounting frustration with experts who do not foresee dramatic changes.

It needs to be underscored that the problem is not declining competence itself. Denis Healey put the matter succinctly in an April 3, 1970 issue of the *Guardian*: "The fact is that modern government is an immensely complicated administrative job and the task of making it work is a very difficult one. The tasks are infinitely more difficult than those which faced ministers thirty or fifty years ago ... So you come back again to the question of competence."[1] Competence has risen – often significantly – over the last twenty-five years. For example, the tools and techniques of policy analysis are now far superior technically to those available twenty-five years ago. But if the tools and techniques of analysis have increased arithmetically over the last quarter of a century, problems to be analyzed have grown geometrically. It is the outcome of this footrace between competence and complexity that so frustrates both rulers and citizens.

Take the economy as an example. In the mid-1960s economists became increasingly confident of their tools and techniques, finally claiming the business cycle was manageable. The economy could be fine-tuned to avoid major declines. In the succeeding twenty years, the tools and techniques of economics improved tremendously. But during that period, various factors, including OPEC price increases starting in 1973, pushed nations into the more capricious, less controllable, uncharted terrain of double digit inflation, unemployment, and interest rates. By the late 1970s, economists found how fallible were their tools and techniques in contending with these phenomena in the unstable, unpredictable world economy. Alan Greenspan put the problem succinctly in the December 12, 1984 issue of *The New York Times*: "Even though we had an extraordinary increase in our tools, such as computers, we have not been able to keep pace with the growing complexity of economic relationships, both domestic and international."

Analysts themselves contribute to complexity with their jargon and their sophisticated methodologies. But, in the broadest sense, policy analysis (read all policy methods) is more victim than perpetrator in being outrun by complexity. That is, policy analysts did not create problem complexity but rather suffer from it. Compare 1965, just as the information, analytic and complexity explosions were starting in the United States, with today. Policy analysis tools and techniques now are far superior to those of 1965. But the increase in complexity has produced a much wider gap as compared with the earlier year. Policy analysts in 1965 were better able to cope with the *then* existing policy complexities than their current counterparts. However, if only the 1965 policy analysis tools were available *today*, policy analysts would be much further behind than they are now. Analytic advice would be even less sound.

Also important along with complexity and competence are public expectations, size (scope) of government, and attitudes toward government. The first two have soared much like complexity. The public's attitude toward government has, however, soured in recent years, in part because of the growing gap between complexity and competence. These changes are a post World War II phenomenon. Britain's central government was mainly passive in domestic affairs until 1945. Sir Frank Cooper observed: "Until relatively recently [central] government used to be largely about the administration and expense of foreign affairs, defense, law and order and the raising of the necessary revenue."[2] The Labour governments of 1945–51 ushered in the modern welfare state and began the era of rising expectations.

We do not know whether expectations of what government should do began to increase and government action followed or whether government leaders began to increase programs to meet what they considered to be important needs and public expectations grew in response to new programs. But once started the modern welfare state in advanced Western societies grew and expectations grew. Citizens began to look to government for basic security – for a pension at retirement, for maintenance funds when children were born, for loans or grants when those children went to college, for income when sickness or unemployment occurred, and for burial expenses at death. Further government was called upon to be concerned with community development and economic development and a host of other responsibilities that either were found before the war only on a small

24

scale at the local level or simply did not exist at all. Increasingly these expectations focused upon the central government, if not as the main actor as the main source of funds.

Expectations became a driving force. As expectations push more and more responsibilities on government, problem complexity increases. If we expect government to eradicate poverty or maintain full employment or hold down inflation, the policy equation becomes increasingly complicated. Complexity rises in part because of the specific expectations at hand, say lowering unemployment. But what expands complexity so much is the interaction when several inter-related problems must be confronted. The results often are unpalatable tradeoffs. For example, keeping full employment may bring undesirable inflation. Expectations are not fulfilled. The result is a simple equation: Expectations drive up complexity and complexity outruns competence. Suddenly, government is no longer part of the solution. It seems to be the problem.

POLICY/POLITICAL LEADERSHIP

Despite all the complexity, despite the coming of computers and the many policy experts, leaders at the top of the government still give shape and tone to their administrations. Margaret Thatcher has made clear, perhaps uncomfortably so, how much her ideology, the way she decides issues, the information she wants, and her style of interacting with cabinet ministers and civil servants, have molded her administration. Thatcher's highly visible active style underscores how much the individual at the top counts. But earlier prime ministers and their Cabinets in deciding *not* to change also were shaping their administrations through inaction. They were not helpless victims, trapped by institutions that would not yield, however much they may have thought so. Both action and inaction, when change is possible, are choices even though inaction often may appear as acceptance of institutional inevitability. If British government is to be modernized, there must be leadership from the top. Here is where change must start.

Power has to do with getting things done. It is not just winning elections, not just formulating policy and moving it through Parliament, but mastering the machine to put policy in place and running as

25

desired. In the power equation political leaders need the capacity to influence *both* the *formulation* and the *implementation* of policies. At question is the degree to which these leaders can have an impact upon *delivered policy* – an impact not only on top level decisions but on what happens to participants in central government funded programs. Policy leadership has two key elements: political mastery and organizational mastery. *Political mastery* has to do with the capacity of the leader to exercise influence over the party, Parliament, other politicians, interest groups, the media, and the people. *Organizational mastery* refers to the capacity of the leader to exercise influence over the *entire* machinery of government responsible for the administration or operation of central government funded programs.

Political mastery is the crucial *first* element, the fundamental requirement for an effective elected politician. Maintaining political mastery is the first goal among several when things are going well; it may be the only goal when political standing is threatened. Political mastery may reach a critical point at which only organizational mastery can keep it going. Part of the leadership equation is sufficient knowledge about those to be led – their strengths, their weaknesses, their institutional codes and customs – so that the intangibles of leadership can be applied effectively. Politicians wanting to influence delivered policies need knowledge about how large public bureaucracies work. The "anthropology of the machine" must be fathomed before organizational mastery can be exercised. Such knowledge is a fundamental aspect of the politician's responsibility.

Top leadership has a fundamental responsibility to guide the strategic process. Governments need a road map showing the direction the nation should take and the means for getting there. Vague promises will not do. Governments need a carefully crafted, realistic strategy.

Strategy – the strategic process – has three key elements. The development of broad objectives, the grand vision of what a nation is to be, is the first necessary step in evolving a strategy. The second element is a careful analysis that determines the internal consistency of the broad goals and the feasibility of their implementation. These broad objectives that start the analysis should undergo rigorous testing and well may be modified and refined. It is not enough to ask where one wants to go, one must also seek to determine how to get there and may find that changes are necessary because certain

26

elements conflict internally and necessitate tradeoffs or because some goals cannot be implemented in the form proposed. Only through hard analytic effort can objectives be hammered into a reliable directional guide and a realistic starting road map be developed. The third element of strategy is the logical extension of the second. As time passes, circumstances change. No one has a sure course. The initial road plan is certain to need tactical revision over time. And in cases where the environmental changes are dramatic, fundamental rethinking about the broad objectives may be required.

Such thinking and planning are demanding. A real danger is that planning will go too far and develop a map that is too detailed and rigid. But strategic analysis can give strong directional guides and a coherence that allows reasonable flexibility. Effective governance is unlikely without a realistic strategy.

Top leaders face no more difficult task than reconciling competing pulls and pressures in the political/policy process. The search is for a viable balance. How to find the "just right" point is the operational issue. It is the same problem that faced young Goldilocks, lost in the woods, and hungry, who stumbled upon the Three Bears' house, found that house unoccupied, and further discovered three bowls of porridge. Taste testing showed one bowl too hot, a second too cold, and the third just right. We might call the principle at issue the "Law of Creative Balance" but it seems better – and less portentous – to label it the "Goldilocks Theorem." How is the search for the "just right" point to be carried out? Goldilocks doesn't give much of a hint. This lack of precision has not diminished the story for a countless number of children. However, if the Goldilocks Theorem holds in terms of many of the public (and private) sector activities and functions that are of great interest to us, lack of precision is a critical matter.

Strategic thinking illustrates the problem. In their book on excellent American companies, Peters and Waterman argue that formal long-range strategic planning almost always leads to an overemphasis on techniques and then observe: "But the problem is not that companies ought not to plan. They damn well should plan. The problem is that planning becomes an end in itself ... [T]he plan becomes the truth, and data that don't fit the preconceived plan ... are denigrated or blithely ignored."[3] In a Rand study of innovations in criminal justice, the researchers found a similar result: "Premature certainty represents the opposite of an adaptive and evolutionary innovation process ... [A]n overemphasis on planning *prior* to implementation was its most common precursor ... [P]rojects that sought premature certainty prolonged the initial planning period in a vain attempt to resolve more questions than could be reasonably addressed in the absence of actual implementation."[4] These two statements not only illustrate the Goldilocks Theorem, but cast it as a dynamic process. Unlike Goldilocks, the person or organization seeking the right amount of planning cannot simply measure at one point in time as Goldilocks in testing three bowls of porridge. The "just right" point must be sought in a process that involves numerous variables acting over time.

Nowhere is the question of balance likely to be more critical over time than in the case of politics and policy. The politics/policy imbalance is an inherent problem for central governments. As Ben Heineman, Jr., a lawyer who served in key political and policy analysis positions in the Carter administration, has argued: "Reconciling the tensions, even antagonisms, between the world of policy ... and the world of politics is ... the supreme act of [presidential] political leadership."[5] To let policy dominate politics at the top is a fatal flaw. The government of the day's first and most compelling concern is its political standing. Sound policy demands a strong political base – first things first. Sound policy, however, requires more than politics. It requires a significant investment in strategy, management and analysis.

The politics/policy imbalance looms as British central government's most pressing institutional problem. Key arguments in the book are that the political/policy balance is skewed towards politics; that more attention to strategy, management and policy analysis are needed in British central government to correct the imbalance; and that these issues are insufficiently understood and discussed. The latter leads to a much greater emphasis on policy analysis and management than on politics – on organizational as opposed to political mastery. Because the imbalance is attacked, the excessive political focus decried, and organizational skill and experience emphasized, the reader may think this indicates a view that politics is dirty and destructive whilst policy analysis and management are pure and desirable. Nothing could be further from the truth. To argue that there is an imbalance towards politics away from policy is not to claim that policy or analytic considerations should dominate politics at the presidential or Cabinet levels, but rather that politics ought not be too dominant.

Britain's economic decline relative to other Western nations concerns us not in the sense of considering specific economic policies but because the British Disease is crucial to the issue of central government modernization. There are two points of clear agreement about Britain's economic woes. First, Britain's economic problems go back to the last century. Second, it has been the weakest of the Western European economies during much of the post World War II period, at least until the 1980s. Less clear are the implications. How sick the patient is, what brought the illness, and what can be done about it are critical unresolved questions. And, as indicated earlier, since 1982/3 when Britain recovered from its recession, Britain's economic growth has led to a claim that the British Disease has been conquered or at least will be in Mrs Thatcher's third government and perhaps a fourth one. A quick look at Britain's economic record over the last century will help put the issues in perspective.

England and Wales in 1895 were at the top of the world with income per capita over twice that of Germany and about a third more than France and the United States.[6] In 1899 Britain produced one-third of the value of world exports of manufactures.[7] Britain entered the twentieth century as the dominant world economic power, but as Desai points out: "By the 1870s it was clear that the British economy was no longer the most dynamic capitalist economy. Its growth rate, its rate of innovative activity, its international competitiveness had all suffered, and it was facing competition from the United States and Germany in all markets to which it exported. The response of the political and economic community in Britain in the years 1870–1900 determined the course of the long-run stagnation."[8]

In the years between 1900 and 1945, Britain remained a world economic power even though the relative trend line continued downward. Andrew Gamble could point out both that "the Great War of 1914–18 marks the beginning of the collapse of British military, financial and industrial power" and that "in 1931 Britain was still one of the strongest states in the world economy and better able to ride out the depression than most."[9] In 1932 Britain had 2.8 million people unemployed, 13.5 percent of the work force.[10] The United States in contrast experienced unemployment of a fourth of the labor force. Although declining, Britain's share in the value of world exports of manufactures was still above 20 percent by 1937.[11]

The postwar boom and collapse

Britain entered the postwar era as the most powerful Western European country. That period can be divided into two segments. First were the boom years that ran well into the 1960s. Even though Britain was declining relative to the OECD countries, these years were ones of extremely rapid growth. Economic growth was particularly strong until the early 1960s and in retrospect was fairly strong until the early 1970s.[12] After that comes a decline so visible that British columnist Peter Jenkins finds apropos the statement of a seventeenth-century Spanish observer who claimed Spain's decline had become so rapid that "one can actually see it occurring from one year to the next."[13]

Emerging from World War II after an industrial effort that had met Britain's wartime needs and with its major European rivals having been decimated by the war, Britain appeared strong. The nation grew faster than she had ever grown before in her industrial history.[14] Britain's share in the value of world exports of manufactures rose from 21.3 percent in 1937 to 25.5 percent in 1950.[15] This outstanding growth when measured against earlier periods in British history is a point to emphasize because of its relevance to the British Disease issue.

The British decline in GDP and manufacturing since 1973 has been precipitous as shown by data from before the Thatcher years. Britain's share in the value of world exports of manufactures that stood at 25.5 percent in 1950 had declined to 9.7 percent by 1979.[16] The manufacturing drop was so great it threatened deindustrialization. Eatwell indicates the following percentage increases in manufacturing output in the decade of the 1970s: United States (37), West Germany (23), France (35), Italy (38) and Japan (56); and then observes: "[Britain's manufacturing output] was an incredible three percent *lower* in 1980 than in 1970. *Three percent lower.* So in the last ten years Britain has had no companion in failure. She stands alone."[17]

Britain's income per capita that in 1895 was over twice that of Germany and a third greater than that of France by 1977/8 had fallen to slightly over half that of West Germany and a little under two-thirds that of France.[18] By 1979 when Sir Nicholas Henderson retired as ambassador to France, he observed in a dispatch: "We are scarcely in the same economic league as the Germans or French. We talk of ourselves without shame as being one of the less prosperous countries of Europe. The prognosis for the foreseeable future is discouraging. If present trends continue we shall be overtaken in GDP (Gross Domestic Product) per head by Italy and Spain well before the end of the century."[19]

The Thatcher years: economic miracle or failed revolution

Although I believe the weight of evidence strongly supports the argument that Mrs Thatcher's economic policies in her first two governments have failed to turn the British Disease around, the mid-1980s have made the question legitimately debatable. As *The Economist* observed:

A fictitious Conservative spokesman boasts: In the four years to 1985, the British economy has grown by an average of 3% a year, compared with average growth of less than 2% during the Labour years of 1974–79. Exports are running at record levels. In 1985, Britain's exports of manufactured goods rose 15%, increasing their share of world markets. This government has reduced the rate of inflation by 40% since 1979.

The Labour spokesman counters: Since the Conservative government came to power in 1979, growth has averaged a mere 1% a year – only half the average rate achieved by Labour. Yet, despite their deflationary policies, the rate of inflation has fallen by a mere four percentage points. British manufacturers are being squeezed out of world markets: last year, as world trade boomed, Britain's exports grew by less than 1% in volume.

Who is lying? Neither, each figure is correct. The trick is to choose from the many possible measures the one which is most favorable to your argument.[20]

Start on the positive side of the ledger. By 1987 Britain had experienced the longest run of sustained growth in the postwar period, a marked reduction in inflation, and a large increase in annual productivity gains. Significantly, *The Economist* reported in 1986 that Britain in the last four years has had the fastest growth rate in Western Europe.[21] The climate for private effort appears improved because of the government's privatization of nationalized industry, its

31

successful steps to reduce the power of the trade unions, its elimination of income and exchange controls, and its reductions in marginal tax rates. The Thatcher government privatized nationalized businesses valued at over 7 billion pounds (net proceeds) in the period 1979–85.[22] As for entrepreneurship Barnaby Feder has observed: "The brightest omen ... is the record rate of formation of new businesses, with 54,000 created in the first six months of this year [1985], up 10 percent from a year earlier. Britain now has 140,000 more businesses than when Mrs Thatcher took office six and a half years ago. The figures do not include uncounted thousands of people who have set up small businesses and who did not register with the tax authorities."[23]

Alan Walters, Mrs Thatcher's economic adviser, in a book entitled *Britain's Economic Renaissance* stresses productivity gains: "In the first three or four years of the 1980s Britain experienced a more than fourfold increase in the annual productivity gain. The figures suggest that at last, Britain may be starting to catch up with her great European rivals and partners. *They may be the first signs of a cure for the British disease and may even herald a minor 'economic miracle'.*"[24] In his cautious, carefully qualified optimism, Walters suggests a possible "Thatcher effect" because of increased stability and freedom, recognizes that it is too early to render a final judgment, but speculates that "if the productivity gains persist, and we do come near to the productivity in Germany and France, it will be difficult to attribute causation to any other source [except Thatcher]."[25]

The negative side of the Thatcher revolution includes the worst of the postwar recessions, slow economic growth over the entire period of her premiership, a severe decline in manufacturing, unemployment worse than that of the Great Depression, a poor public investment record, and growing disparities between the "haves" and the "have nots." Britain's real GDP declined 2.7 percent, industrial production fell 9 percent, and unemployment rose from 1.4 to 2.5 million persons between the first quarter of 1980 and the second quarter of 1981. Manufacturing dropped 15 percent in eighteen months and still has not regained its 1979 levels.[26] The recession was so deep that real GDP did not return to its 1979 peak until the third quarter of 1983. Further, in the first Thatcher term real growth was even below that of the previous Labour government's of 1974–9 and only one-third that of the period 1960–73.[27]

32

The OECD in 1986 observed that "the present level of unemployment, about 3.2 million or 13 percent of the labor force on the official count ... is almost equivalent to the degree of unemployment witnessed in the 1930s, *although the problem today appears to be more persistent and deep-rooted.*"[28] Long-term unemployment (over a year) was a critical factor. By 1986 its rise represented "all of the increase in unemployment since 1981"; at 40 percent in mid-1986, long-term unemployment stood far higher than most of the other big industrial economies (e.g., U.S., 12 percent; Japan, 15 percent; West Germany, 33 percent.)[29] Moreover, the Thatcher government since 1979 made eighteen changes in how unemployment is counted, generally lowering that number and "by the end of 1986, [with] fiddles and measures combined had removed up to 1m[illion] from the count" so that the true number of jobless may have reached well over 4 million.[30] Nor was the million person growth in new jobs since 1983 nearly as positive as the raw figure suggested because half the jobs were taken by the self-employed and half by part-time women with full-time male employment remaining flat.[31]

Thatcher's first two governments pursued public investment policies that undermined competitiveness. As Pratten observed: "In many trades, the substitution of new and improved products which is a vital ingredient of competitiveness requires research and development, new capital equipment and engineers, technicians and craftsmen to set up production. Here the record of Mrs Thatcher's government is bad. She has not provided the conditions for creating new products and investment ... R & D expenditure has stagnated, investment in UK manufacturing industry has fallen."[32] Not only have real resources been wasted in high unemployment, training has failed to increase worker's skills and experience.[33]

Of equal importance may be the disproportionate distribution of unemployment among males (16 percent) and among regions with a male unemployment rate at 20 percent or more in the North and North-West of England, Northern Ireland, Wales and Scotland.[34] Since 1979 when Thatcher came to power, factory jobs have declined 27 percent overall with 94 percent of those losses in the Midlands and Northern Britain.[35] Britain may be moving rapidly toward being two nations, a prosperous southeastern area dominated by London and an impoverished remainder typified by the northern industrial cities. In his disturbing *Sunday Times Magazine* article comparing Liverpool and Turin (the two competitors in the Brussels football disaster), Ian Jack writes of Liverpool, which is experiencing a 25 percent unemployment rate: "No other city in Britain, and possibly in the world, has declined so steeply and absolutely in the last two decades ... The traveller from Liverpool to Turin finds the hardest thing to adjust to is not so much wealth as optimism."[36] Moreover, it is worth noting that Sir Nicholas Henderson's prediction was half fulfilled in the 1980s as the average Italian became richer than his British counterpart.[37]

There is little question that Mrs Thatcher's socioeconomic policies have caused much misery and have intensified social conflict. Has that pain been justified? Was it purposeful or inadvertent? Marquard argues that "the long-term economic improvement of which short-term pain was supposed to be the harbinger does not seem to have transpired ... [I]t is not at all certain that the pain has been worthwhile, even in her own terms."[38] Finer, Pratten and Krieger claim ulterior motives. In discussing the Conservative manifestos, the former argues that "behind the manifestos there lies a 'Hidden Manifesto': to dismantle, to disperse, if possible to destroy, any citadel of Labour votes, money, patronage, and power" and offers as examples industrial privatization, the sale of council houses, the assault on trade unions, and the efforts to abolish the Greater London Council and the metropolitan counties.[39] Krieger goes further to posit greater racial polarization and further yet in arguing that "politics in the age of Reagan and Thatcher leaves much doubt about the contemporary compatibility between capitalism and democracy."[40] Such a claim goes too far. However, the actions or inactions of both leaders increased class disparities and the potential for severe social conflict, and, in the Thatcher case, created a geographic split that makes the poor North including Scotland and Wales radically different from a well-to-do South (Southeast). These cleavages loom as one of the most disturbing legacies of the first two Thatcher governments.

The Thatcher years also had a fortuitous bounty when North Sea oil came on line making Britain alone among the major OECD countries self-sufficient for fuel supplies.[41] Eatwell argues that "the maintenance of living standards [were] primarily the responsibility of North Sea oil."[42] The future without this oil may be grim: "When the oil runs out, or nearly does, I despair of a country that has de-industrialized as we have," said former Labour Cabinet minister, Roy

Jenkins. Peter Jenkins, a leading newspaper columnist, is even bleaker. "No one has a convincing explanation," he wrote in October 1985, "of how we are going to afford to import the food and raw materials we need to eat and work when the oil is no more."[43]

The British Disease and Western Europe in the 1980s

The British Disease yields a seeming paradox depending on whether economic growth comparisons are made by contrasting current British results with earlier postwar years in Britain, or by contrasting British economic performance with that of OECD or EEC countries during the same time period. The 1980s have made the paradox more vivid.

The 1980s so far have been a difficult period for most of Western Europe. On the good side, rapid inflation was halted. But then came what has been labeled as "Eurosclerosis" and might be described as "stagnonflation" as economic growth rates plunged and unemployment surged bringing Western Europe the worst economic growth of the postwar era. The 1980s have not so much brought Britain up – economic growth compared to earlier periods was generally worse – as it dragged Western Europe down by a greater factor. Britain was joined on the sick list as abnormally low growth and double digit unemployment plagues Western Europe in the 1980s. France's experience has been so bad that the French fear both Italy and Britain may pass them in the growth league.

Britain's economic growth for a few selected years in the 1980s, which the Thatcherites can use as the base to show better performance than the last Labour government, is hardly spectacular compared to earlier periods in Britain. The few selected years of the 1980s have brought lower economic growth than other selected years in earlier decades including the 1960s and 1970s when British growth was viewed by almost everyone as unacceptably low. Recall also that Britain's "good" years of the 1980s followed a devastating recession in the beginning Thatcher years. As unexpected as British economic growth leadership may strike us, even for a few selected years, it must be remembered that Britain looked relatively bad in a very rapid economic growth footrace of the early postwar period and now looks relatively good during a segment of the 1980s amid the slowest growth of the postwar era. It is a shaky base for claiming a Thatcher "Economic Miracle."

35

Summing up and looking forward

Although British industrial problems can be traced to the nineteenth century, Britain until the 1960s was still a world power and experienced high growth during the worldwide postwar boom. We might think of a long race in which Britain in the last century took a gigantic lead, weakened during the period of the two great wars, but has been passed by numerous other runners only in the last few years. *The British Disease did not take on its virulent form until the 1960s as visible relative poverty* vis-à-vis *its European rivals emerged.*

The recent relative economic poverty has no historical analogue in this century. Recall Britain fared relatively well in the Great Depression. *Relative impoverishment is a new phenomenon.* Negative reactions to it cannot easily be shrugged off with the claim of coming through bad patches before. British and foreign observers before the recent economic surge increasingly stressed the negative consequences of the continuing economic problems. Keith Middlemas claimed that "the sense of [economic] decline has become a pervasive nightmare."[44] Professor Ralf Dahrendorf, the German scholar/politician who once headed the London School of Economics, painted the most pessimistic picture of all in claiming that "a mood of gloom and a sense of hopelessness have become so widespread in Britain that one can almost speak of a clinical depression of the British public."[45] Has Britain in Thatcher's "good" years thrown off the gloom that so marked the nation through the recession beginning in 1979? Has Prime Minister Thatcher in her commitment to free market forces and her tenacity in pushing it overcome what American historian Martin Wiener has called "the decline of the industrial spirit"?[46] There are some positive signs. William Pfaff argues that "the morale of British business and of the country's leadership has been transformed."[47] In the July 9, 1987 issue of *The New York Times*, Steve Lohr in a grim portrait of Newcastle still claims "it is hard to escape the conclusion that elements of Thatcherism have been embraced in the Northeast ... [T]he region's new crop of entrepreneurs certainly looks like a page out of her book." But it is premature to claim that Thatcher in her first two governments has overcome the failure of industrial spirit that traces back to the last century. As *The Economist* observed: "After seven years of living with the pro-private enterprise governments of Mrs Thatcher, the attitudes of Britons to the financial success of their entrepreneurs has changed little. While the self-made men want to be proud of their success at taking risks, they still find themselves apologising for it."[48]

Britain, however, is not doomed to economic decline, at least not in terms of its underlying economic structure. And this was true long before Thatcher and Thatcherism. As Eatwell has argued: "All the ingredients for economic success are present in abundance. If Britain were a company, she would be a striking example of unrealized commercial potential – ripe for a takeover!"[49] Gamble is equally optimistic: "Britain has all the conditions and advantages necessary for sustaining industrial development and for smoothly adjusting to new patterns of social organization. There are none of the unsuperable obstacles to development found in so many Third World countries."[50]

GOVERNMENT AS PART OF THE SOLUTION

Surely one of the great ironies of the Thatcher era is that she who cried "get the government off the backs of the people" became the most statist postwar premier.[51] But it is not a surprising outcome. Central government now is pivotal. The active involvement of government in interrelated social and economic policies is the distinguishing feature of the postwar welfare state era. Competing political, bureaucratic, economic and sociocultural forces all are reflected in the governmental policymaking process.

Even though the welfare state has its origins in the nineteenth century, World War II is the dividing line marking the period of intensive, continuous, active government involvement in a host of socioeconomic issues. World War II catalyzed national governments driving them from the problems of unemployment and economic collapse to those of mobilizing every resource to survive as free nations.

In Britain after this war came the remarkable Labour governments of 1945–51. The Prime Minister, the (until recently) much underrated Clement Attlee, was a master of the machine – the last competent *managerial* prime minister. He led an extremely talented group who put the modern welfare state in place. However, that government left mainly unchanged the creaky machinery of British central government that was so inadequate to run the modern welfare state, *except in*

37

the hands of an organizational virtuoso like Attlee supported by an exceptional Cabinet.

Looking back today, the question arises "Did the welfare state sink Britain?" However appealing that notion may be in the current conservative climate, the aggregate data on welfare outlays indicate that Britain is well down the list of heavy welfare spenders. OECD data, using total tax receipts as a percentage of Gross Domestic Product, show Great Britain fourth among OECD nations in 1955 but only a single percentage point below the leader (West Germany). The thesis of an initially heavy burden, however, does not hold in that the top handful of nations, which were all closely bunched together in 1955, contains some of the outstanding examples of growth in later years. A quarter of a century later, Great Britain had fallen to ninth among the OECD nations, had recorded the third *lowest* percentage increase between 1955 and 1980, and trailed the leading six nations (all relatively high economic growth countries) by 5 to 15 percentage points. For example, Sweden, the current leader, had tax receipts at almost 50 percent of GDP; Britain was slightly below 36 percent.[52]

The welfare burden in some crude sense of aggregate outlays or average or marginal tax burdens did not debilitate or destroy the British economy. At the same time there is a more subtle impact that suggests interaction between the welfare burden and the British governmental structure. Ashford has argued: "The British political system may be unable to accommodate what is in many ways its most creative accomplishment, the welfare state itself."[53] Wilks more pointedly singled out economic policymakers in observing that "the real interpenetration of state and economy involved in a complex, interdependent welfare state has simply not been recognized by economic policymakers."[54]

The mark of the 1980s has been a growing disquiet in the advanced western nations with the direction of the welfare state. Controversy centers on the financial burden of the public sector claim on national resources and the heavy hand of government – principally national government – in managing the welfare state and the economy. Margaret Thatcher and Ronald Reagan took the lead in calling for reining in government. Government was no longer the solution. It was the problem. That is wrong just as government only as a solution is wrong.

38

Any analysis of central government must start with how pervasive it has become in the postwar years. Current central governments engage directly in fiscal and monetary management, business regulation and industrial development. They create the physical infrastructure (e.g., roads, airports, etc.) central to commercial activities, own industries, and in the aggregate claim a significant proportion of national product. Pervasive central government is a brute fact.

The large-scale organization (or organizations) called government can be successful problem solvers. Extreme threats of which war is the best example have called forth both leadership and the national resolve of the citizenry to work together. One part of the peace time "Battle of Britain" is to recognize how dire is the economic threat, a second is to make the needed changes. Government's role should be to sell the idea of the urgency and to take the pivotal role in leading change. Its biggest task of all may be to make the needed changes in central government structure and capacity in that government's own pattern (to recall C. P. Snow's warning) is a critical element of the problem.

A stronger central government, which is not the same as a larger central government, will be needed whether the government's rhetoric is free-market or managed economy. The argument is not ideological. Be the objective more or less government – the journey from the here of Britain today to the desired goal demands strong central government leadership and competence. A dramatic redirection of central government takes great effort and crucial to that effort is *the implementation capability of the central government itself.*

2

AN AMERICAN'S VIEW OF BRITISH GOVERNMENT

Coping with the modern welfare state and the managed economy demands a strong central government. Such a statement for Britain is an argument neither for greater centralization nor for a presidential prime minister. Crucial to my thesis is the notion of strong government at all levels. At the same time various national and international pressures that create the complexity-expectations-competence conundrum drive modern governments toward dominance by the national government and by a single leader. Great effort will be needed to resist such pressures. A clear danger is an imbalance with too great a dominance by a prime minister or the central government.

Such imbalance often comes about either because of a basic misunderstanding of government power or because of efforts at personal aggrandizement. If the test of governance is policy performance, the distribution of power is not a zero sum game (a gain being precisely offset by a loss). A strong prime minister does not imply a weak, dominated Cabinet; strong central government does not demand docile local authorities cowering before the Treasury. *Effectiveness requires a strong prime minister, ministers and ministries, and local authorities where strong encompasses the notion of competent.* Only under such circumstances is relatively good performance (policy outcomes) a reasonable likelihood. With good policy performance there can be multiple winners. How efficiently and effectively can weak ministers carry out the strategy a strong prime minister wants followed, or weak local authorities provide the needed services central government desires? Only if performance is turned on its head to be equated solely with spending reductions or personal dominance does weakness appear as a virtue. In the policy performance game, winning is unlikely to occur *without* strong government at all levels.[1]

Much too often, a prime minister wants to dominate ministers, pull power up to No. 10, and keep departments weak. Parliament is an arena where the opposition seeks to embarrass the government of the day and mandarins arm ministers to parry attacks and score points. Politics and policy performance are hopelessly intertwined requiring a delicate balance for effectiveness. If politics is too dominant, a premodern government structure can continue. In the British case Parliament is the starting place for seeing the imbalance between politics and policy performance.

PARLIAMENT

In this section I am going to ignore the House of Lords quite simply because it is not a key factor in the British central government policymaking process. To do this is not to deny that the House of Lords on occasion adds to public debate or that its committees may have more expertise available among members and more time to deliberate than the committees in the House of Commons. Still what is written about powerlessness is even more appropriate to the House of Lords than to the House of Commons while the former has almost none of the power of the latter. So in the rest of the book the term "Parliament" is used interchangeably with "House of Commons" except where a distinction between the two Houses is demanded for purposes of clarity.

From the American perspective the British Parliament and individual members, even in the so-called golden age of the House of Commons between the Reform Acts, were relatively weak, and since then have grown even weaker. There is nothing in the British experience to compare with American congressional government of the nineteenth century or with the powerful individual committee chair of today who can defy both the president and the rest of Congress. Parliament is a legitimizing, not a legislative, body. There is much truth in Bruce George's remarks made during 1983 debate on the Exchequer and Audit Department (now National Audit Office):

If we look at the 150 legislatures of the world, we see the two ends of a continuum. There is on the one side the United States which has a genuine

41

legislature and on the other side there are the minimal legislatures of the Eastern bloc and legislatures within dictatorships.

If I were asked on which side of the center of the continuum we are, I should say that we are nearer the side of the minimal legislature than the genuine legislature.[2]

Power and powerlessness

Two images of Parliament emerge – power and powerlessness – seemingly in direct conflict. Yet both images are real. Parliament turns out to be a relatively powerless body that has real power because it is perceived as powerful by the prime minister, ministers, MPs and mandarins. All focus an inordinate amount of attention on what goes on both on the floor of the Commons and in terms of what backbenchers say and think. Parliamentary centrality flows from a myopic perspective, not from the raw power to impede the government of the day that wants to act. *Parliament's primary source of power is the overreaction of governments to what happens in Parliament because Cabinet members and mandarins alike have been socialized that way during their careers.*

Parliament is the centripetal force that dominates the attention and concern of ministers and mandarins. Here political careers are made or destroyed. Prime ministers, cabinet members, and junior ministers focus intently on the views of party backbenchers and on how the opposition may interpret and attack their statements and actions. Philip Norton argues that "Government backbenchers are the most important Members in the House as far as the Government is concerned."[3] Top mandarins and high flyers devote much of their considerable talents to helping the ninety to a hundred members of the government to carry out their parliamentary duties, which disproportionately consist of answering the opposition. In this image, Parliament dominates the British political/bureaucratic world. It is not only powerful but too powerful.[4]

The second image is of weakness. The Mother of Parliaments is primarily a formal debating society where the government and the opposition stake out clearly different positions that enhance adversarial politics and Westminster games but have little to do directly with policymaking. However, as George Jones has pointed out to me, there can be an indirect impact on policymaking flowing from the "law of anticipated reaction." What is so difficult to discern is whether the government's reaction is to expected policy criticism or to possible personal or party embarrassment.

Parliament (derived from the Old French *parlement*) by its very name is supposed to talk. It is a talking shop and so are most legislative bodies. But legislatures can talk or debate in committees and sub-committees. *The issue is whether or not the debate is informed and that depends in part both on available information and analyses and the debaters' capacity to use such information and analyses.* Information availability often depends on the government's willingness to provide it and the pressure brought to bear to pry it loose. The latter is not simply a function of power or prerogative but of analytic capacity to delve into what information is available. Yet Parliament has gone out of its way to restrict available information and analyses by providing members and select committees with limited numbers of staff, by avoiding meaningful dialogue with civil servants (somewhat changed with the new select committees as discussed shortly), and by support-ing secrecy legislation making it the most closed government among advanced Western nations.

In the case of a government with a clear working majority the duality of parliamentary dominance and weakness yields a virtual monopoly on policymaking by an elite handful of ministers and mandarins. At any one time there is policymaking by a one party oligarchy of ministers and their top mandarins insulated against constructive policymaking pressures because of their monopoly con-trol over information. *The duality produces a relatively uninformed, ineffective Parliament combined with a small ruling elite of ministers and mandarins who have a near monopoly on decisionmaking yet have neither the will nor the tools and techniques to engage in effective policymaking.*

In this stark portrait of Parliament, no effort has been made to paint in the grey shadings. Parliament has become less docile in recent years. Philip Norton has admirably documented the changing mood of Parliament such that "the Government knows that it cannot rely upon the *unthinking* loyalty of backbenchers to see it through."[5] The departmental select committees and an upgraded National Audit Office reflect a growing parliamentary concern for scrutiny. Ministers and mandarins do not see themselves as an all powerful oligarchy – a small ruling elite in control. On rare occasions Parliament will defy the government but usually there are mitigating circumstances. Take the

Shops Bill to remove restrictions on stores being open on Sunday. The government lost by fourteen votes with over sixty Tories against that bill. *The Economist* on April 19, 1986 argued that "it was the government's biggest Commons defeat," but went on to observe: "In truth, the failure of the government has less to do with Westminster politics and more with campaigns in the churches, village halls and high streets of the country ... It was Britain's most notable example of successful single-issue politics, and its first taste of the political power of moral fervor." Having watched U.S. Congress members in panic over an attack from the radical right (particularly its religious wing), parliamentary fear seems the overriding factor rather than newfound parliamentary power. The stark portrait is essentially accurate. *The duality of Parliament's power and powerlessness lies at the heart of Britain's problem of pre-modern, anti-modern governance.* We need to explore further this odd beast the British Parliament.

What is Parliament's role in governance?

However much disagreement there may be on what Parliament should be doing, one point is clear: Parliament does not govern. It has neither the *legislative* nor the *policymaking* functions. These are on the "executive" side. For an American, a legislature without either of these functions is a most limited body. What then is Parliament supposed to do? Norton points out that

the main functions of the House of Commons may be said to be those of providing the personnel of government, of representation, of sustaining and providing a forum of debate for the Government and Opposition parties, of legitimizing the Government and its measures, of scrutinizing and influencing the measures and actions of Government, and of performing a number of minor ... functions ... If one were to seek to provide a simple, one-word description of the central role of the House of Commons derived from [these] functions ... then the most apt word would probably be 'watchdog.'[6]

Of Norton's five functions, only staffing the top of the government (a crucial function discussed separately later) is not a watchdog activity broadly construed. Representation, except in serving constituents, implies MPs "taking the pulse" of their constituencies in order to bring voters' views to their deliberations. Legitimization can be seen as the final result of the watchdog effort in putting the stamp of approval on legislation. The two key related operational aspects of

44

the watchdog effort are debate and scrutiny. The central issue is whether "watchdogging" can be made more effective in the constrained setting where Parliament has no legislative or policymaking functions.

The most traditional watchdog effort is debate between the government of the day and the opposition. Yet Smith and Polsby argue that "[parliamentary question time] is the modern political equivalent of the medieval tournament ... [A] flash of wit is worth an hour of administrative wisdom. Question time is therefore an opportunity for a fair amount of political knockabout humor and entertainment."[7] If calling the government to account is the goal, question time – or more generally the adversarial style that has so long characterized the Parliament – does not do the watchdog job. It is an unfair game. Individual MPs have minimal staff support, really none for probing policy issues. In a battle of pre-modern forces, the government simply has far more people and ammunition.

In no way is the power of Parliament better symbolized than by question time. It is a kind of perpetual test given over and over again to political executives to demonstrate their political manhood (Thatcher included). In that sense, question time is all important in Britain, and worth committing mandarins to the joust in the role of arming their knights. West Germany copied Britain by introducing question time in 1951 but answers are seldom given by ministers or the chancellor. As Mayntz points out: "Neither the public nor the media are much interested in what happens in question time, and no member of the government need feel that his reputation depends on his performance."[8]

The new select committees and the National Audit Office

Two recent steps have aimed at redressing the imbalance between the House of Commons and the government of the day. First, departmental select committees were established in 1979. Second, Parliament strengthened the Comptroller & Auditor General (C&AG) through the 1983 National Audit Act that took effect on January 1, 1984. Both changes are not only important in themselves but well illustrate the great difficulty of major institutional change in British central government. Philip Giddings in the excellent volume of essays, *The New Select Committees*, has captured this theme:

The leader of the House of Commons when the committees were set up spoke boldly and perhaps rhetorically in terms of a radical constitutional innovation. He, and other advocates of the new system, saw it as shift in the balance of power between government and Parliament, an episode in the Commons' historical struggle to control the executive. But what has actually happened is rather different. It is a *marginal, incremental adjustment* to one of the features of the complex web of inter-relationships between the House of Commons and Ministers of the Crown in a system of parliamentary government.[9]

The fourteen departmental select committees, composed of back-benchers from all parties, hold hearings with the remit to call witnesses including ministers and mandarins, issue reports and generally track the assigned departments and associated public bodies. A typical select committee will be served by a small number of permanent staff members, one or two of whom are likely to be administrative clerks with Oxbridge credentials and will have been tested with similar procedures to those of civil service administrative trainees. For all of the departmental select committees, there are roughly sixty to seventy outside part-time special advisers, some of whom may be national experts working on a limited consulting basis.[10]

In the Giddings and Drewry assessment chapters at the end of *The New Select Committees*, the former stresses greater ministerial accountability; the later, more civil servant accountability. Giddings points out: "What might ... pass unchallenged on the floor of the House is not so likely to slip through an alert select committee, particularly on an issue which has excited the attention of interest groups ... Though it may be accountability rather than control, after rather than before the event, the new system has substantially increased the liability of decisionmakers ... to answer Parliament, to explain, justify, defend, and to do so (largely) in public and on the record."[11] While recognizing the rather severe constraints put on what civil servants can say before select committees, Drewry argues that bringing civil servants into the picture is a critical contribution: "This small dent in the minister's personal monopoly of departmental answerability is probably the most significant constitutional by-product of committee development over the last two decades, and the new committees have considerably deepened the dent."[12]

Weakness and problems abound. Although nearly 200 select committee reports were an increasing source of information generally and hence contributed to openness, Lock pointed out that only nineteen reports (10 percent) in the period 1979/80 to 1982/3 were debated directly or indirectly by the House.[13] Several committees complained that staffs are too small for the government departments to be monitored and lack sufficient specialists.[14] At the same time the select committees have made only limited use of National Audit Office staff thereby not drawing on Parliament's only big staff.[15] Indeed, an administrative clerk told me: "The lack of staff comes more from lack of demand [from MPs] than from stringency on the supply side." Moreover, there is no demand for in depth scrutiny so select committee staffs seldom engage in extended policy analysis.[16] MPs do not think in terms of hard analysis and may not do much thinking at all about the select committees. An interviewee told me that committee members sometimes "break the seal" on the envelopes providing background material for a committee meeting when they sit down for the meeting.

While the claim that backbench members are either "has beens" or "never will bes" is overstated, the quality of the committees leaves much to be desired. More critically, upwardly mobile MPs do not expect to make their careers on a select committee. High turnover may be the real problem. Lock shows an overall turnover rate for 1979–83 of roughly 40 percent (range 11 to 77 percent) and notes that of eighty-seven members originally appointed, fifty-three were either promoted to ministerial positions or the opposition front bench.[17] Status and power of the kind flowing to a U.S. congressional committee chair do not exist. Still, Beloff and Peele report: "[T]here have been some cases of opposition MPs preferring work on a select committee to being a front-bench spokesman ... John Golding preferred to be chairman of the Select Committee on Employment rather than seek a Labour opposition front-bench portfolio."[18] Committee service, however, will be central only for "has beens" and "never will bes."

The overall judgments on the select committees' experience thus far are discouraging. The new select committees are a minor appendage to the main efforts of the House of Commons and the departments. Drewry argues that "the interconnection between committee activity and proceedings on the floor have been *disappointingly patchy*"; Giddings finds that "the effect of these committees on ministerial and departmental policymaking has been *indirect, and marginal, contextual rather than substantive*."[19] Drewry offers the analogy that "the select committees are a small squad of Davids facing an army of departmental Goliaths."[20] The analogy is much too kind in suggesting that the select committees like David might win or that the sling shot contains pebbles that can do real damage rather than ink pellets that can only embarrass.

A House of Commons staff interviewee suggested that "the set up now is about as powerful as the select committees are likely to get." The implication is that the government of the day – not only currently but in the future – will let them go no further because select committees are potential attackers of government policies. Parliament in this sense is a creature of the government of the day.[21]

Finally, critics of the new departmental select committees argue they may be doing harm in misshaping Parliament. One claim is that the "select committees are based on American models which are inherently incompatible with a system where Parliament exists to sustain the government."[22] Second, the new committees distract attention from the House of Commons chamber which is the appropriate forum for parliamentary affairs. Third, the committees create a superior class of backbenchers who have much more information than the nonmembers.[23] Fourth, as George Jones argues: "Policymaking is a matter for Government and the parties. If MPs wish to engage in policymaking, and they are not in Government, they should operate through their party organizations."[24] Policymaking is not the function of Parliament as an entity separate from the government. Fifth, select committees add to the burden of already overburdened MPs who could spend their time far more constructively engaged in party efforts at scrutiny and challenge.[25]

The tale recorded in *The New Select Committees* is a classic British example of how what appears to be dramatic changes end up as minimum incrementalism. The National Audit Act experience to date offers more of the same. The act freed the Exchequer and Audit Department from Treasury funding control, gave it the new name of National Audit Office (NAO), and made value for money (economy, efficiency, and effectiveness) audits part of the NAO's stated remit although such audits had been performed in the past with the approval of the Public Accounts Committee. Edward du Cann, Chair of the Public Accounts Commission, claims "that Parliament now has an instrument, a method by which activities of government can be brought under a closer and more informed scrutiny. That's a revolution."[26] If revolutions were measured as earthquakes are on a Richter scale, this one would be faintly perceptible thus far.

The key change well may be that the NAO now has the authority and the money to upgrade its staff. Once made up of school leavers with no accounting credentials, NAO now hires bright university graduates and requires that they acquire outside certification as do private auditors. There is no substitute for competence. But its effective use demands stong leadership not just from the top of NAO but from Parliament. By British standards NAO has a large staff numbering 827 with roughly 600 professionals.[27] In the value for money audits concerned with effectiveness, NAO clearly is into a major policy analysis area. But two qualifications are needed. First, the NAO staff is composed of accountants, not policy analysts. Accountants bring a different kind of thinking to effectiveness compared to policy analysts, focusing far more on costs and financial questions than on policy outcomes.[28] Second, neither the Public Accounts Committee nor NAO delve into policy issues by challenging the correctness of objectives. Such a concern is considered a partisan policy issue. Objectives are taken as given; then the question is how well a given objective is being pursued. But taking objectives as given means not undertaking the policy formulation and analytic questions that are critical to analytic thinking. Thus, it might be said that NAO's current remit allows it to tiptoe toward policy analysis but holds it back from major aspects of analytic thinking.

How is the new effort working out? Probably the fairest answer is that it is too early to tell. One early assessment is worth mentioning. After looking at the NAO's first twelve published reports, *Public Money* underscored the low key approach being taken and observed after recognizing a case could be made for going slow: "[T]here is also a case for adopting a more robust approach, particularly now that the Comptroller & Auditor General is entirely free of the Executive, and particularly where the 'gently, gently' approach has clearly failed to work in the past."[29] There is little question that over the last decade Parliament has become more serious about scrutiny. Still, "gently, gently" captures the situation. More tools are available. But whether Parliament has the political will to move the long distance it needs to go to use scrutiny effectively, is far from clear. To obtain greater insight on this question, we need to look more closely yet at Britain's most exclusive club.

Parliament writ large

Thus far, Parliament has been treated as separate from the government of the day. For example, asking what are Parliament's functions in the previous subsection casts Parliament either as a single body separable from the government (as in the case of select committees) or as the main vehicle by which the opposition challenges the government. Now we need to think of Parliament broadly as including the ministers – prime minister, ministers, and junior ministers – in their executive roles. The first thing to note is that Parliament has as members all the major active politicians involved *directly* in the national governance effort. The second is Parliament's exclusiveness. A former member, Edmund Dell, has categorized one of Britain's most anachronistic animals quite aptly: "The House of Commons is not just an exclusive club, it is a club one of whose objectives it is to exclude."[30] One outcome of exclusiveness – ministers being members – is treated later in the chapter. At this point the focus is on how this exclusive club really operates.

Earlier the adversarial style of Parliament was stressed. The Westminster game often is a classic debate setting where the two sides try to score points. Insults, name calling, and misuse or distortion of information are all "fair" and likely to be sound tactics. But things are more calm below the surface. Indeed, Professor Richard Rose has pointed out that a study of the whole legislative record shows roughly 80 percent of legislation is not the subject of divisions of principle and argues that there is more a consensus than an adversarial model.[31] Parliament is really a rather tame place because the government pulls its punches: "The government of the day denies itself much of the power nominally granted by its absolute majority in order to ensure that most measures it introduces will receive the tacit support of the opposition party, as well as the active support of its own backbenchers."[32] Parliament's tameness comes from the behavior of the party in power, not the party in opposition. What blocks the government from "controversial" bills is fear (anticipated reaction) of backbencher revolt, of opposition party disagreement, some combination of these two, or of a black mark for the next election.

Rose offers a "conspiracy" theory to explain why the government is so timid. It is the mutual self interest of those *currently* in power and both the frontbenchers and rising young stars *likely* to be in power later. Rose argued:

The fundamental political conflict is ... between the inveterate backbenchers, whether Conservative or Labour, and frontbenchers enjoying the powers of office ...
If House of Commons reform was simply caught up in Adversary conflict between the Conservative and Labour parties, the swing of the electoral pendulum would sooner or later give a majority to the reformers. In fact, the adversaries are not evenly matched. The proponents of reform are *permanently* condemned to being on the "outs" with government. Quondam supporters turn into opponents of reform once they enter government and enjoy all the advantages of dominating an unreformed House of Commons.[33]

Even though not necessarily a safe arena, the House of Commons is well-travelled terrain where parliamentarians and mandarins know the rules and have a store of precedents built up over many years. The world avoided is that of serious policymaking. That arena is both unsafe and unknown where neither parliamentarian nor mandarin is likely to have had much experience. Skills will not have been tested. It is an uncharted sea full of unknown risks. Better the joust.

It is well not to be entirely negative in light of the steps Parliament has taken. Still "gently, gently" is unlikely to convert Parliament to an effective watchdog. *If Parliament remains a nineteenth-century anachronism, fixated on chamber debate, British government is most unlikely to modernize.* Yet Parliament in more narrow terms is not its own master – or, more accurately, does not see itself as its own master. Major parliamentary reform demands government leadership, or a radically different image of Parliament.

The U.S. Congress offers a good example of legislative independence. Under "normal" circumstances, party discipline holds even though not with the force it does in Britain. At the same time Congress is extremely jealous of its independence. A president who affronts *Congress as an institution* is almost certainly to be punished swiftly and overwhelmingly. For example, in 1974, Congress came to feel that President Richard Nixon was usurping one of its most basic powers by impounding (i.e., refusing to spend) funds Congress had appropriated. Not to spend funds Congress has mandated fundamentally threatens Congress' independence from the Executive. Congress' response was budget and impoundment legislation that passed with a total of two negative votes from both Houses of Congress.

Parliament no doubt can go a little further in enhancing its powers of scrutiny. But making a major jump is likely only if Parliament acts as a body against the Executive. At this point, however, Parliament remains on the government of the day's leash.

PRIME MINISTER AND CABINET

Parliament's strange combination in being both all powerful and powerless produces at the center an exceptionally strong executive (prime minister *and* Cabinet) stuck in the mire of parliamentary myth and mores but relatively unfettered by explicit institutional barriers. Anthony Lester in discussing Parliament's absolute sovereignty cites A. V. Dicey on "the absolute legislative sovereignty or despotism of the King in Parliament" and observes:

The principle of parliamentary sovereignty means that Parliament has the right to make and unmake any law whatever ... [Britain has] laws which may be called fundamental or constitutional because they deal with important principles lying at the basis of our institutions ... [but] there is no such thing as a supreme law, or law which tests the validity of other laws ... *The main safeguards against the abuse of power by the Government in Parliament are therefore not legally enforceable* ... [T]he role of our judges in protecting human rights is closely confined both by the subordinate position of the courts in relation to the omnipotent legislature and by a widespread public philosophy which welcomes the narrowness of the judicial mandate in this country.[34]

From an American perspective with our checks and balances in a written constitution, the absence of explicit institutional constraints in British central government is mind-boggling. Here is raw power – truly an omnipotent legislation unrestrained by defined institutional barriers. Yet in turn Parliament is dominated by the prime minister and Cabinet.

The prime minister as leader and catalyst

The prime minister's leadership role is particularly critical in Britain. Where else can leadership come from? In the United States it can be said that at times Congress or the Supreme Court leads. It even makes sense to speak of state and local leadership. As Richard Neustadt has pointed out, the U.S. Constitution did not create a government of separate powers but rather "created a government of separated institutions *sharing* powers."[35] Neustadt for his purposes emphasized the sharing of power among the separate institutions. The institutions also can act alone. For example, the House and the Senate can change their own internal procedures without presidential approval even if the changes impinge on presidential-congressional relationships. More importantly, the separate and independent institutions sharing power can take the initiative – can take the leadership role. Although the president is the likely leader, leadership can come from another independent center. In particular, Congress can set out on its own, awkward as that may be in this chief executive-centered era.

Where there is real independence of institutions in the United States, the mark in Britain is interdependence. The British central government system is so interdependent and so secret that leadership responsibility is difficult to pin down. At least until Thatcher it seemed to reside in the minister (including prime minister)-mandarin monopoly. Mrs Thatcher, however, makes clear that the prime minister stands atop the entire central government.

Raw power, as discussed, is seldom used because of the timidity of the government of the day.[36] But the power potential is there. In recognizing it, *we isolate the key point for giving direction, not just to the center or to the Executive or to the central government but throughout British society*. In Britain, interdependence keeps leading back to the prime minister. Even if prime ministers cannot force fundamental change, their negative power of stopping change is overwhelming. Although basic change in Parliament is fundamental to government modernization, the power point for change is the prime minister (and Cabinet). Unlike Congress, Parliament will not go it alone. Nor is the center likely to build strong analytic and strategic capacity and utilize it or to engage in positive management without prime ministerial leadership. Who but the prime minister can be the catalyst for major change?

Near dictatorial power

Harold Wilson wrote in *The Governance of Britain* that "it is essential at the outset [of this book] to deal with the great debate that has dominated academic discussion for many years – the question, has the system of Cabinet government described by Bagehot a little over a century ago given way to a *quasi-presidential prime ministerial auto-*

cracy?"[37] Lord Wilson writing in the pre-Thatcher era came down clearly for the Cabinet. He argued that Richard Crossman, who had attacked the Bagehot thesis, was himself the "classical" refutation of his argument in his own service in the Wilson Cabinet of 1964–70 through Crossman's "unfailing, frequently argumentative, role ... in ruthlessly examining every proposal, policy or projection put before Cabinet by departmental ministers – or by the prime minister."[38] Lord Wilson then went on to observe: "John Morley, whose much-quoted *primus inter pares* has led to his frequent condemnation as a complacent Bagehotian, himself rightly described the prime minister as 'the Keystone of the Cabinet Arch,' but went on to refer to 'powers always great and in an emergency not inferior to those of a dictator.' The key here is the reference to an 'emergency.'"[39]

Lord Wilson argues correctly that the experience with Winston Churchill as near dictator during World War II must be discounted. However, the Morley statement points out that the prime minister's nonemergency "powers [are] always great." What Lord Wilson does not discuss because he is focusing on prime minister *or* Cabinet is that prime minister *and* Cabinet usually have powers "not inferior to those of a dictator."

Cabinet itself is part of the exceedingly strong base a prime minister has for being a catalyst and much more. As Hennessy argues: "Cabinet government remains a putty-like concept. A prime minister can make of it very largely what he or she will, provided colleagues do not baulk at their treatment."[40] Ezra Suleiman writing in 1980 argued that "the President of France is, in many respects, probably the most powerful executive in the western world."[41] The last several years have qualified that statement when Socialist President Francois Mitterand was forced to share power with the neo-Gaullists for the first period of "cohabitation" in the short history of the Fifth Republic. While the "imperial presidency" in France has been diminished recently, events in Britain have underscored that the small group at the top has far more power to bring legislative change than an American or a French president. Mrs Thatcher in 1984 made clear how close British central government can come to near dictatorship. Donald Shell observed in his review of the 1984 Parliament: "Mrs Thatcher's government of 1984 was unusually strong. 'Elective dictatorship' [the key phrase of Lord Hailsham's 1976 lecture] is, of course, an over-simplification, but if ever the phrase had been applicable, it was appropriate now. *Parliament could be a nuisance to government*; but if so, this was more likely to be in expressing the views of groups to whom the Conservative Party was naturally sensitive."[42]

The discussion so far has been cast in relative power terms – the prime minister relative to the Cabinet and the two together relative to Parliament. Care must be taken not to confuse relative power within a government and the absolute power of a government. The latter has to do with policy performance where the pre-modern nature of the British structure intrudes and significantly reduces the exercise of absolute power. In his critical evaluation of the Cabinet, Hennessy wrote:

My own prejudice ... is that a 1916-model Cabinet machine is, despite later modifications, not up to the stresses and strains of the economically and socially disturbed eighties – let alone the post-North-Sea-oil nineties; that, even if we had paragons placed around the Cabinet table instead of ordinary human beings, they would still be hobbled by the flawed instruments at their disposal; that ... it is time for a prime minister to do a Lloyd George on the machine and to commission ... an inquiry which tackles the system as a whole examining both the Cabinet and the departmental structure which buttresses it."[43]

THE SECRECY SYNDROME AND CLOSED GOVERNMENT

Cockerell, Hennessy and Walker charge that the parliamentary press Lobby is spoonfed willingly through mass, nonattributable briefings from "sources close to the prime minister" rather than engaging in hard investigative reporting and close their harsh critique with this statement:

At the end of 1984 the Conservative *Mail on Sunday* bemoaned the increasing tendency of the government to be more and more secretive and claimed that it daily misused the Official Secrets Act ... Britain is the most backward country in the whole of the Western world both in the ability of the press properly to investigate the "great and the good" and in the refusal of all governments actually to trust the people with the information to which they are fully entitled.
The newspaper did not add that part of the remedy lies in the hands of journalists ... [who] must not allow themselves to be used as ... accomplices in concealment.[44]

The recent withdrawal of a few newspapers from the Lobby may signal the start of basic change, but I fear my recent claim still holds: "Blend together the 1911 act, the Lobby, and Mrs Thatcher's skillful news management and the result is the most consistent, most effective government information manipulation in memory, likely ever in Britain."[45] In Britain, those who have followed the Iran-Contra affair and watched the behavior of the American press, led by such prestigious newspapers as *The New York Times* and *The Washington Post*, may fear an active press.[46] Britain's counterpart, however, by almost any measure is at the other extreme with the Lobby, as presently constituted, ill-serving their nation's need for greater openness.

That secrecy is central to the minister/mandarin monopoly is of critical concern in the next section. Secrecy may be a symptom rather than a cause of Britain's problems. But once in place, secrecy becomes the shield that protects Britain's rulers from being held responsible for governance, the mandarin's information and advice monopoly, and the oligopoly power of a handful of policymakers at the top. Given all of these "benefits," secrecy has its adamant defenders. Cockerell, Hennessy, and Walker have observed: "Secrecy is built into the calcium of every British policymaker's bones. It is the essence of his – or her – concept of good governance."[47] But of late secrecy has been challenged by establishment figures including former permanent secretaries, Sir Patrick Nairne and Sir Douglas Wass; just as surprising, the First Division Association of Civil Servants has supported the principle of freedom of information.[48]

There is a case to be made for secrecy beyond guarding national security or protecting proprietary business information. Inside advisers need to know their advice will be privileged lest they hold back speculative ideas and comments. Open deliberations can force political advocates to forsake compromise and fight for extreme positions that please a constituency or interest group. Too much openness can cause public servants to worry excessively about how they appear not what they do. But Britain goes much too far. Secrecy – more broadly closed government – shuts out the information, advice and interaction that puts ideas to the test. It sets up a weighting system that overvalues the people, the ideas, and the information on the inside. Clive Ponting illustrates the point by drawing on experience at the Ministry of Defense where "the published studies [of outside institutes on strategic and defense issues] were usually greeted with amused contempt within MOD."[49] Ponting may be suspect, a disgruntled victim, but his case is substantiated from the top of the Ministry of Defense in this statement by Sir Frank Cooper, the permanent secretary at MOD from 1976 to 1982: "[Defense and foreign affairs] are not areas where there is a great deal of widespread expertise in this country. In defense in particular there are very few other experts and [the Ministry of] Defense has a near monopoly. In terms of foreign affairs? Well, people certainly write history and write pieces about foreign affairs. But again there is a limited knowledge of the real relations that one country has with another."[50] How revealing a statement. *Those poor, uninformed fellows on the outside may write in their amateurish way but the best and the brightest (civil servants) have an information monopoly and no doubt superior intelligence.* The insiders do not need outside help.

The great cost of secrecy is that it reduces or eliminates the kind of competition that improves information, analysis, and ideas. Strong competition improves the players and hence the game. Assume two young tennis players, both with much natural talent but A clearly superior to B at age eighteen. Suppose A restricts himself only to those British tennis tournaments where the top international players do not compete while B plays on the international circuit. It is likely that A will be unbeatable in the minor tournaments whilst B well may lose frequently in international competition. At age twenty-one, however, I'd pick B with his tools sharpened in the international arena against A. The mandarins are much like A – ever so talented and untested in open competition.

Both Ponting and Cockerell and his colleagues stress that secrecy is the enemy of democracy in barring people from the decision process. But democracy is a separate issue. Secrecy is to be rejected on more pragmatic grounds – it hampers effective governance. As *New York Times* columnist Anthony Lewis observed so pointedly: "Can anyone really believe that repression of criticism leads to efficiency in a society, to new ideas? Look at the Soviet Union. Or look at Britain, which despite its democratic character has the most repressive press laws of any major Western country – and the worst record of failed government policy."[51] Lewis well may go too far both in judging British policy and in his cause and effect assumption but it is hard to argue against the deadening impact of secrecy. And in this sense, secrecy does threaten British democracy.

57

MINISTERS AND MANDARINS

Four basic points need to be discussed about the ministers and mandarins who monopolize British central government. First, government departments are large-scale bureaucracies with all of the advantages and disadvantages associated with such entities. Second, neither through party nor parliamentary experience are ministers prepared to lead the large public sector organizations they head. Third, the mandarins are not prepared for modern management, particularly to be the modern generalists demanded by the complexity of the advanced welfare state. Fourth, people from the outside need to be brought into British policymaking but the supply of capable persons is thin.

Bureaucracies

The term "bureaucracy" has negative connotations with "bureaucrat" having an increasingly pejorative ring. This tendency is unfortunate. A large-scale organization in either the public or private sector must have a specified structure, functions, and hierarchies. Some must lead and others follow. There would be chaos without organization. Changing an organization is a major means of solving problems. At the same time organizational or bureaucratic pathologies such as red tape, means becoming ends, and turf battles, can debilitate a public or private organization. Not to understand the nature of large-scale organizations – the potential for solving problems and for pathological behavior – is a debilitating flaw for any leader of a complex private or public entity.

What marks the public sector organization is the coming together of politicians who may have limited organizational experience generally and little or no experience in the organization to be led and permanent civil servants who have long service and know the bureaucratic game in their organization. Further, support of the status quo is characteristic behavior for career staff in bureaucracies – public and private. Be that as it may, part of the leadership equation is sufficient knowledge about those to be led – their strengths, their weaknesses, their institutional codes and customs – so that the intangibles of leadership can be applied effectively. That means politicians wanting to influence policies need knowledge about how large public bureaucracies work.

The anthropology of the machine must be fathomed before organizational mastery can be exercised. Such knowledge is a fundamental aspect of the politician's responsibility.

Political masters and career officials do not always agree. Such clashes can have desirable aspects. As Dell argues: "[T]he last thing it must be is a deferential civil service. If the sky gets darker and darker and Ministers sail on as though through the calmest sea, civil servants should have something better to do than provide good briefs protecting Ministers from good arguments."[52]

Ministers as managers

Ministers are not equipped to manage large-scale organizations. Nor generally speaking, do they want to manage. Even if they do, the task is made difficult by the existing structure of British central government. The British reader well may remark that the last two statements are correct but irrelevant. Ministers are not supposed to manage. Barbara Castle, when Secretary of State at the Department of Health and Social Security, wrote in her diary: "[B]ecause Philip Rogers [DHSS Permanent Secretary] has got touchy about our doing things behind his back, I said he must be informed first. *After all, as overall manager of the department, he has his rights.*"[53] Whether Mrs Castle is more condescending towards Rogers or toward managing is unclear, but that management is an inferior task – not performed by a Secretary of State – is most clear.[54] The management function in this book, however, is not a minor task to be shunned by the leader but rather merges with the leadership function at the top. Those at the top should not be engaged extensively in micro-management tasks but they must give direction to the organization if it is to succeed in its organizational objectives.

Neither party nor Parliament prepares ministers to govern. They are not "organization-men." Few ministers even have any experience working in large organizations. To make matters worse, the Cabinet minister is overloaded with duties. He remains an MP with the usual constituency and parliamentary duties plus being a government spokesman. He is charged with collective responsibility for what his government does so he participates as a member of Cabinet and Cabinet committees that handle national and international issues.

Finally, he is charged with leading a department with thousands of staff and a host of complex functions.

What does the new minister shunt aside to make the overload manageable? He is familiar with constituency and parliamentary activities. Cabinet puts him with colleagues he has worked with before. Only the department throws him into an unknown environment. And here he can find an escape – the mandarins standing ready to care and feed the minister. As Young and Sloman have pointed out aptly in *No Minister*: "Academics, journalists and backbench MPs may castigate the bureaucracy, doubt its competence, question its energy, jealously observe its pretensions to power, but ministers give little hint of this. *They tend to marvel at the civil servants' industry, integrity and sheer availability*."[55] The Thatcher government's efforts call this statement somewhat into question, but it remains generally accurate.

Lacking is the concept of strong ministers with enough organizational flexibility to develop their own management teams and sufficient institutional knowledge to provide managerial direction. This problem extends to the basic approach to government appointments where the evidence indicates that the government of the day either does not want managerial control or else does not appreciate its specific demands (again the Thatcher years are an exception). First, the game of ministerial musical chairs, which has ministers serving on the average of two to two and a half years, suggests that political factors, not executive or management capacity, is the main reason for ministerial appointment. Second, there often is outright wastage of the precious few political spots in the departments through making the appointment of junior ministers mainly a party political exercise with little regard either for the needs or sensitivities of the secretary of state or for the substantive or managerial skills of the appointees. Junior minister positions still seem to be conceived of as "finishing school" training for potential cabinet ministers, in essence preparing them mainly for roles in the cabinet team and as departmental spokespersons in Parliament. Indeed, the junior minister position is an almost perfect creation for seeing that ministers do *not* have people serving them they can call their own in the sense of sharing a basic commitment. As Klein and Lewis have pointed out in comparing junior ministers and special advisers: "Junior Ministers are usually picked by the Prime Minister. They are not dependent on their

60

departmental Minister, may not necessarily be congenial to him and may even see themselves as long-term rivals to him ... MPs are unlikely to offer the unreserved personal loyalty which ... is the hallmark of the special adviser."[56] The argument is not that these appointments should have no political overtones, but surely there must be a more sensible way to build a departmental team. Third, there is the lack of almost any appointments of additional (nonelected) outsiders to serve the minister directly. Further, the few political advisers chosen generally have been people with party political, not policy and organizational, skills.

Fourth, Britain places permanent civil servants closer to the top than almost any other country and makes it difficult to remove a permanent secretary. Of critical importance, the status of the permanent secretary is unclear. Is he the number two person in the department ranking above junior ministers? If not, where does the permanent secretary fit in the chain of command? What is the relationship between the ministers and the higher civil servants below the permanent secretary? What commitment do these civil servants have to the ministers and to the permanent secretary? Even if career civil servants are nonpartisan, either having no strong party commitment or submerging such commitment to an even stronger commitment to professional public service, a basic tension remains between the commitment to political masters and commitment to the department as continuing organization, the public interest, and the career civil service and civil service superiors. It should be thus. But if so, the case is compelling that ministers should be able to bring in outsiders they have vetted for personal commitment, a vetting inappropriate for career officials.

My point, is not that a new minister necessarily inherits a bad permanent secretary and acquires inept junior ministers. But the new minister who really wants to exert political control has limited maneuvering room if he is dealt a bad hand. *The structure is anti-management*.

Mandarins

Although the British civil service exhibits the classic bureaucratic traits of conservatism (small "c") and a bias toward existing policies, it is *not* as obstructionist as suggested in recent books and crystalized in the Kellner and Crowther-Hunt subtitle labeling the British civil service as "Britain's Ruling Class."[57] Their detailed analysis conjures up a civil service that moves purposely and skillfully to render minsters powerless with political control taken overtly from them. One of my most perceptive interviewees – a mandarin but an irreverent one – argues that higher civil servants are extremely constitutional in their thinking. They want leadership from the political executives. So often they do not find that leadership, but rather a minister deeply concerned with his parliamentary performance, yet uninterested in managing an organization (in truth having only the vaguest notion of what managing is). A vacuum at the top is created. Civil servants are sucked into it willing or not. The end result is that the British system provides too much power to the high civil servants and in turn magnifies their deficiencies.

The highest level civil servants are among the best and brightest of Britain's traditional professional elites. Their strongest suit is maintaining stability and "fixing things" (to use the descriptive term of a mandarin interviewee) including shoring up weak minsters or keeping imprudent ones in bounds. *What the mandarins have done so well, however, has been performed with the traditional (pre-modern) tools of the trade honed over many years.*

Particularly for the real flyers who eventually reach the highest positions, the early plums are positions such as private secretary to a minister or a secondment to the Cabinet Secretariat – i.e., those that focus *upward* toward the top away from managing policy. Frequent position changes for high flyers mean they become highly competent in Westminster games yet often do not accumulate either program-specific knowledge or experience in managing policy, especially in local affairs where domestic policies get executed. Managing major departmental programs on a daily basis is a job for junior personnel or "failed" administrative class people who are seen by the mandarins as not being able to make it to the top levels. Garrett put the matter bluntly arguing that the mandarins consider management "a second-rate occupation for practical men, in esteem well below the all-around good chap, the natural top administrator and policymaker."[58] Historically management in the British departments generally has stopped in the middle with final responsibility resting with "outcast" under secretaries who will never make it to the key policy jobs.

The higher civil servants are masters of bureaucratic politics both within their departments and "outside" in inter-department negotiations. This capability is so often the fine art of palace intrigue rather than the mundane mastery over large organizational units. What has been created is a man for all seasons in parliamentary and highest level bureaucratic politics but one who is not much exposed to implementing or managing policies as they move to the field. Using a military analogy, it is as if all the emphasis is upon developing staff personnel who along the way to the top will be aides to headquarters generals, but with no emphasis upon leading men in battle. The latter are what we in the United States label "line" skills. *These line and staff skills are not necessarily interchangeable capabilities.*[59]

The term "policy-mongering" is used to describe the kinds of high flyer jobs that lead to the top of the civil service.[60] A more accurate term is "politics-mongering" since these positions focus mainly on parliamentary and top-level bureaucratic politics, not policy itself. The main emphasis is not on policy formulation, strategic planning, performance assessment – the domain of policy analysis. As Plowden notes in discussing mandarin skills: "The apt answer to the parliamentary question, the aggressive yet noncommittal speech, the emollient negotiating brief to deal with a difficult delegation, the appropriate concession to resolve an impasse on a draft bill ... are all examples of achievements that are highly valued and that can help to secure promotion. All are highly *political*."[61] Mandarins are such broad generalists because these skills are in demand. Nobody at the top wants hard analysis.

The mandarins are classic generalists. They enter after a general education, albeit not quite as general as in the past. In 1982 history, economics (including philosophy, politics, and economics or PPE), and English were the most popular subjects for Administration Trainees without a single classics graduate.[62] Once in the career civil service, outstanding high flyers are likely to spend less time in training than their more ordinary fellow workers because their time can less easily be spared. Fry argues that "a new lease of life seems to have been given to the British belief that actually *training for administrative work is inimical to virility*."[63]

Although drastic changes are needed, we must be careful not to throw the baby out with the bath water. Politics is a critical aspect of policy formulation, implementation and management. The greatest need in government is for generalists who can blend together political, organizational, programmatic, and technical factors – the last three generally being subsumed under the term "policy." The typical mandarin is good in politics and some of the components of policy but is *overbalanced* toward politics in the complex politics/policy equation. The Goldilocks Theorem again applies, but does not mean that an Oxbridge background is incompatible with being a modern generalist.[64] *What is wrong is taking a generalist straight from university and exposing that person to training (or lack thereof) and experiences that make him or her more of a generalist.* Oxbridge types who are the best and the brightest of university graduates can become competent modern generalists. It is pre-modern, anti-modern government that wastes this valuable human resource.

The minister-mandarin relationships problem has been exacerbated by the bombastic, anti-bureaucratic style of the Thatcher government, but a sourness in the relationship existed before that. As Plowden has pointed out: "A vast gulf separates ministers and officials, whose feelings towards their masters and their masters' profession range from the uncomprehending, through the politely sympathetic, to the contemptuous."[65] This distaste of the professional civil servant for the professional politician does not fit easily with the earlier argument that the civil service stands ready to follow its political masters. There is no denying a tension where the strongly held principle that the duty of civil servants is to carry out the wishes of their ministers conflicts with their assessment of ministers' capabilities. Mandarin ambivalence, however, is something a minister must take into account in confronting the problem of asserting political control. In practical terms, this would mean that a minister should not grant absolute trust to civil servants but should build upon their principle of loyalty to develop a professional relationship.[66]

The thin supply of competent people

Several interviewees told me that at any one time there are likely to be roughly a hundred members in the two Houses from the government party who are even marginally competent to staff the ninety to a hundred government executive positions. Even if twice that number are in some respect competent, it is a thin supply of political executives. The supply problem goes beyond the ministers and junior ministers at the top. A frequent argument is to bring people into the government as advisers to individual ministers or the Cabinet. Outsiders have been brought in systematically on a small scale in the Cabinet Office (Central Policy Review Staff), the Prime Minister's Office (Policy Unit), and in the departments (special advisers). But on the outside too the supply is thin. The skills and experience needed simply may not be available. One of my most perceptive interviewees, a former minister, said in response to my argument that outsiders need to be brought into government: "Whom do you bring in? God knows. University and research institutes don't prepare such people. Businessmen often are hopeless."

Two final comments on competence. First, no question will loom larger *if* Britain undertakes a concerted effort to modernize government. However sensible the plans on paper, they will not work without competent people in place. This proposition has escaped many a government as it rushed to new programs and policies without the people needed to do the job. Second, particularly in light of the supply problems, the career civil service is a valuable resource that should not be wasted in reckless "Whitehall bashing" by the politicians.

LOCAL GOVERNMENT

As the recent Thatcher government experience amply reveals, local government can be a quagmire of conflict for the national government. Beloff and Peele point out: "[M]any of the changes which the Conservatives wished to see introduced in the most important domestic policy areas such as education, housing and social services necessitated intervention from the center, and could not be reconciled with a local authority's freedom to resist them ... Improvements in communications have made possible a degree of centralization impossible to contemplate in earlier periods; what previously had to be done locally can now be performed by central government."[67] The problem is simple to state: Central government provides a significant portion of the funds spent by local government – roughly one half now, down from around two-thirds under the last Labour government. At issue is the extent to which central government should become involved (i) in formulating national policies for local efforts funded at least in part by central government funds and (ii) in assessing how efficiently and effectively central government funds supporting local activities are spent. Should he who foots the bill call the shots?

What to do about local government, even if we restrict discussion to spending rather than public borrowing problems, is a thorny one ultimately coming down to the central question of responsibility. At issue are not simply questions of fiscal responsibility involving the proper accounting for central government funds spent but basic matters of objectives, performance, and competence and responsibilities among governments. This shared governance that has become such a vexing problem in most if not all of the advanced welfare states will be considered at length when treating management issues in Chapter 5. However, the issues of confused responsibilities and comparative competence need to be emphasized. As to the former, Jones and Stewart in discussing a 1977 Labour government Green Paper on the Layfield Report point out: "Whereas the analysis of the Layfield Committee has shown the need to reduce confusion by separating the roles of central and local government, the Green Paper increased confusion by a re-assertion of the notion of partnership, but as the Layfield Report has shown, partnership was not shared responsibility but shared irresponsibility."[68]

Competence also is a key issue. There may be a central-local mismatch when Whitehall generalists come up against senior local government officials who are likely to be specialists and have a very different attitude. As Rose observes: "The higher civil service has an almost Durkheimian sense of moral solidarity; it is bad form or it is just not done for higher civil servants to compete against each other. In cricket terms, what counts is not whether one wins or loses, but how one plays the game. But local government officials are footballers: They want their team to score the most goals."[69] The British civil service may lack the orientation and experience needed in order for the central machinery to exert a resonable level of control over central government funded domestic policies. Even with strong commitment to follow political control, the capacity to exert such control may be missing. Such a charge – even if correct – in no way suggests civil servant obstruction although civil servants may prefer to be viewed as obstructionists rather than as deficient in managerial terms.

3

EXPERT INFORMATION AND ANALYSIS

The information and analysis explosions have created a fundamental dilemma for policymakers. On the one hand, they are confronted with more and more complex information that needs to be analyzed and interpreted. There is a growing dependence on expert help. One requirement is for the reduction of masses of information to manageable size for busy policymakers. More important is making policy sense out of available information and analysis. The demand is not simply for data technicians, but for persons who can interpret conflicting data and analyses. On the other hand, it is becoming increasingly clear how difficult it is to do sound analysis and how often the experts are in error. In the last quarter century, problem complexity has increased far more than analytic competence. Fallibility is the mark of the available analytic tools. At the same time there is no turning away from the complexity that demands the development of expert information and analysis.

Policy analysis is very much an American product. Spawned in the late 1950s at the Rand Corporation, the first of the U.S. military "think tanks," policy analysis was introduced into the federal government at the Department of Defense with Secretary Robert McNamara's "Whiz Kids." These young, bright analysts were mainly brought into Defense from the outside. Four years later the Office of Economic Opportunity established the first domestic policy agency analytic office. In October 1965 the Bureau of the Budget (now Office of Management and Budget) established the Planning-Programming-Budgeting System (PPBS) throughout the federal government, mandating analytic offices and establishing an outcome-oriented system as the base for U.S. policy planning.

Britain using American PPBS rhetoric started a somewhat similar process under Prime Minister Edward Heath in 1970 by establishing the Central Policy Review Staff (CPRS), an analytic office in the Cabinet Office, and Program Analysis and Review (PAR), a system to some extent resembling PPBS. While the U.S. and British systems had surface similarities, the differences explored in this chapter are significant. Lessons can be drawn from both experiences. The U.S. effort, however, was far more serious so that most of the lessons come from America.

HARD–EDGED POLICY ANALYSIS: THE AMERICAN FRAMEWORK

Richard Nelson has observed: "The normative structure of 'rational [policy] analysis' rests on the logic-of-choice approach to decision-making, drawn from economics, statistical decision theory, and operation research."[1] I have defined policy analysis as "a means of synthesizing information including research results to produce a format for policy decisions (the laying out of alternative choices) and of determining future needs for policy-relevant information."[2] These statements capture policy analysis at its origins in the United States with the strong emphasis on policy problem solving using "hard" quantitative techniques.

Policy analysis at its early stages mainly involved the application of the normative framework of economics and statistical decisionmaking techniques to problems not traditionally treated by economists. The quantitatively oriented economist was the prototypical analyst. Hence American practices are labeled "hard-edged policy analysis."

American policy analysts today still emphasize quantitative techniques, a rational framework focusing on choices at the margin, and a strong research base. However policy analysis is not simply applied microeconomics. It has become more sophisticated, adding political and organizational (implementation) analysis to the economics/operations research base. Analytic units have passed through a number of stages at different times emphasizing evaluation and experimentation, organizational studies, and efforts to integrate policy and political factors. The biggest gains have been in the more technical areas of analysis where there are increasing numbers of journeymen who are competent to carry out specialized analyses.

PPBS was designed to be the formal basis for both agency (roughly equivalent to a British department) and central government-wide policymaking. The system was to start in the agencies with the government-wide effort being a by-product of the policy structure and formulation developed at the agencies. What differentiated it from earlier systems was the new program structure, the emphasis upon program outcomes, and the creation of high-level, "hard-edged" analytic staffs serving at the top of the agencies.

PPBS, like PAR, died rather ingloriously. However, PPBS left a critical legacy of analytic thinking and analytic offices in federal agencies, the Executive Office of the President, and Congress. The Reagan administration has often been anti-analytic so the role of policy analysis in the federal government is decreasing. At the same time both major analytic offices and numerous policy analysts on other staffs remain prominent in the federal government.

Two closely related factors have been important for the growth of policy analysis in the United States. The first has been the emphasis upon openness. Freedom of Information legislation was first passed in 1966. The legislation itself was not the most significant factor since it contained both important loopholes and could be ignored if the principal parties were not favorable toward open government. *The key element has been a bias against secrecy supporting a process that both legitimized openness and facilitated the development of institutions necessary to support openness.* The atmosphere of openness fosters a competition that stimulates the search for information and the challenge of information and analysis. Increased search and challenge have raised the level of that information and analysis available to top policymakers.

The second closely related development over the two decades has been the growth in the number of policy analysis and research organizations that engage in policy-oriented work. While the non-governmental research and analysis sector has organizations of greatly varying competence, a number of prestigious institutions produce a relatively high level of policy research and analysis. Organizations on different sides of the political spectrum such as the Brookings Institution and the American Enterprise Institute turn out studies and analyses that have contributed constructively to public policy deliberations. Moreover, these institutions provide a base for people to go in and out of government so that experienced analysts are available with new ideas and with the appropriate policy/political credentials when administrations change.

Before turning to some generalizations based on the American policy analysis experience, the story of Britain's efforts at policy analysis needs to be told. Many of the words (the rhetoric) are American, but the experience is distinctly British with its pre-modern elements.

The Heath era

"Edward Heath," one civil servant who had served a number of prime ministers told me, "was the only prime minister who wanted policy analysis." He saw that the British government lacked an "[analytic] capability at the center for assessment of policies and projects in relation to strategic objectives."[3] The quote is from the 1970 White Paper that announced both CPRS and PAR to launch the British government's search for policy analysis and strategic thinking.

When the Conservative party was in opposition in the 1960s, the Conservative Research Department began to think about establishing analytic capability at the top of the government. At that time the rhetoric of PPBS was in the air. The White Paper observed that "the basis of improved policy formulation and decision-taking is a rigorous analysis of existing and suggested government policies, actions and expenditure," and then went on to say "the necessary basis for good government is a radical improvement in the information system available to Ministers."[4]

PAR and CPRS – the two main elements of the "Heath Revolution" – in general terms sounded much like PPBS. A main difference was that CPRS had a longer-term strategic role:

[Government policy] needs to be reinforced by a clear and comprehensive definition of government strategy which can be systematically developed to take account of changing circumstances and can provide a framework within which the Government's policies as a whole may be more effectively formulated. For lack of such a clear definition of strategic purpose and under the pressures of the day to day problems immediately before them, governments are always at some risk of losing sight of the need to consider the

70

totality of their current policies in relation to their longer term objectives; and they may pay too little attention to the difficult, but critical task of evaluating as objectively as possible the alternative policy options and priorities open to them.[5]

Heath's grand vision on paper emerged in practice in a much watered down form with a tiny CPRS and a PAR structure that bore little relationship to policymaking reality. Moreover, Heath became frustrated with his creatures. Nor did the civil service find much of use in the new approach – better the old ways. No later prime minister has had Heath's appreciation of policy analysis and strategy.

The remainder of this sections looks first at the now departed PAR and CPRS and the No. 10 Policy Unit added by Wilson, and then asks where the ministers and mandarins are today in policy analysis. The former is made easy by two excellent studies that permit a brief stressing of key points.[6] Where we are today calls forth the first concerted blast from off-the-record interviews.

The first death: PAR

PAR and PPBS, both long dead, offer an interesting comparison yielding a number of useful lessons. Both systems in their grandest terms had similar soaring, overly ambitious, unrealistic prose. In particular, both promised extremely broad-gauged analysis thereby exhibiting a most restricted understanding of the grave limits of available analytic tools and the dearth of competent analysts. Implementation in both cases was poor at best. As grand government-wide systems, both simply never got off the ground and both were moribund before deservedly being put to rest.[7]

Differences, however, are more important than similarities. PPBS fostered analytic offices throughout the federal government and a policy research and analysis structure inside and outside of government that yielded both relevant policy research and analysis and a supply of experienced analysts. Further, the ferment around PPBS brought competent analysts in sufficient quantity to stimulate the needed scrutiny and challenge of analytic results. PAR also stimulated analysis to a degree but the impact was small.

PAR, in contrast to PPBS, was not outcome-oriented. It did not pose the hard question of whether a policy or program delivered the outcomes it promised either implicitly or explicitly. Not asking this question let politicians off the hook. One of the bitter political fruits of America's analytic explosion has been finding that many federal programs were ineffective. Needless to say, members of Congress, presidents, political executives, and civil servants have tried to hide negative findings, discredit them, or walk away to escape blame. Escape is not always possible. Overall, the use of outcome results has eliminated some bad programs and saved a few good ones.[8] Focusing on outcomes – on policy performance – has brought a needed, if uncomfortable, reality to decisionmaking. The level of sophistication in considering policies has risen.

PAR was not a top level decisionmaking or analytic system. It belonged to the civil servants; ministers were excluded. Admittedly, British civil servants are much closer to the top than their American counterparts, but without politician involvement the exercise was trivialized. PAR became mandarin business as usual. As Gray and Jenkins observed: "[G]iven the bureaucratic requirements of consultation and negotiation ... the departmental management of PARs often fell to generalist administrators best known for their consummate skills as essayists ... [T]he final product was often just that – an essay with little evidence of rigorous appraisal or of prescription for action."[9] Worst of all, PAR had no real client. No ministers strongly supported it. Top level leadership simply was not interested – a fatal flaw. There was no political commitment.

In the United States, PPBS ran out of political commitment and died too, but analytic offices found commitment from the top of agencies. American cabinet secretaries saw the value of policy analysis. So later did both presidents for their own use at the White House in relations with the agencies and the Congress, and the Congress for use in its internal and external relationships.

Policy analysis at the center

Britain has lacked both the demand for and the supply of policy analysis. If there is an exception, it is the Central Policy Review Staff that often bore the label of the "Think Tank" or simply the "Tank." For our purposes the early CPRS is the most interesting. CPRS was the chosen vehicle for meeting the analytic needs of cabinet government. Its charge was to serve the prime minister and Cabinet in their collective roles. Physically, CPRS was located in the Cabinet Office, not No. 10 Downing Street. This location was in keeping with support of the entire Cabinet in executing their collective responsibility for decisions.

The first head of CPRS, Lord (Victor) Rothschild, a senior scientist just retiring from the Shell Oil Company and a member of one of England's most distinguished families, was not political in the partisan sense but was well tied in to the British establishment. He was a power to contend with in the decisionmaking process at the top.

The relatively small CPRS (it was never to exceed twenty professionals) was a mix of *career* civil servants seconded from their departments for a two-year period and nongovernment outsiders, mainly from universities and industry and hired on two-year contracts. In their backgrounds and orientation, Pollitt points out: "If there was a systematic bias in the mix of disciplines it seemed to be in favor of economics and business experience ... Compared with the old Administrative Class as a whole the Staff contained a high proportion of members in their twenties and thirties, and seemed to display an even more elitist, Oxbridge ethos."[10] CPRS had some of the flavor of the early U.S. analytic offices with their "whiz kids" reputation. *But the British version had Oxbridge generalists, not hard-edged policy analysts.*

CPRS was seen as a counter-bureaucratic presence at the center, expected to offset to some extent both the more parochial perspectives of the ministries and the Treasury's desire to cut expenditure. A main vehicle was a series of relatively short papers called "collective briefs" that commented on specific departmental recommendations and were intended to offer a broader government view.

At least in the early Rothschild days, CPRS was charged with seeing how the strategic vision of the government's manifesto was faring. The strategic reports for a period became a feature of Cabinet meetings and meetings of junior ministers. But as Plowden noted: "These strategy meetings were launched with some enthusiasm in the early days of Mr Heath's administration. They became less frequent during the developing crisis of 1973–4."[11] Such meetings faded in the Labour government and were not revived under Thatcher. So died the most innovative aspect of the "Heath Revolution."

Rothschild was anti-bureaucratic – grit in the machine rather than oil. His successor, Sir Kenneth Berrill, was a man of the machine. One Berrill effort, the CPRS *Review of Overseas Representation (ROR)*, merits discussion. The report took six CPRS staffers eighteen months working both in London and on extensive fact-finding trips overseas. The ROR was an unwise study for so small a staff. It would have been foolish even if the staff had been much larger, being too "researchy" (primary data gathering) and too showy for a unit at the center of the British government. At the same time the questions posed needed to be asked. The ROR experience leaves a nagging question. If not CPRS, then who should, would, and/or could do such a study? The Foreign Office was not willing to undertake the effort and indeed seemed to practice its traditional talent of knocking the study. Nor is it clear that any outside research organization had the resources on its own to undertake such a study. It seems unthinkable that the British government would have given an outside organization the charter to do what CPRS did. There is a hole in the center of the British government stretching into the departments.

Berrill was followed by Robin Ibbs. Hennessy and his colleagues rendered a widely held opinion: "[Ibbs] was judged in Whitehall to have done well in his pleasant, undemonstrative but pertinacious fashion." As one insider puts it: "On industrial matters, it's a matter of 'Call for Robin.'" Sir John Hoskyns reckoned CPRS "came to its full or as near as it has possibly got to its full potential, under Robin Ibbs."[12] Ibbs was at the center but CPRS's mandate was far more constrained than in the days of Rothschild and Berrill. This constraint arose in part because Mrs Thatcher is anti-analytic and in part because she was never comfortable with Ted Heath's creature. John Ashworth, once Britain's chief science adviser who served under both Berrill and Ibbs, caught the essence of Thatcherism: "Of its very existence it [CPRS] sort of encapsulated a view about government for which she had no great sympathy. She was what she called a conviction politician. *There is a difference between being a conviction politician and being a rationally guided politician.*"[13] After Ibbs came John Sparrow; after the 1983 election came execution. Mrs Thatcher, surely with some joy, killed the last institutional vestige of the Heath Revolution.

In looking back at CPRS, two points need to be underscored. Although CPRS had some excellent staff people (a number of whom were interviewed), what finally stands out is the general lack of hard-edged analytic capability. One CPRS analyst, who did so qualify, told me that the British government had done almost no analyses in the years he served in it and later watched it. He said "the big issue in the U.K. is where we can find anyone who can do reasonable analysis." *Routine Punctuated by Orgies* had two equally condemning quotes from former Think Tank members:

They were very thinly spread over a lot of areas. The stuff was not very good ... The members of the Tank were very ordinary. They had no real experts ...
We were interfering a lot on a fairly superficial plane. I always felt frustrated at second-guessing without the depth of knowledge that made it fully justified. More often than not I wondered what I was doing.[14]

The strongest institutional lesson to draw from CPRS is that the personal relationship between CPRS's head and the prime minister was the dominant factor in how CPRS was used. Lord Rothschild in a letter to Prime Minister Thatcher observed: "One thing is, however, perfectly clear: it is that if a Prime Minister does not feel the need for CPRS in the Cabinet Office, whether there is its partial analogue in No. 10 or not, there is no point in the existence of a CPRS. It depends crucially for its success on the confidence which the Prime Minister has in it."[15] Hennessy and his colleagues finally argue: "The main lesson of the CPRS 1970–1983 is that its chief customer is the Prime Minister whatever ... [the 1970 White Paper] says about being the servant of the Cabinet."[16] The first necessary requirement for a strong analytic office is support from the top and that ultimately boils down to the relationship between the political leader and the analytic unit head.

If CPRS was a failure, it was an extremely instructive one. Its mix of insiders and outsiders is appealing. That the mix of broad generalists and more substantive types was skewed toward the generalists should not obscure the fact that CPRS had a number of capable people who did useful work and tried to meet analytic needs now clearly not being met at the center. CPRS still stands as a useful experiment for determining how policy analysis can be used at the higher levels of British central government.

A key innovation of the Labour government was the establishment of a No. 10 Policy Unit under Bernard (Lord) Donoughue, a political historian and biographer from the London School of Economics and Political Science, who had strong ties to the Labour party. His small office (it never exceeded ten) was staffed with people similar in training and expertise to those members of CPRS who came from outside the government. To distinguish it from the already existing CPRS, the Policy Unit was charged with mainly short-term policy work while CPRS was to concentrate on longer-term issues. In No. 10, the Policy Unit was more likely to be called on for immediate problems. Donoughue was a close adviser to the Labour prime ministers, especially Wilson.

For Harold Wilson (at least Wilson 1974–6), "the long run" was a week. Except occasionally in the area of economics, the demand for policy analysis was not strong in the 1974–9 Labour government. A former Policy Unit member interviewee said "the main task [of the Policy Unit] was indicating the political implications of policy proposals." The Policy Unit of the Labour government did not bring hard-edged analysis to the center.

Under Thatcher the Policy Unit was cut back immediately in line with her views on small staffs. Once CPRS was abolished, the unit grew with staff specializing in policy areas and ultimately exceeded the Labour government unit in size. However, it was still a small staff. Nor was its head a key Thatcher insider.[17] Policy analysis in the main is still missing from the center of British central government.

"Analytic Cripples"

Policy analysis is not a valued commodity among the British political policymakers in No. 10 and the ministries. A mandarin interviewee said: "Go to a minister and say I am going to do analysis, he turns off. If they [ministers] don't want to know, civil servants don't tell them. If Mrs Thatcher says that she is going to make civil servants more efficient, she is on good political ground. But if she calls for analysis that would seem odd." Ministers are not just indifferent, they are intolerant of policy analysis. And here ministers dominate mandarins. The interviewee just quoted also observed: "The civil service comes to feel that policy analysis is not quite the thing for a gentleman to do. Policy analysis is not in the kit of tools." A former high civil servant (Oxbridge, of course, but also a competent analyst) observed even more savagely that so many of the Oxbridge types are "cripples in the analytic sense." Neither the two people quoted nor I are questioning the mandarins' intelligence or arguing that they are serving ministers poorly in terms of what ministers demand. The problem is worse:

Ministers and mandarins alike are poorly serving Britain by using outdated techniques.

Not only are the top mandarins *not* policy analysts, *they generally lack the capability to be good users of policy analysis*. Another mandarin said that the top civil servants have "no numeracy, are not problem solvers. The Oxbridge types who major in classics or the arts really don't think in number terms." I did not find much evidence that matters are improving either at No. 10 and the Cabinet Office or in the spending ministries.

The exception, if there is one, surely would be the Treasury. *But, Chancellor* quotes Cambridge University's Michael Posner, many years a Treasury consultant, on the Treasury's "special brand of cleverness": "The Treasury has always been the power-house ... Treasury has always contained very clever people, at least as clever as one meets at High Table in an average Oxbridge college. They're well-read, they're accomplished, they're intelligent, they're know-ledgeable, they're powerful."[18] Apparently, the only higher accolade would be to be more clever than dons at High Table in an above average Oxbridge college.

But is clever enough? Sir Frank Cooper has argued that the Treasury mandarins "live in an isolated world and a different world from the rest of humanity. And until you change this, you're never going to get an effective Treasury."[19] Let us, however, defer for the definitive description to a much more famous Cambridge don using Lord Keynes' 1939 description of the Treasury:

There has been nothing finer in its way than our nineteenth century school of Treasury officials. Nothing better has ever been devised, if our object is to limit the functions of Government to the least possible and to make sure that expenditure, whether on social or economic or military or general administrative purposes, is the smallest and most economical that public opinion will put up with. But if that is not our object then nothing can be worse. The Civil Service is ruled today by the Treasury school, trained by tradition and experience and native skill to every form of intelligent obstruction.[20]

Nearly fifty years has not dimmed the relevance of Lord Keynes' statement.

This kind of obstruction, which is charged to almost any budget office by spending departments all over the world, is not the only sin. The Treasury does *not* ask the right questions; not is it equipped to do so. As Plowden has observed: "If the financial management initiative can progress beyond the mere assessments of inputs, then the Treasury's part in the whole system should be to evaluate programs in relation to their objectives. This would be a major job of policy analysis. It would be a completely different task from the Treasury's present task, and one which it is certainly not yet equipped to perform – even if it can bring itself to relinquish its traditional concern with candle-ends."[21]

For the top mandarins, who well may be the best and the brightest of traditional British professionals, the problem is not only lack of knowledge of hard-edged policy analysis but the absence of competition. Brains alone are not enough. The monopoly of ministers and top mandarins in the decisionmaking process diminishes the rigor of challenge and scrutiny. Competition is not used to drive out preconceptions and poor ideas or force in fresh thinking. Sir Frank Cooper shortly after stepping down as Permanent Under-Secretary of State in the Ministry of Defense observed of his peers:

I doubt whether the management culture of the civil service has changed all that much at the higher levels of the service ... [T]hey still are *insufficiently armed with those technical skills which are required for efficient management* ... There is still a gentlemen-players view, in which the former make policy and the latter implement it. These attitudes are wrong in themselves and *changing technology will increasingly expose their inadequacy.*[22]

Cooper speaks broadly of the lack of modern managerial techniques, discussed in the next chapter, and so goes well beyond hard-edged policy analysis. It is a most condemning general comment.

A brief note on the Cabinet Office

The Cabinet Office thus far has been mentioned only in passing as the home of CPRS. It merits scant attention in a discussion of British policy analysis efforts to date because the Cabinet Office has had almost no role in analysis except for CPRS. At the same time the Cabinet Office looms large in future thinking. First the cabinet secretary may be first among mandarins challenged only by the Treasury permanent secretary in ascribed status. He clearly is the top mandarin reporting directly to the prime minister. Second, he heads some of the best and the brightest senior civil servants who are seconded to service in the Cabinet and its committees. As Michael Lee has pointed out: "The Cabinet Secretariat ... is now more prominent in public affairs as the administrative support given to Cabinet committees ... It is recognized that the agenda of the Cabinet has been extended to cover the greater complexity of interaction between different policies, and that the position of Britain in world affairs requires the prime minister to act 'presidentially.'"[23] The Cabinet Secretariat itself could be a major point of analytic coordination in servicing the Cabinet government structure. Third, the Cabinet Office is an extremely flexible vehicle which has made it a home for various efforts including CPRS. Were a prime minister to want to build a powerful analytic unit without going through the political battle of creating a Prime Minister's Department, the Cabinet Office would be the logical place. Here is perhaps the most inviting location for a real effort to upgrade policy analysis at the center when we look to prescription.

British brilliance versus policy analysis

My criticism of mandarins as lacking in a hard-edged analytic orientation must be juxtaposed against their brilliance – a quality few would challenge – since the two are opposite sides of the same coin in the British case.[24] An American academic Martin Trow, who has worked extensively on British higher education, observed in a piece that emphasized the lack of policy analysis and research in that area:

For a very long time the British have put a high premium on a certain kind of brilliance, the capacity to speak with style on a variety of subjects. It is in part the cult of the amateur and in part the cult of the "first class mind" ... [T]he inordinate admiration for this kind of brilliance distracts many Englishmen from the awareness that brilliance is almost independent of knowledge. On the contrary, to educated Englishmen, brilliant talk appears to be wisdom. And consistently the British see wisdom as a good cheap substitute for knowledge ...
This I think is in line with the long standing elite notion that if three or four really top flight knowledgeable people can come to some agreement on the nature of a problem and how to solve it, that is superior to the kind of grubby research that on the whole intellectually inferior people do.[25]

My only quibble with Professor Trow's insightful statement is that at least in the case of the mandarins, they are not amateurs, albeit quite different professionals from the American policy analysts. But this British style is very much the cult of the first-class mind. It is this very orientation and this particular style of brilliance that explains the seeming incongruity of obvious cleverness and superior intelligence and the failure to ask the most basic kinds of analytic and policy research questions. The mandarins simply do not think in analytic terms because the system does not reward such thinking and indeed may punish it.

The cult of the first-class mind puts British brilliance and hard-edged policy analysis in conflict in the world of Westminster and Whitehall. Logic, however, would seem to go in the opposite direction towards intelligence and analysis being linked together. So conflict is cultural, not logical. British brilliance turned to policy analysis should produce first-class analysis. There is nothing in the broad generalist training or experience that logically rules out doing sound analytic thinking. As we turn next to the American policy analysis experience, the argument is not about relative brilliance of American analysts versus British mandarins but about the kinds of thinking that facilitate sound policy analysis and policymaking.

LESSONS FROM THE AMERICAN POLICY ANALYSIS EXPERIENCE

The American analytic experience is a mixed bag so discussion is marked by on-the-one-hand and on-the-other-hand arguing. However, the main point needs underscoring that *the American policy analysis experience is positive*. Hard-edged policy analysis has contributed to policymaking in general and specifically to policymaking in the White House and at the top of the federal agencies. We now know enough about how to develop strong analytic capacity in support of policymaking to be able to indicate what has worked, what has failed, and what are some present dangers and opportunities.

Sound policy analysis does not automatically lead to better policies. The tie between policy analysis and policy is almost always indirect. Policy analysts are staff advisers to policymakers, not decisionmakers themselves. The main function of the policy analyst is to improve the basis of decisionmaking – to enhance the quality of information, analysis and advice available to those making major policy decisions. The analyst's most important contribution may be exposing bad policy ideas and poor analytic reasoning. The dilemma of recent years is that choices so often boil down to no palatable options or at least to each option having significant negative features. Decisionmakers need

to understand expected negative outcomes and see potential unintended consequences. Analysts fail if they do not expose bad ideas and
make the consequences of choices as clear as possible. But they do not
decide. The politicians do.

Before turning to specific lessons, two points from Chapter 1 need
to be recalled. First, since policy complexity has outrun analytic
competence, analytic problems abound despite real improvements in
analytic techniques and thinking. Second, the Goldilocks Theorem
holds. American policy analysis may have produced too many analysts
in the federal government, yet not gone far enough in developing
policy generalists and strategic thinking. Such criticism should not,
however, mask the value of the road map for modernizing British
central government.

Top-level support and a power base

One point is clear: *Analysis will flourish only if strongly supported from
the top and provided with a real power base*. Prime ministers and
ministers must want sound analysis, understand the costs of obtaining
it, and be willing to pay those costs. It is not enough for the leader to
mouth homilies about the wonders of policy analysis. What I wrote
after serving in the Office of Economic Opportunity (OEO) central
analytic office during the Johnson administration still holds:

[Nothing] suggests that a central analytic office deep within the bowels of the
agency will have much impact on policy ... [A] viable central analytical office
(one that has a chance to use analysis effectively) in a ... policy agency requires
an institutional relationship in which the agency head: a) recognizes the
importance of analysis as a means of strengthening his hand in the policy
process *vis-à-vis* the lower tiers of the agency; b) gives the analyst high status
in the agency, including a direct tie to the decisionmaking and implementation
process; and c) provides sufficient personnel positions to support a major
analytical operation.[26]

In particular the leader (or someone in the leader's inner circle) and
the analytic unit head must be able to work together. We finally come
down to a one-on-one relationship – a personal chemistry.

The OEO analytic office offers a good example of an analytic power
base with top level support, high status, and sufficient staff. The head
of the office was one of the handful of high officials in the agency
reporting directly to the agency head. In the final two years of the

Johnson administration the analytic office director was the agency head's most important policy adviser. The office engaged in policy formulation, strategic planning, and program budgeting and was responsible to the agency head for the development of all of the agency's policy and budgeting submissions to the Bureau of the Budget (now Office of Management and Budget) and hence to the president. At its largest the office had roughly forty high level professional staff, a number of whom were economists coming to the government from different research organizations or universities. There was a larger cadre yet of experienced career civil servants with strong budget, financial, and program analysis backgrounds and with extensive knowledge of public programs and organizations.

A strong analytic unit needs a critical mass of policy analysts with hard-edged techniques. These techniques are part and parcel of the American analytic process required for the kinds of interaction that go on within the policy analysis and research communities. But hard-edged analysts, unless they themselves have such knowledge and skills, need to be combined with persons having significant program-matic, organizational and political knowledge and skills. The available evidence points towards the usefulness of combining insiders and outsiders with the needed skills and experience.[27]

The supply of competent analysts

The growing number of policy analysts and analytic units within and outside the U.S. government has led to the increasing challenge and scrutiny of information and analysis. Such competition has the beneficial effect of reducing flawed information and argument. It does not produce answers where there are no answers, but competition does tend to raise the level of the debate.

The United States has no general shortage of policy analysts and researchers. They abound in government, in for-profit and nonprofit policy research and analysis operations, and in universities. At a change of government large numbers of analysts stand ready to join federal agencies. Numerous policy analysts are on congressional staffs. There is a large supply of experienced policy research and analysis organizations outside the government ready to do work directly for government agencies under grant or contract, or to do their own independent policy research and analysis. In the latter case a growing

82

number of prestigious institutions with various political colorations make their policy presence felt both by offering new policy ideas and by challenging those of the government of the day.

There has been much less of an increase in competent generalist policy analysts who can synthesize across substantive policy areas (e.g., education and manpower) or between policy and politics in a single substantive area. At the same time the growing sophistication of policy analysis in more specialized areas and the broadening of analytic issues has placed more demands on generalist policy analysts. Beyond analytic techniques, these generalists now need in depth knowledge about substantive policy and about organizational and political issues relating to that policy. Generalists heading policy units also need to know how to use staff and organization to fill in where they themselves lack knowledge or skills.

Complexity has made obsolete the "generalist-generalist." Today, the need is for the "generalist-specialist." In this classification the term "generalist" comes first because the ability to generalize across broad areas is the critical first demand. We can also think of a "specialist-generalist" to define a case where special knowledge is the first and foremost need – a good example is the head of a technical laboratory. But our concern is only with the two classes of generalist.

The policy generalist must know more and more and be capable of working with a broader range of specialized information and analyses. The generalist-specialist needs a strong technical base so as to be skilled in the uses of the product of specialists. At the same time the policy generalist must still have the capacity to cope with the big picture that seems to become larger and larger. Such breadth is hard to find. There have been virtuoso policy analysts with a high level of generalist skills, but these generalist-specialists remain in short supply.

A critical problem that reflects a clear failure in the U.S. policymaking process has been the lack of development of a strategic approach. With a few exceptions, U.S. policymaking and the underlying policy analyses have been micro-oriented, confined to a single policy issue without enough concern for broader objectives and with too short a time perspective. It is beyond the scope of this book to discuss at length the debilitating effects of the lack of a strategic approach on U.S. policymaking, but this point needs making: The first necessary step in a strategic approach is the political leader's will and commitment to pursue a realistic longer-term perspective. After that, and only after that, can hard-edged analysis of the internal consistency of objectives and the feasibility of their implementation become a central element of strategy.

Analytic excesses

Policy analysis and policy research are simply a different order of magnitude in the United States compared to the rest of the world. From the mid-1960s until the Reagan administration, federal government analytic staffs grew larger and larger. In this period many staffs were hardly "lean" and may have been too big, overburdening the policy process with analysis and analysts.[28] Even though the buildup of analytic capability in the United States contributed toward improved decisionmaking, it may have reached a point of diminishing returns. But even that is not clear. Given the present stage of analytic development, the "just right number of analysts" will not close the gap between problem complexity and analytic competence. Modern tools such as policy analysis and strategic planning are not panaceas, but they increase the probability of more effective governance. That is hardly inconsequential. *The grim message of the information dilemma is that developing the needed techniques and structures will be difficult and risky without sure gains; the failure to modernize, however, carries an even more certain likelihood of ineffective governance in the modern welfare state.*

A negative by-product of U.S. policy analysis is the exclusionary aspect of high-powered techniques. Rivlin points out that analytic specialists use *coded languages* not only to facilitate analysis but "to create a prestigious professional fraternity whose membership is restricted to those who speak a separate and arcane language."[29] Thurow notes caustically: "Occupying the high technical ground with a boldness and confidence that to me is not justified, economists have been able to cow the public, press, policymakers and politicians in ways not usually open to academics and technical people."[30] Policy analysts revel in their high-powered tools that separate them from politicians and managers. The analytic framework derived from economics also can be used to exclude analysts from other backgrounds. One result is to block information and variables that do not fit well with the predominant analytic techniques and orientations.

The greater danger may be that the broad analytic framework, which in conceptual terms can integrate wide varieties of information, is going to be in the hands of "narrow" policy analysts who have neither the necessary knowledge to cope with certain kinds of information nor the orientation to see that such information is important.

The quality and relevance of expert information and analysis

The secrecy that permeates British society shapes both government behavior and that of the media and the research community which is made up of universities and freestanding research organizations. Similar arguments are made in the United States for a level of secrecy that shields the vast government bureaucracies from detailed scrutiny and stems the flow of policy information to the media and the research community. Admittedly, U.S. institutions are more oriented to openness than those in Britain. But the press toward secrecy is clearly a factor. *Openness demands effort and vigilance.*

In the United States there are two main arguments for openness. First is the central place of citizens' right to know in democratic theory. In this sense openness is an end in itself – a fundamental element of American democracy. Second is the positive contribution of knowledge to governance. Openness facilitates scrutiny. Information fuels analytic competition. Yet whatever the rhetoric about the critical contribution of openness to American governance, political executives and career bureaucrats are uncomfortable with it and offer numerous reasons to make information and analyses off limits.

There are valid reasons for secrecy. But at the same time the prevailing pressures in the United States just as in Britain are toward too much secrecy in government. The openness that exists today did not come easily nor will it remain without steady pressure. Two undertakings in the last quarter century have contributed significantly to the availability of relatively sound and relevant policy information. The first chronologically was started in the early 1960s by policy-oriented federal government staffs to stimulate policy research and analysis in the research community. Second was the congressional effort that produced the Freedom of Information Act in 1966 and tightened it significantly with amendments in 1974.

The early policy analysis offices were dominated by "outsiders" coming directly from universities and research organizations. These analysts had previously operated in a climate of openness where publication was the norm. Expert information became the preferred weapon of the policy analysts. They often turned to their peers in the research community. In contrast to the defense area, where much policy research capacity existed in 1961 when the Department of Defense analytic office was set up (but here secrecy reigned for national security reasons), the social policy analytic office found little useful policy research: "At the start of the War on Poverty there was almost no serious academic community interest in the many areas of antipoverty concern such as manpower, urban ghetto problems, income maintenance, education ... [T]hese areas were much more the domain of professional journalists than professors ... [O]ne needs to be clear how close we were to ... zero [policy relevant research] in early 1965."[31] The analytic offices funded policy research projects to increase the flow of outside social policy research and analysis. What marked this outside research was its availability because the researchers pressed for publication. The availability also was consistent with analytic needs where research results were seen as support for policymaking and where such policymaking often was in a broad arena. Not only did the research effort grow, it generated information available to other researchers, media people and the public.

The federal agency analytic offices were the forerunners of such offices in the rest of the federal government and in states and localities. These offices have been both users and generators of information, in part through outside research. Expert information became a key raw material fueling analytic competition. The production of information by outside organizations created a supply of policy researchers and analysts who could execute external studies or staff government offices. Finally, the flow of policy information and analysis stimulated further research and analysis. Even a concentrated attack on social science research by the Reagan administration has not turned back the tide.

Openness is so critical because of the fallibility of the available policy analytic and research tools and techniques. Were the tools and techniques far more powerful, analysis behind closed doors without scrutiny and competition might be highly effective even though it did not fit well with basic democratic principles. *Hard competition among strong analytic units helps avoid two key dangers—policy analysis*

*shrouded in secrecy and information and analysis generated through pre-
modern techniques.*

The Freedom of Information (FOI) Act passed in 1966 had
enormous loopholes that were exploited by the federal agencies to
avoid making information public. In 1974 Congress strengthened the
FOI Act significantly, overriding President Gerald Ford's veto to do
so. President Ronald Reagan has often attacked the FOI Act but the
law is still on the books and the federal agencies generally comply in
opening their document files for inspection upon the request of
American citizens. The House Government Operations Subcommittee on Information recently examined how well eight agencies
complied with the FOI Act. Representative Glenn English, chair of
the Government Operations Subcommittee, argues, based on the
study statistics showing roughly a 92 percent "success" rate (i.e.,
meeting the requirements of the law), that the FOI Act is "successfully accomplishing its primary purpose: making government documents available to those who want them."[32]

Several comments on the FOI Act experience are in order. First,
the early experience was not good and more stringent legislative
amendments were necessary. Success today is after almost two
decades of effort. Second, the failure rate of roughly eight percent may
keep hidden the really damaging information. Indeed, for the deepest
secrets no outsiders may know what to ask. But much information is
obtained. More importantly, the clear direction of the law is toward
openness, toward federal agencies making information available to
citizens. Third, the FOI Act generally has been of more benefit to
investigative journalists that policy analysts, thereby reaching a broad
general audience. Fourth, Congress has been the driving force behind
the FOI Act effort. The Executive Branch often has been unenthus-
iastic. *But Congress' independence from the executive has allowed it to
persist in the face of the strong bias in the executive agencies toward
secrecy.* Fifth, the sky has not fallen. Sometimes a FOI Act request has
turned up past injustice or embarrassing facts. Even the Department
of Defense can exist with a 90 percent plus success rate. The British
departments compared to U.S. departments are hardly hotbeds of
illicit activities.

Britain has much more of an uphill climb to openness both because
of its stronger secrecy tradition than the United States, or seemingly
most other advanced democracies, and because of the relatively

limited supply of policy analysts and researchers. But a tracing of the American experience back two decades indicates both strong opposition to the FOI Act and the dearth of available policy researchers. Unlike the American case where leadership came in one instance from the Executive Branch with a strong agency role and in the other from Congress, there is but a single source of the needed leadership for Britain. The ball falls in the prime minister's court (an issue pursued in later chapters).

4

TOP LEADERSHIP

This chapter and the next one turn to leadership/management issues. Chapter 4 focuses on the top leader or leaders considering the approach likely to create and/or maintain the kind of strong government that is a prerequisite of effective performance. We start where the process of strong governance must start at the top with the leader of the government.

The Attlee, Eisenhower and Thatcher governments provide a basis for spelling out key dimensions of top-level leadership. First, an Attlee-Eisenhower comparison shows the similarities of the last two leaders in the United States and Britain who were masters of the machine. There are two critical differences, however, that justify including the American president. Eisenhower was a much more dominant figure than Attlee, the latter's less assertive role fitting well with the classic British Cabinet government model. Also, Eisenhower was an extraordinary decisionmaker who could handle the big decisions where Attlee was a master of the ordinary decision. An interviewee said Attlee was expert at getting the routine job done and liked to clear his desk. Attlee was an implementer par excellence. Second, I look at Mrs Thatcher, who has been the most ideological British leader in memory. She also is the first anti-government, anti-bureaucratic prime minister in rhetoric and yet highly interventionist. There is much similarity between Prime Minister Thatcher and President Reagan, and comparisons and contrasts will be made. Third, drawing on the Attlee, Eisenhower, Thatcher and Reagan experience a framework is presented for analyzing leadership approaches. Finally, we return to the Attlee years to consider the relationships among top leadership, national confidence, and governmental competence. The Attlee governments are particularly interesting both because a handful of leaders rather than a single person were dominant and because that administration in such contrast to recent British experience performed so well.

ATTLEE AND EISENHOWER: THE ORGANIZATION-MAN LEADERS

Almost a quarter century after he stepped down, scholars have rescued Dwight David Eisenhower, drawing on much new material to show Eisenhower's consummate leadership skill in working behind the scenes to dominate his administration.[1] Shortly after Eisenhower left office, a poll ranked him close to the bottom in presidential ratings. Recent polls put him ninth and Ambrose speculates that "his reputation is likely to continue to rise, perhaps even to the point that he will be ranked just below Washington, Jefferson, Jackson, Lincoln, Wilson and Franklin Roosevelt."[2]

Why? First, twenty years after Eisenhower's presidency ended, the 1950s look better and better. Ambrose argues that "Eisenhower gave the nation eight years of peace and prosperity. No other President in the twentieth century could make that claim. No wonder that millions of Americans felt that the country was damned lucky to have him."[3] Second, not only were the outcomes good, the inputs, Eisenhower's organizational and management skills, were too. General Eisenhower was the last American president with real organizational mastery, so masterful in fact that few if any outsiders recognized his prowess.

Attlee's image may have been even worse. Hennessy and Arends captured that image perfectly in observing: "A deeply underwhelming figure, even at the zenith of his titular power he had no physical presence and on the equivalent of the Richter Scale for oratory, the needle scarcely flickered. He seemed dwarfed by Winston Churchill on the Opposition benches, not to mention the big man beside him at his own Cabinet table, Ernest Bevin."[4] Attlee too is being rescued by history. What stands out is his ability to handle men and institutions. Harris succinctly sums up Attlee's success and his skills in this long statement:

When he came to power in 1945 he assembled and managed a team of ministers which carried out a program of legislation so massive and so radical that, however controversial, it entitles him to be regarded as a great Prime

Minister. The nationalization of the basic industries, the foundation of the Welfare State, and the establishment for the first time of the Labour Party as a plausible party of government had an impact on Britain and the world which no British government had made in the twentieth cenutry ... [I]t is inconceivable that any of the Labour Party leaders but Attlee could have controlled the Cabinet, led the party and satisfied the public opinion which was a prerequisite for the success of his legislative program. Had any of the other possible leaders become prime minister – [Aneurin] Bevan, [Ernest] Bevin, [Herbert] Morrison, [Stafford] Cripps, [Hugh] Dalton – there would have been conflicts, more likely than not because of personal clashes, that would have hampered the action and possibly have brought about a debacle. Attlee's patience, self-control, self-effacement, sense of timing, feeling for what was possible, and his unique knowledge of party and governmental techniques gained in forty years of public work, were his strength – a combination of personal qualities and professional expertise which none of his colleagues could rival.[5]

Other reviewers of the 1945–51 period do not give Attlee such fulsome praise as Harris.[6] However, the emerging consensus is that the 1945–51 governments were remarkable, surely the most effective of the postwar period, if not the century. Looking back, the economic growth starting in that period and lasting until the early 1960s is stronger than any other segment of the postwar years.

Both Attlee and Eisenhower had visions of where they wanted to go and could think realistically about how to get there.[7] Both understood power and how to use it, particularly in its institutional dimensions. In this age of politicians who are so lavish in their promises but whose results fall so disconcertingly short of their vision, it behoves us to look hard at what made these men tick.

Style versus substance

Effective leadership is an elusive, slippery notion. Too often the image is dominated by a particular style, usually bound up in a somewhat idealized personification of a great leader. It may be Roosevelt in a fireside chat, with booming patrician voice, or Churchill, who seemed to typify the steel of the British people in calling Britain to stand fast in the darkest days of World War II. But all successful leaders are not ringing speakers or a man among men. Indeed, style so often hides far more than it reveals. In looking at effective leadership, the critical point to note is that personal stylistic factors may differ dramatically;

so may national customs and circumstances; and yet the underlying functional demands for getting the job done are likely to be similar. Three separate, but interrelated, phenomena must be distinguished: the style of doing things, what is to be done, and the effectiveness in doing it.

Style can be used broadly to describe one's "equipment" including not only skills and knowledge but temperament. And the last so often shapes the external image of the person. It also affects how the game is played. For example, Attlee was sparse in language and shy while Eisenhower was outgoing and preferred to bring people together before him in the give and take of discussion. These traits were fundamental to their styles.

There is no question that these stylistic factors shape how one goes about doing the job, but how they contribute or detract from effectiveness is far less obvious. Tennis fans have no trouble with a hot-tempered John McEnroe and his aggressive play and the cool Bjorn Borg and his often cautious back-court game, both being champions. In the game of leadership, too, individuals will hone their strategy and tactics to their underlying skills and temperaments. Stylistic differences tend to be a kind of epiphenomenon that mislead if confused with the substance of getting the job done.

The job to be done will depend both upon custom, circumstance and personal preference. National customs will be a powerful factor, both in shaping what needs to be accomplished and in setting ground rules for accomplishing it. At the same time that circumstance and custom set boundaries for goals, the choice of goals, except in extreme cases such as cataclysmic war, remain fairly broad. Here, individual leaders have real choices in where they could take the nation.

It is the area of performance that history now gives such high marks to Attlee and Eisenhower. What did they do right? And more importantly, are the skills and knowledge that marked their success ones that have relevance to the future?

The needed traits of leadership

Getting the job done demands personal, institutional and strategic knowledge and skills. Three summary statements indicate the nature of these attributes:

1 Eisenhower and Attlee had the interpersonal skills and confidence to be good judges of people, to lead without appearing to do so, to choose persons who compensated for their own personal weaknesses, to put together strong teams of persons and to work comfortably with outstanding individuals.

2 Both had sufficiently deep knowledge and understanding of the workings of formal and informal institutional structures, processes and behavior to permit them to use the available organizational means and processes in pursuing their objectives.

3 Eisenhower and Attlee were pragmatic men of broad vision who subjected their most fundamental objectives to rigorous testing for internal consistency and administrative feasibility.

Both Attlee and Eisenhower had the capacity to choose good people and use them effectively. Ambrose observed that Eisenhower "wanted competent, proven administrators, men who thought big and acted big. Completely free of any need to boost his own ego, or to prove his decisiveness or leadership, he wanted to 'build up' the men who worked with him."[8] Eisenhower not only picked good people individually but could assess each person's strengths and weaknesses and combine individuals to increase their strengths and minimize their weaknesses. An interviewee told me that Attlee was "strong in seeing things to be done, in understanding the dynamics of those things, in finding exactly the right person to do the job and in seeing that the job was carried out."

It is one thing for leaders to be reasonable and realistic about clear subordinates; the real test is their ability to view realistically both themselves and others at the top. Leaders need to know what they do not know and to recognize necessary tasks to be done that are beyond their skills, knowledge or temperament. Such a capacity requires that a leader has both deep introspection in knowing his own weaknesses and a good eye for talent in others. It is a capacity sadly lacking in recent leaders, in part because they do not have sufficient organizational knowledge either to perceive the traits they lack or to recognize them in others. There may be no sterner test of leadership than to work successfully with men of great skill and reputation. Attlee was an absolute master at this task, as underscored in the earlier quotation from Harris. Eisenhower was also, and did it with studied effortlessness, a critical aspect of the hidden hand that served him so well both as general and president.

What best illustrates Attlee's and Eisenhower's abilities to work with extremely talented individuals is the foreign policy area where each formed very close relationships with men who were seen by others as far superior to the leaders. In looking at these relationships, it should be noted that Eisenhower was primarily a foreign and defense policy leader with much less interest and active involvement in domestic policy. Domestic issues, such as the development of the welfare state and the nationalizing of industries, dominate Attlee's concerns, although he did take a strong interest in India (an area of special competence) and nuclear affairs. The basic point is that Attlee had a much fuller plate than Eisenhower and less personal concern and investment in foreign and defense areas so that he worked out a fundamentally different relationship with his Foreign Secretary, Ernest Bevin, than Eisenhower did with his Secretary of State, John Foster Dulles.

Attlee neither wanted to turn foreign policy over to a cabinet committee nor to dominate it himself. As Hennessy and Arends report in a personal conversation with Lord Bullock on March 4, 1983: "What Attlee did in reality was to say 'I'm going to hand over my prerogative on foreign policy to Bevin. So I'm certainly not going to hand it over to a committee.'"[9] Rather than simply turn foreign affairs over to Bevin, Attlee formed a strong working relationship with Bevin that involved both foreign and domestic issues. Lord Bullock reported in a BBC Radio Three broadcast on October 3, 1982: "There have been few if any partnerships in British Government as close or successful as that between Bevin and Attlee. Attlee discussed the whole range of government business with Bevin as with no other minister."[10] The Attlee approach is caught succinctly in his explanation of why he did not interfere in foreign policymaking: "You don't keep a dog and bark yourself; and Ernie was a very good dog."[11]

Eisenhower's main mission was to strengthen American defense and foreign policy, and he took a most active role. Greenstein argued that "Eisenhower had chosen to be his own defense secretary."[12] His Defense Secretary, Charles Wilson, who had been president of General Motors, was seen by other members of the Eisenhower Administration as stronger than the president. Wilson, however, was

94

dominated by Eisenhower and had the main job of running the department efficiently after Eisenhower made policy.

The Eisenhower-John Foster Dulles relationship was far more complex and subtle than that of Eisenhower and Wilson. Dulles himself was a much stronger figure than Wilson and brought a store of knowledge to foreign policy that Wilson did not have in the defense area. There was a partnership between Dulles and Eisenhower. Dulles had strong views and expressed them. The two were in constant contact even when Dulles was overseas. However, the direction of the relationship was the opposite of what people thought at the time. As Greenstein observed: "They jointly perfected policies, but Eisenhower made the final decisions and Dulles executed them."[13] Eisenhower's ability to lead strong leaders stands out. In his assessment Ambrose captures the essence of this trait: "What the [new] documents show, in my opinion, is how completely Eisenhower dominated events. Eisenhower, not Charles Wilson, made defense policy; Eisenhower, not Foster Dulles, made foreign policy; Eisenhower, not Ezra Benson, made farm policy ... *Eisenhower kept all power in his hands.*"[14]

Both Eisenhower and Attlee were organization men in the good sense of that term. Eisenhower was a master at blending formal and informal institutional processes. His military career shaped his appreciation of formal structures and the need to take account of institutional mores. He also was a strong believer in competent staff work, appointing persons with great professional skill and experience in key staff positions and building up strong analytic capabilities in the National Security Council to support foreign and defense policy-making. At the same time, Eisenhower recognized the critical place of informal channels and of the importance of hearing a diversity of views. Again, the stereotype of Eisenhower at the top being handed a formal document, which gave him the option his staff had chosen, appears to be wrong as are so many other of our impressions of Eisenhower.

Attlee's skills are captured by Harris:

No prime minister has been on better terms with his civil servants, and few, if any, as good. This was partly due to his moral rectitude, which led him to respect men whose profession was not to seek power but to serve the state, and partly due to his view that the objective opinion of an official who occupied his job by merit of intelligence, training and experience was at least as worthy of consideration as the aspiration of a leading politician. It was not a matter of weighing the assessments made by civil servants against the proposals made by politicians, as much as considering any view put forward entirely on its merits. Some of his civil servants, looking back on their days with him in Number Ten, recall that he was quite oddly "apolitical." His instinct was to find what was a truly national policy.[15]

That Attlee was apolitical is indeed odd since he had been a professional politician for most of his adult life. Eisenhower, it will be recalled, was approached by the Democrats at one time to run for president and without a political career was viewed as apolitical. The point, of course, is not that national leaders can ignore political issues. Attlee and Eisenhower both had pragmatic political skills. Both men, however, could step back from party politics "in the small" to take account of institutional and strategic considerations. Attlee and Eisenhower were highly political in the large sense of that term, but were not unduly concerned with the kind of party political issues that can so misshape decisionmaking by forcing concern on extremely short-run, often ephemeral issues.

What made these two men so different from the politicians that followed them is that they took the next critical step in strategic thinking to worry about whether or not the objectives made sense pragmatically. They subjected their cherished objectives to the harsh light of reality. In a letter to Harold Laski in 1944, Attlee wrote:

Whether the postwar government is Conservative or Labour it will inevitably have to work in a mixed economy. If it is a Labour government it will be a mixed economy developing toward socialism. If a Conservative government it will be an economy seeking to retain as much as possible of private enterprise. But both governments will have to work with the world and the country as it exists. There are limits to the extent to which the clock can be put forward or back ...

I hope you will ... believe that because I am face to face every day with the practical problems of government I am nevertheless firm in my Socialist faith and that I have not the slightest desire to depart from it.[16]

Attlee was pragmatic taking the world as it was and doing the hard work of figuring out how to get as far as he could. He never believed that wishing would make it so.

Eisenhower's pragmatism is best seen in his domestic objectives where he was reactionary. If he had had his personal choice, Eisenhower would have cut away the still rather minimal welfare structure that had emerged in the postwar period. However, Eisenhower recognized that the existing reforms could not be abolished and wrote to his brother: "Should any political party attempt to abolish social security and eliminate labor laws and farm programs, you would not hear of that party again in our political history."[17]

Extraordinary and ordinary decisions

Eisenhower was an extraordinary decisionmaker willing to make the big choices. Although he masked his dominance of his administration, Eisenhower was ready to confront hard issues and take the lead decision. Attlee was much more the ordinary decisionmaker. He lacked the brute force to push decisions through. He would hang back from big decisions where no clear Cabinet consensus existed. Attlee was much more the convener, the backroom operator. In part this was an Attlee tactic. He believed holding back was a good procedure because the problem may solve itself. But some problems did not, e.g., the 1947 convertibility and 1949 devaluation crises. Under the great pressures of extraordinary decisions, Attlee in some cases seems to have panicked.[18] He simply was not an Eisenhower or a Churchill or a Bevin comfortable with making the extraordinary decision.

At the same time Attlee was the super manager/implementer who knew how to drive the machine once direction had been established. Most decisions are ordinary in the sense that reasonable discussion can bring a near consensus on what to do. Attlee was masterful in getting such a consensus in Cabinet. And, after that, he knew how to move from the decision to its implementation. Extraordinary decisions yield no such consensus. Here Attlee has been accused of dithering. He neither forced consensus nor took the lead without it. But no one else in that Labour government, save Herbert Morrison, could have engineered the machine as Attlee did.[19] It seems likely no leader of the postwar period was in his class as a "nitty-gritty" implementer, even Eisenhower.[20]

The key lessons

Praise of Eisenhower and Attlee, could be viewed as being nostalgic, even reactionary, yearning for an earlier, simpler time. Moreover, different types of leadership style may be demanded in the mass-media world of the 1980s. Nor should the chinks in their institutional

97

armor be ignored. The title of Greenstein's book, *The Hidden Hand Presidency*, indicates the manipulative nature of Eisenhower's eight years in office. Attlee may be faulted because he did not go further in modernizing British government to meet the demands of the modern welfare state and the nationalized industries that he had brought into being. Attlee, after forty years in the system, was able to bend it to his will without significant institutional changes because he had such a deep understanding of the political and organizational structures and processes. But the welfare state was passed on to successive prime ministers who lacked Attlee's organizational skills. Because Attlee was so much a product of his experiences as an "insider," we should not write off his great accomplishments that have been eroded by his failure to see the need for fundamental institutional changes in the British central government. There also remains the issue of effectiveness in achieving the wrong objectives. Much of the criticism of Eisenhower was of his regressive social policies and of his cold war foreign policies, while the Attlee brand of socialism was viewed as wrong-headed by many Conservatives.

Recognizing all the dangers of drawing any kind of lessons for the future from earlier periods, I would still underscore that the functional imperatives of success remain the same today as they did then, and that the personal, institutional and strategic capabilities that Eisenhower and Attlee brought to government are still essential to effective governance. The problem appears to be less that these men's capabilities would be out of style and more that it is damnably difficult to find people with such qualities for political leadership. As Greenstein observed: "The capacity to think organizationally ... [is] far less transferable than the specific instruments and arrangements he [Eisenhower] employed."[21]

THATCHERISM: THE GOVERNANCE APPROACH

This section looks at how Prime Minister Thatcher approached governing, her relationships with ministers, and her mode of decision-making. It is interspersed with comparisons and contrasts with President Ronald Reagan. Besides her governance approach, "Thatcherism" includes three other elements: managerial style, substantive policy preferences, and personal traits and style. Managerial style could be subsumed under governance approach, but is sufficiently important for our purposes to treat separately. Substantive policy preferences, which, for example, include monetarism and privatization, are to be distinguished from governance preferences. Personal traits and style, e.g., a good political nose, shrillness and toughness, cut across the other categories. Indeed, her traits and style often dominate everything. As Peter Riddell of the *Financial Times* has written: "Mrs Thatcher's views, prejudices and style have determined the Government's actions more than any other single factor."[22]

The first anti-government, anti-bureaucratic prime minister

Politics being politics, a jab or two at government in general or the civil service has been acceptable for a long time. Still, generally, prime ministers before Thatcher (i) saw a pressing need for central government action viewing the central government as a positive force and (ii) were comfortable with civil servants without major reservations about working with the top career officials.

To argue that Mrs Thatcher is Britain's first anti-government, anti-bureaucratic prime minister is not to claim that there were no precedents whether in Britain or internationally. As to the latter, both Richard Nixon and Jimmy Carter made all out attacks against the federal government and its bureaucrats in three presidential campaigns. Even more broadly, by 1979 the complexity-expectations-competence conundrum had begun to sour advanced Western nations on the excesses of the modern welfare state. In Britain itself, Heath had seen an urgent need to revamp the central government but lacked Thatcher's "sense of conviction."[23] From the Fulton Report on, the mandarins were fair game.[24]

Thatcher's all-out attack on government and bureaucracy, however, was a quantum leap reaching a level surpassed, if at all, by President Reagan. Her posture, symbolized by the notion of getting the government off the backs of the people, was a fundamental attack on the postwar consensus aimed at "rolling back of the carpet of bipartisan politics that had developed in the 35 years since the end of the war."[25] Moreover, Whitehall was a big part of the problem and had to be brought to heel by a strong outsider. Anthony King underscores Mrs Thatcher's "penchant for talking about the government as though she were not a member of it."[26] Only Ronald Reagan could equal or better her in the rhetoric of dissociation. And the enemy within was the civil service and particularly the mandarins who in her eyes had come to symbolize the evils of big government.[27] Her rhetoric worked well on the campaign trail but became a hindrance as she tried to make policy. Over time Mrs Thatcher backed off direct criticism but continued to extol the private over the public sector and to praise the civil service with gritted teeth. The latter is critical for our purposes. After attacking the civil servants mightily in the earlier years of the Thatcher government, the Conservatives became concerned with the low morale of the civil service and the exodus of high flyers since those officials were the main means of carrying out Thatcher policy.[28]

Central to understanding Thatcher and Reagan is that both came to power with limited comprehension of how to use analytic staff and organizational structure to serve their purposes and of how large-scale public organizations actually work. Both came to leadership distrustful of analysis. Thatcher cut back the Policy Unit, reduced the number of ministerial special advisors, and according to off-the-record interviews had to be talked out of abolishing the Central Policy Review Staff at the outset of her premiership. Reagan was the most anti-analytic president in memory downgrading several analytic staffs in the Executive Office of the President by putting them lower in the structure and reducing both the size and quality of staffs.[29] Mrs Thatcher's organizational weaknesses are treated in the next chapter. President Reagan, as indicated earlier, has even outdone Prime Minister Thatcher on anti-government, anti-bureaucratic rhetoric and has almost no understanding of large-scale organizations. Indeed, he is the too perfect case with views so strong they seem unreal having no element of grey to sully the black-or-white appearance.[30]

Surely an anomaly of the Thatcher anti-government approach is that she has become the most interventionist prime minister of the postwar period, indeed since Lloyd George. But getting the government off the backs of the people itself involves government action. Admittedly, the argument can be made that in the transition period from the activist welfare state to the desired more passive central government there needs to be much government effort to unravel and dismantle the welfare structure. But such activism brings an uneasy marriage of philosophy and action and colors much of what follows.

Cabinet dominance

The MP Julian Critchley is quoted in *The Times*, June 21, 1982, as saying of Mrs Thatcher that "she cannot see an institution without hitting it with a handbag." There may be exceptions among institutions but Cabinet government is not one of them. No postwar prime minister has sought with such zeal to dominate the Cabinet. It was a struggle. As Rasmussen has observed: "[T]his supposedly dictatorial prime minister probably has lost more cabinet battles than any other prime minister in recent history ... But the longer Mrs Thatcher's time in office, the fewer seem to be the battles she has lost."[31]

Mrs Thatcher's tenacity in bringing the Cabinet to heel flowed from two sources. The first was style. Interviewee after intervieweee emphasized her toughness and combativeness. One interviewee said in comparing Thatcher to the other postwar prime minister who treated Cabinet members with contempt: "Ted Heath was mean and not very likeable, but he was not tough in the sense that Thatcher is tough." She is a brute force in much the way Lyndon Johnson was (but without the physical aggressiveness), creating fear. Such fear can yield an unfortunate relationship between the prime minister and her ministers: "Ministers are reluctant to consult her too frequently because, if they do, they are liable to be accused of not being on top of their job; but, equally, they are reluctant not to consult her for fear of doing the wrong thing, incurring her wrath and possibly finding themselves countermanded."[32]

Second was her "conviction" politics. Believing she had to appoint a number of "wets" to her first Cabinet, she fought to force her views on those wets and the rest of the Conservative party. It was a difficult battle as Simon Jenkins observed in *The Times*, March 31, 1983: "From the moment the [Falklands] task force sailed, Mrs Thatcher emerged from the morass of factional government to achieve an extraordinary dominance over her colleagues and the government machine ... This sense of Mrs Thatcher as a Prime Minister in absolute command – a command she never achieved during 1979–81 – was communicated swiftly both to those involved in the war and to the wider public."

Win she did. After the Falklands, Mrs Thatcher came to dominate the Cabinet as no other prime minister in recent times. As Peter Hennessy noted: "One experienced Whitehall figure reckons that 'temporarily we don't have Cabinet government ... We have a form of presidential government in which she operates like a sovereign in her court,' which is just about the most toughly worded formulation of the case of Mrs Thatcher as Queen Boadicea driving a chariot of conviction politics through the conventions of collective Cabinet government."[33]

Does it matter that Mrs Thatcher is presidential? The answer is far from clear. "Presidential" when employed by the British almost always refers to the American president and is used either pejoratively to describe a premier who treats the cabinet as lackeys or much less frequently in a rather idealized way to describe a leader who takes charge. If "presidential" is used in the former sense, I think it wrong for both nations as described shortly.

The distinctive Thatcher (and Reagan) decision-making approach[34]

Mrs Thatcher has a decisionmaking approach that can be labeled as "ideological/intuitive." It is a difficult notion as quotations from perceptive Thatcher watchers underscore. David Lipsey, *Sunday Times* economics editor, in the March 27, 1983 issue observed: "What distinguishes an ideological from a pragmatic politician is a disposition to adapt the facts to the theory rather than the theory to the facts. By that definition, this is arguably the most ideological British government since Cromwell's." Less than a week later in *The Times*, March 31, 1983, Simon Jenkins, political editor of *The Economist*, took exactly the opposite view: "Despite some appearances, Mrs Thatcher is not an ideological politician: such leaders are very rare and act from deeper reserves of intellectual self confidence than she possesses. She is the anti-thesis, a leader of intuition." Peter Riddell makes a similar argument: "Thatcherism is essentially an instinct, a series of moral values and an approach to leadership rather than an ideology."[35] Jenkins and Riddell are correct in pointing out that Mrs Thatcher is not a classic ideologue whose world view is based on an internally consistent, well-articulated, intellectually satisfying theory. Painstaking conceptualization is not her strong suit.[36]

The mark of Thatcher's thinking is that grand visions and first principles have a profound influence, yet have not necessarily been subjected to the rigorous analysis needed to determine internal consistency and real world feasibility so as to provide a realistic guide to choice and action. Knowing that one is right does not necessitate thinking about it. "Not thinking about it" can be important before a decision is made and afterward in staying the course.

As discussed in Chapter 1, strategy has three elements: the grand vision (the big objectives), the determination of feasibility, and feasibility reassessment over time. The conviction politician – as the true believer – does only one-third of the job. As King has observed: "[Thatcher] is probably unique among 20th-century British prime ministers in having a policy agenda – a set of views and a set of priorities – that is peculiarly her own and is in no way merely an emanation of her government or party."[37] Strong views are not necessarily views thought through as to implementation. As one interviewee put it: "Mrs Thatcher has made a virtue of postulating objectives and walking away from them, completely ignoring management questions and expecting some mysterious force to work its will." Another interviewee argued: "The Thatcher government is terrible in terms of the capacity to implement. This is a government of brute force (and then some hasty retreats) with little or no appreciation of organizational issues either at the center or in local authorities." When the grand vision and the first principles underlying it are seen as unchallengeable and unshakable, not needing scrutiny, ideology can rule out options but provide neither coherent strategic guidance nor much operational detail. Such governance can produce the worst of the two worlds of ideology and intuition.

Prime Minister Thatcher combined traits that exacerbated the negative aspects of her decisionmaking style. She is highly intelligent but also inflexible and arrogant. As to the latter, Sir William Pile, who was her permanent under-secretary at the Department of Education and Science, said "She is ... the only person I know whom I don't think I ever heard say I wonder whether."[38] Combining dogmatism and arrogance with intelligence and hard work can produce a virulent strain of the ideological/intuitive style.

Care must be taken that pejorative labeling does not mislead. Good judgement and intuition remain essential for effective decisionmaking at the top. There is no fixed road map for choice and action. Even after the best analysis, irreducible uncertainty will still be high. Leaders need the ability to go beyond critical intelligence – to *sense* how to proceed after facts run out and analysis has been carried as far as it can go. Intuition, more than judgement, is an art, the mysterious capacity to pick the right course of action when matters are murky. Both luck and intuition loom large in top-level decisionmaking. What analyst still has the hubris to claim that the thinking of a president or a premier should correspond to analytic thinking? In a most uncertain world, who would trade good analysis for good luck or intuition? But it is critical to emphasize that judgement and intuition are likely to work much better after the needed homework is done and what remains is the irreducible uncertainty.

The notion of doing homework is especially pertinent because Mrs Thatcher is noted for such effort and for "getting it right" about facts. John Newhouse cites a critic of her: "She is the eternal scholarship girl, wanting to study and get on."[39] The critical aspects of homework are at what stage it is done and whether it is approached with a rigidly held view or an open mind. Before a decision, the true believer may ignore or block out facts that could contradict first principles. After an intuitive decision is made, there may be an almost frenzied effort to find corroboration with negative information and analysis conveniently submerged.

There is a world of difference between a decision made on the spur of the moment, then justified with selective facts and analysis afterward, and careful judgement based on an open-minded effort to look at the issue at hand. Now those of us who have studied decisionmaking surely should be sobered by the fact that the purely intuitive decision may turn out in retrospect to be right and the "careful judgement" prove wrong. But intuitive decisionmaking often involves a high level of capriciousness and may set in motion behavior, including future decisions to justify the basic gut decision, that can have grave repercussions. *The essential problem of the ideologue in this book is not that of the policy or political desirability of the vision (the first third of the strategic equation) but that of the next steps involving analysis and implementation.*

A brief note on Reagan and Thatcher

In an earlier draft where I purposely minimized the treatment of President Reagan because he and Mrs Thatcher are so much alike, an anonymous reader for the Cambridge University Press complained and observed that "few British people can begin to understand why Reagan is so successful a president." Just so. Few Americans do either because the "Reagan Phenomenon" – his great popularity before the Iran-Contra scandal – is to be found deep in the American psyche. He came to symbolize the American dream, making much of the nation happier, more proud of America and more confident (I would argue overconfident) than it had been since racial unrest and Vietnam began a particularly difficult time in American history.[40] Fascinating as the Reagan story is, and tempting as it is to pursue it, most of it simply is not relevant to a critique of Mrs Thatcher. What is relevant is that these two people so different in style and capacity were so similar in their use of ideology, the specifics of that ideology (anti-government, anti-bureaucratic, anti-analytic, anti-tax, pro-defense and hard line anti-communism), and ultimately in decisionmaking approach.

Two differences loom large for our purposes. First is President Reagan's style and political mastery flowing from his likeable nature, his optimism and his embodying of the American dream. She in contrast was not likeable, seldom optimistic and so often came across like an avenging fury scolding the nation on its failure to stay on the straight and narrow path. Mrs Thatcher has had to work much harder for political impact and has been willing and able to do so. The second critical difference is capability. In commenting on the appointment of Howard Baker as White House chief-of-staff and Frank Carlucci as the new national security advisor, *The New York Times* columnist John Oakes wrote: "President Reagan's *inherent incapacity for the presidential office has become so strikingly clear* in the recent revelations ... that even his most devoted supporters must feel relieved that the White House management has been effectively delivered into a different style of hands."[41] Can President Reagan really have been so inept all along as the Iran-Contra scandal reveals? If we are speaking of capability itself, the answer is yes. But there are two offsetting factors – Reagan's "handlers" (about which more will be written in the next section) and Reagan's good intuition and luck. Somehow he was able at times to sense the right direction with limited evidence. And most of all there was his good luck. Writing before the Iran-Contra affair, Professor Neustadt observed that "Reagan's luck might be a natural resource on a par, at least, with something like Great Britain's North Sea oil – a pity it can't last even as long!"[42] Alas, depending on intuition without sound analysis and management is a risky game. Long ago Machiavelli wrote: "[A] prince who depends entirely on Fortune comes to grief immediately she changes."[43]

While President Reagan employed so easily his charisma and charm to gain quick dominance, Mrs Thatcher has had to strive mightily for it by combining confidence and toughness with high levels of energy and intelligence. There is also her longevity as prime minister with her now heading her third government and indicating a possible fourth one. What has emerged over time is not only the dominance achieved by Mr Reagan but her greater capacity to learn and to grow.

Two points relevant to later discussion need making about the Reagan presidency. First, his performance shows clearly how critical the individual leader is and how he and his key people dominate structure and staff factors. Put differently, strong structure and staff in place will not save an inept administration. Second, we see how any good principle if carried to the extreme can do much harm. Prior to the Iran-Contra scandal Reagan often was praised for his delegated presidency in direct contrast to President Jimmy Carter's hands-on approach. But it is clear that Mr Reagan's delegation carried no residual control with it as did that of Eisenhower and Attlee. Such residual control as will be discussed later demands knowledge about policy substance and process – a knowledge President Reagan simply did not have. The best of principles taken to the extreme is at least as dangerous as when it is mainly or entirely absent.

LEADERSHIP APPROACHES

The main messages of the discussions of the several leaders are illustrated by Figure 1 showing four possible leader-cabinet relationships. Leader dominance or lack of dominance is not to be equated with strength or weakness. Both Eisenhower and Attlee in their ways

Figure 1. *Leader-Cabinet relations*

		Leader	
		Dominant	Non-dominant
Cabinet	Strong	Eisenhower	Attlee
members	Weak	Thatcher/Reagan	Carter

106

were strong leaders in understanding power and in having the organizational mastery to get the job done. Rather it is a question of giving direction as opposed to being a facilitator (convener). The latter fits well with British Cabinet government, less so with the American presidency.

Both the direction-giving and the facilitator approaches are leadership styles that in general terms seem equally appropriate. However, in today's complexity, particularly as more and more action takes place on the international scene, the leader might need to be more dominant. It is easier to see a person with Eisenhower's leadership style (but likely to be less dominant behind-the-scenes) as a future president than another Attlee as prime minister. But Attlee was an "accidental prime minister."[44] In addition, Attlee had a rare relationship with Bevin that made him comfortable with Bevin's foreign policy dominance (so there was a powerful international presence).[45]

"Strong" as applied to cabinets means capable of doing the job, of leading the ministry and not being totally dominated by the head of the government. Much depends on whether the leader looks for people with the stature and skills to run their own departments. Eisenhower sought men (white men to be specific) who could run the show in their departments. Even in the defense area where Eisenhower wanted to set the objectives, he expected Charles Wilson to have the organizational mastery to implement.

Jimmy Carter is an interesting example of the leader who was not dominant with what appeared to be a weak group of Cabinet members. The qualification is important since Carter not only did not dominate but was a technocrat who did not understand Washington and who came across as a weak, ineffective leader.[46] Such leadership weakness will be likely to make Cabinet members seem weaker than they actually are. The revelations of the Iran-Contra scandal suggest that President Reagan might be placed in the same category as Mr Carter and that view is supported by the evidence that what have been termed his "handlers" must guide Mr Reagan to a degree not witnessed in the modern presidency. Can anyone imagine speaking of Franklin Roosevelt's or Lyndon Johnson's (or Margaret Thatcher's) "handlers," implying staff carrying out critical leadership functions as might happen with the weakest minister in a mandarins' cocoon? At the same time Reagan with adroit handling has been so dominant as to lead perceptive critics such as *The Washington Post*'s Haynes Johnson to observe that "[Reagan] dominates the American political scene as no one since Franklin D. Roosevelt."[47] That political dominance clearly placed him (or more accurately him and his top White House staff) in a stronger power position *vis-à-vis* his Cabinet secretaries.

Dominance by the head of the government is not the same as strength. Leaving aside the constitutional issue of Cabinet government, Mrs Thatcher can be faulted on the pragmatic grounds that she failed to choose strong Cabinets. She did not understand large-scale organizations and hence did not pick ministers with the ability to master the machinery of central government. She did not find managers. Both Attlee and Eisenhower did. They understood that the leader cannot manage the government directly but that those who head the great departments must be managers. My argument, it should be noted, is not that all the members of the Thatcher Cabinet (or the Carter Cabinet for that matter) were weak or poor managers. Michael Heseltine had the reputation of being both strong and a sound manager. Also, the Thatcher style may have made ministers appear weaker and less competent as managers than they actually were. But with the needed caveats, the characterization of the overall Cabinets as weak still holds generally and overwhelmingly so in comparison with the great Attlee Cabinets.

LEADERSHIP, CONFIDENCE AND COMPETENCE

George Jones has called the 1945–51 Attlee governments "the most effective of all Labour governments and possibly of any [British] government since 1832."[48] It is a particularly interesting government given the current importance of the "presidential" prime minister versus the Cabinet government models of British governance. It was truly Cabinet government at its best. And most interesting of all, Prime Minister Clement Attlee, the only ordinary man in Labour's Big Five, was able to hold together and keep on course the often volcanic prima donnas – Ernest Bevin, Stafford Cripps, Hugh Dalton and Herbert Morrison. It also was a confident government in a confident nation.[49]

Confidence, not just of leaders, but of the led, is essential in war and peace. Greenstein quotes General Eisenhower from an unpublished chapter about the 1942 invasion of North Africa: "Without confidence, enthusiasm and optimism in the command, victory is scarcely

108

obtainable."[50] For a nation confidence alone is not enough for positive change; national apathy however is sufficient to block essential changes. *If a new leader does not find a solid base of national confidence as he enters office, his first task is to restore it.*

Britain among all the wartime allies was the only one to take part in both world wars from beginning to end.[51] World War II "deprived her not only of manpower ... but a loss of material possession in the form of damage to the housing stock, loss of shipping and above all exhaustion of financial resources and disruption of trading links."[52] Lord Keynes was to send the most pessimistic of messages to the new Labour government in its first week writing of a "financial Dunkirk."

Britain faced a terrible economic crisis, but faced it with confidence, probably overconfidence since without the U.S. and Canadian loans, "the welfare state, built up between 1945 and 1951, would not have been possible."[53] But there was reason for confidence. First, Britain had won the war showing great courage and fortitude both by those in the military and those on the homefront. The nation emerged from the second World War with strong agreement about reforms and a better nation. Second, Britain was still a world power with a clearly earned second spot in the West, hence making it first in Western Europe. As Morgan argued: "Attlee's Britain was a conservative, cautious land, reflecting the reassuring cricket-loving, downbeat style of its Prime Minister. But it did not feel itself to be a declining one. *There was a rough strength about post-war Britain which contrasts with the declining self-confidence of the 1970s and the 1980s.*"[54]

The base for takeoff

Along with the confidence borne of victory and of Britain's high place in the immediate postwar period, several other factors formed the base for takeoff for the Labour government. First was the work of the Labour party when not in power, particularly in the 1930s, and that of individuals such as the two towering Liberals, Keynes and Beveridge.[55] Second, the time was ripe and Labour was the party capturing public support. As Morgan has argued: "Labour was uniquely identified with a sweeping change of mood during the war years, and with the new social agenda that emerged ... To a degree unique in the history of British Labour government, and indeed unusual in the record of any administration this century, there was a background of consensus for the British variant of 'socialism in one country.'"[56] Indeed, Britain was casting aside Winston Churchill, who had been ideal in wartime but was not perceived as the person to lead the peace. It was not that he lacked the leadership skills in a general sense but that he opposed much of the Labour program. Equally important, Labour for once was without the usual split between the demands for pure socialism from the party's left and for gradualism from the leadership – everything came together in the years 1945–51.

The third element for the takeoff is what can be labeled "general readiness and competence" to distinguish it from the specific competence and power orientation of the Labour government leaders which are discussed in the next section. The nation had experienced controls and rationing for much of the war. The control devices in the ministries were in place and people were accustomed to them.[57] Moreover, war had mobilized the population.[58] The home front shaped by the demands of war became the model that drove and inspired the peacetime reorganization effort.[59]

Whitehall had changed too between 1939 and 1945. There was an influx of outsiders, some of whom stayed on after the war.[60] Also wartime itself had demanded not only higher levels of performance but a much more outcome-oriented effort in Whitehall. *Muddling through was not enough.* People, material and capital were combined so that a needed product emerged. What came forth was a "can do" spirit that would serve well the difficult task of putting the welfare state in place.[61]

Competence and the zest for power

By 1945 Labour had the experience, the competence and the zest for power to staff a truly remarkable government. Its leaders had benefited from the wartime years in the Coalition government that had showed them both the limits and the potential of flexible government.[62] And just as the case with Whitehall that experience was performance-oriented. Beyond experience was competence and the zest for power. As Morgan observed:

It was a gifted administration, a government of prima donnas in many ways, but one in which the broad vision of Bevin, the managerial skills of Morrison, the spartan intensity of Cripps, the ebullient authority of Dalton, the charismatic appeal of Bevan, the intellectualism of Gaitskell ... and others, all welded into some kind of coherent whole. The socialist ideal still retained its validity ... But this ideal was combined with executive competence in most areas and a zest for power rare in the annals of the somewhat innocent world of the British left.[63]

Labour's Big Five of Attlee, Bevin, Dalton, Morrison, and Cripps was an unusually talented group. Bevin was the superstar. He was a bold leader, a man from the same mold as Churchill. Bullock quotes an article from *The Times* written at Bevin's death: "Like Mr Churchill, he seemed a visitor from the 18th century; he was of the company of Chatham and Samuel Johnson. His place, one felt, was among big men, men of strong hearts and strong opinions."[64] He was a man of great imagination combined with tremendous common sense. His confidence and capability were the foundation for his decisiveness, his readiness to make the bold, extraordinary decision.[65] He was an implementer too as witnessed by his role in the Marshall Plan and NATO. Attlee considered Stafford Cripps the second big man in the Cabinet.[66] A powerful intellect and a star as chancellor after he replaced Dalton, Cripps' political judgment was at times suspect.[67] But he was a powerful leader "regarded [in 1947] as the most dynamic figure in the Government: not only brilliant, but scrupulous, courageous and unique in his readiness to place nation before party. He was seen ... as he always had seen himself: as a savior."[68] The other member of the Big Five who at times seemed larger than life, Hugh Dalton, well may have been Cripps' intellectual equal. A man of strong views and enormous industry, he was a former don with a formidable reputation as an intellectual. He also was a man difficult to work with, whose temper could burn, whose judgment also was suspect, and who was never trusted by his colleagues.[69]

The two who made the greatest contribution to the social great leap were the two full time politicians – Herbert Morrison and Clement Attlee. The former displayed mastery of the House of Commons and the Parliamentary Labour Party. The latter held together the prima donnas in his government.

Morrison combined great natural ability with unparalleled party and legislative experience – not just in Parliament but as leader of the London County Council. As for the former, his biographers note: "[Morrison] had a feel for the House of Commons and seemed to know instinctively how it would react. He must have been born with the ability to manage people and to organize them."[70] What distinguishes Morrison is his institutional knowledge – he knew all the tricks and how to use them in the heat of legislative battle. The only comparable figure with such knowledge dominated competence from this half century that comes to mind is Lyndon Johnson, who both as Senate majority leader and as president is considered to be the American legislative master.

Attlee was the one indispensable member of the Cabinet, the only person who could hold the powerful group together. Bullock captured this role in observing: "It was not a way of running a government to satisfy the more assertive characters who sat in Cabinet with him, but by refusing to commit himself to one side or the other, Attlee established not only his impartiality, but his indispensability: he was the one man under whom all the others agreed to serve, the man best suited to hold together a party which contained very different, and at times conflicting views."[71]

Attlee lacked many of the natural talents of his peers in the quantity that makes stardom seem certain and had qualities (shyness, remoteness) that were clear liabilities, but he had honed his skills to reach a level few people reach. He was a master student of leadership and organization. Moreover, he had one quality that few possess – stamina.[72] He used it well. As prime minister his mastery of the Cabinet flowed in part from his mastery of Cabinet documents he read and assimilated in advance.[73] Further, Attlee was extremely disciplined and that trait, combined with stamina and a deep understanding of leadership and organization gained from his careful observation, helped make him a master at getting things done, an implementer par excellence.

Attlee also was the right man at the right spot, even though his biographer labels him correctly as an "accidental prime minister."[74] Yet, once he became prime minister, his strengths and even some of his general weaknesses (e.g. not being a "big man") fitted perfectly with the particular demands of the configuration of ministers who dominated the Labour governments of 1945–51. Attlee's own words ending a long appreciation of Churchill are used by Kenneth Harris at the end of his biography to capture Attlee: "He was, of course, above all, a supremely fortunate mortal. Whether he deserved his great fate or not, whether he won it or had it dropped into his lap, *history set him the job he was the ideal man to do.*"[75]

What marked the leaders of the 1945–51 Labour governments was boldness. There was a zeal for power that drove the government. But this zest for power was a force that needed to be guided and directed. Attlee and Morrison kept the show on the road in their management of the Cabinet, Parliament and the party. Only Morrison appears to have had the managerial skills to carry out Attlee's indispensable role. However, there is doubt because of his bad relations with Bevin.[76] For the Labour government this was a blessing in the sense that Attlee almost certainly could *not* have filled Morrison's shoes in Parliament and party, nor probably could any of the rest of the Big Five.

No British government of recent times has equalled the 1945–51 Labour government's desire for and appreciation of power. Donoughue and Jones observe that "the overriding characteristic of Morrison was his itch to exercise power."[77] The Labour Big Five wanted to exercise power. Attlee captured the notion in writing about Bevin: "Because of his genius for organization and his confidence in his own strength, he did not fear – he embraced power ... And power was given to Ernest. Men recognized in him a national leader, someone to lean on ... At a time when the Labour Movement had all the hopes, aspirations, ideas and saints necessary for Utopia, Ernest helped bring its feet to the ground by insisting that these things without power were useless."[78]

First, power must be won. But power won is not power used for policy. Some may be content with the rewards of office itself. Others may settle for party political power. Still others may want policies pushed through but be unwilling to make necessary compromises. Even those who can get their policies enacted may lack the skills to have them implemented effectively. The Labour governments of 1945–51 understood these various aspects of power including implementation as no other British government coming after it. The leaders of this period also understood that power in performance terms was not a zero sum game.

The Labour leaders generally, and Attlee in particular, might be faulted for not modernizing British government. But that structure worked for this remarkable group. Indeed, Labour's accomplishments seem to have provided a sound base for the relatively high economic performance that began in the Labour years.

Good fortune, to be sure, played a key role. Labour could not have built their base for takeoff without the financial resources provided by the United States and Canada, a bit *deus ex machina* as it were. It is easy with hindsight to pluck out golden truths to explain success. Even with all the necessary caveats, critical elements of that Labour government success are relevant to Britain's current crisis. And none seem more relevant than bold leadership that has a powerful vision of a better Britain and a deep appreciation of the commitment, competence and confidence demanded to move in the desired direction.

5

PUBLIC MANAGEMENT

This second chapter on leadership/management shifts attention from the top leader or leaders to the institutional structures and processes that stretch from the top to deep in the organization. The earlier chapter emphasized political leadership; the current one stresses executive management. While the separation of leadership and management is useful for discussion purposes, it is also potentially misleading because politics, policy and management are intertwined. Organizational reality is a seamless web. In particular, political leadership and executive management merge at the top.

MODERN MANAGEMENT

Management has become an "in" word taking on nearly mystic qualities. *The Economist* observed in a review of two new management books that "like pop-sociology and psychiatry in the later 1960s, management bears all the signs of a fad so absurdly superficial that one day people will cringe with embarrassment that they ever took it seriously ... [Management] now means not management itself, but the study of management – a field which will grow many gurus for the gullible before fashions change."[1] Just so. But the term "management" remains the preferred word to describe the bundle of activities undertaken to move an institution (using this term so broadly as to include a nation) toward its objectives. Mintzberg makes "the manager" his overarching concept specifying ten managerial roles: "*figurehead, liaison, and leader* (interpersonal roles), *monitor, disseminator, and spokesman* (information roles), *entrepreneur, disturbance handler, resource allocator, and negotiator* (decisional roles)."[2] Unlike the British, Americans do not speak of "mere management" implying a lower level task carried out by lesser figures in the organization. Relatedly, I use "public management" instead of "public administration" in part because management has become such a central issue of late in both the United States and Britain and in part because public administration carries the baggage of the discredited notion of a politics/administration dichotomy with the latter being something political executives or ministers do not do.

No definition is likely to capture the notion of management for several reasons. First, management is dynamic and involves an irreducible element of discretion. The manager acts; a follower reacts, often requiring manager reaction. Complex situations often allow neither "going by the books" (following specified rules, regulations, and procedures) nor "going to the boss." Effective performance demands discretionary behavior by someone *on the ground* handling the situation directly. Modern management is people- and process-oriented. The good manager needs to look down, see subordinates as a key resource, and respect the specific knowledge of the front-line person. Middle level managers to be effective must both use discretion to treat complex problems directly in their purview and cope with the discretionary behavior of subordinates. Second, management is an ongoing process that involves setting the organization's direction, determining any necessary modifications in direction and redirection (new objectives), fixing and maintaining lines of responsibility, and developing a base of resources (e.g., financial and human capital) to meet future needs as yet unknown. Third, management is more art than science. Despite the plethora of books on management and the vast number of schools (at least in the United States) professing public and private sector management, there is no sure fix and few purely technocratic solutions. This is not to say that managerial techniques and approaches cannot be learned. Indeed, one of my strongest condemnations of ministers and mandarins is that they have not mastered these techniques. Modern management techniques can aid a strong leader and even help shore up a not so strong one. Still, managerial excellence ultimately depends on the person (art), not the approach (science).

Management involves figuring out where to go and how to get there, how to put together different resources and delegate responsibility, how to motivate people to move in desired directions over time, and how to build, maintain or repair an institution to make it capable of coping with changing circumstances and uncertainty. Figuring out where to go and how to get there is the strategic management function. In the broadest sense, top management must ask what the organization is to be over time. Determining lines of responsibility (delegation) and direction setting are primary tasks of the top. But setting direction is merely a wish until the further question is posed as to whether the organization can gain the capacity needed to move in the desired direction. Beyond determining the mix of resources is putting those resources in place. Once resources are in place, motivating people becomes the primary management task. Mobilizing resources and motivating people involve the management of implementation. Finally, management is also responsible for institutional maintenance and development. What works today may not tomorrow.

The mark of modern organizations – be they public or private – is growing structural complexity in response to an increasingly difficult external environment. Moreover, as Mintzberg has observed: "Managers' jobs are remarkably alike. The work of foremen, presidents, government administrators, and other managers can be described in terms of ... basic roles and ... working characteristics."[3] The top political leader and the low-level line manager are both part of an institutional structure with guiding rules and precedents; both must try to combine available human and nonhuman resources to induce behavior in subordinates that leads toward specified objectives.

Differences are important too. Providing effective political leadership in Britain requires different skills, experience and style than providing effective leadership at ICI. At the same time the managerial demands in a small ICI production unit are much closer to those in a local government office than those of a multinational corporation. As we move toward the top, the remit becomes broader. There is a great distance between Winston Churchill motivating Britain with his own courage and soaring rhetoric during World War II to the corporation line manager of a small assembly operation. The higher managers are in both public and private institutions, the less bounded are their responsibilities. The people at the top are more likely to operate at critical points of interaction that stretch not only across their organizations but into the complex political/operational world.

117

Current operations and strategy

Managing has two related but separable aspects – current operations and strategy. American corporations separate the tasks functionally with a Chief *Executive* Officer (CEO), the higher position, and a Chief *Operating* Officer (COO). The CEO is the big picture person charged with looking at the future for possible redirections. The CEO is the person of vision; the COO is the organization's chief implementer. The COO is responsible for keeping the organization on course for current objectives. The COO, however, is not a nuts and bolts manager like those at much lower levels of the organization and surely appears to be a broad generalist from below. Further, the COO may become the CEO. The differences are not necessarily in experience, skills or styles of leadership but rather in organization function. The separation makes sense for organizational purposes as long as it is clear that the two functions of formulation and implementation are necessarily interlocked. The ultimate test of top leadership is putting the two together.

Delegating responsibility

A critical element of positive management is developing and maintaining a framework for the realistic delegation of responsibility. The top executives cannot be expected to answer for whatever happens in a large hierarchical organization. Take the issue of quality control in a vast manufacturing concern such as General Motors. Each manager at the lowest level of the hierarchy will be responsible for the products coming out of his unit. The unit manager should (or would) be called to task if the unit is performing poorly compared to other units or some other comparative standard. So may be the unit manager's immediate supervisor especially if several units under him have poor quality ratings. But, if the quality problem is isolated, there is no reason to hold the CEO or COO responsible. The problem may be one they are at most dimly aware of. In the example at hand, top management is responsible for overall quality control. That means establishing a favorable institutional setting for ensuring high quality. Most important is the delegation of responsibility and the choosing of subordinates who report to the top. One of the top's most critical functions is to delegate responsibility and to create a structure where

118

subordinate managers have a reasonable chance to accomplish the objectives for which they are responsible. In discussing Eisenhower, Greenstein wrote of "his skill and subtlety in delegating power" and observed in reference to both Sherman Adams and John Foster Dulles: "Eisenhower stayed in charge, but he did not try to do everything himself. He was gifted at conveying *general* policies to his subordinates and then allowing them much leeway for specifics."[4]

All of this seems rather elementary until we look below the surface and ask about the conditions for the setting of realistic lines of responsibility and delegation. Those above want a reasonable level of control. A lower level unit manager may have a fixed budget setting out both available financial resources and the number of personnel lines, as well as a significant number of guidelines sent down from above. The problem is that these restrictions can leave a subordinate manager with so few resources or so little discretion that the chance of reaching assigned goals is all but foreclosed. Facing each manager *vis-à-vis* subordinate managers is the task of balancing control, resources and discretion. This balance is at the heart of the delegation of responsibility issue. The subordinate manager can ask legitimately: "What is fair? Am I being given enough resources and discretion to have a reasonable shot at fulfilling my responsibilities?" His superior, if not the person at the top of the whole organization, can ask the same questions of his own superior. The critical point is that delegated responsibility is a two-way street. Superiors must not only seek to retain control so they can fulfill their own responsibilities to their superiors but provide an environment of resources and discretion amenable to meeting responsibilities by their subordinates.

What has been written thus far applies equally to the public and private sectors. That political appointees and career civil servants are involved does not undo the basic laws in the public sector, but it does take a greater effort to get the responsibility equation right.

THATCHER'S "MANAGEMENT REVOLUTION"

Nineteen-seventy-nine marked the start of a new era in British central government where genuine concern about management became an important and continuing focus. Heath tried to incorporate analytic and strategic thinking in British government; Prime Minister Thatcher pushed management. But in her dogged way Mrs Thatcher

119

has stuck with her concept; Heath lost interest in his. Indeed, Jenkins and Gray write of an "obsession with management" in the Thatcher years.[5] The Thatcher tenacity, however, has been a mixed blessing given the direction her attempted management revolution has taken.

Rayner scrutinies, FMI, and other management initiatives

Mrs Thatcher started her management initiative early with the appointment of Derek (Lord) Rayner in 1979 as her special adviser on efficiency. The Rayner scrutinies that emerged were quick studies (first sixty, then ninety days) under strong direction from the center. The Efficiency Unit that under Rayner reported directly to the prime minister is in the Cabinet Office. In the typical scrutiny a small team looks at a rather narrow area seeking to determine a more *efficient* use of resources.[6] "Quick and dirty," the scrutinies aim at improving operations rapidly. They do not consider effectiveness but focus on operations where feasible organizational changes can be made quickly.

The efficiency scrutinies, which have continued, make good sense. Most importantly, as Nevil Johnson has observed: "[T]his kind of analysis of operations ... serve[s] to diffuse widely the thinking underlying it ... [What] this boils down to is a managerialist view of the civil service's function."[7] (These points will be returned to shortly). The scrutinies have another positive feature: in being concerned with operations, they do *not* threaten the top. Finding low level management improvements make top management (ministers and mandarins) look good and appear management-oriented. Such changes may affect lower levels of a ministry adversely but do not penetrate the upper reaches of the ministry. The last statement is not made cynically but to offer a bureaucratic explanation for what success has been achieved while stressing that such success does not mean management really is "in" at the top. This last remark leads to the Financial Management Initiative.

FMI has been a horse of a different color. It is a big, top-level system like PPBS and PAR. The government apparently learned from the sad history of the two earlier systems and allowed much more time for implementation.[8] But FMI is still a major government-wide effort with goals similar to the earlier systems. Gray and Jenkins state that "the FMI's stated purpose is to ensure that managers at all levels ... have (i) clearly defined *objectives* and ways of operationalizing them,

(ii) a distinct *responsibility* for resource use as well as operational effectiveness and (iii) the support, including relevant *information*, training and advice, necessary to achieve these."[9] The FMI started with the departments which were required to draw up a plan for establishing FMI priorities. Departments were to indicate what they would do to develop an information system in support of these objectives, performance indicators, and output measures. But a Financial Management Unit in the Treasury guided and assisted the department. Hence the FMI has many of the features of a topdown exercise such as were found in PAR and PPBS.[10]

FMI threatens the top. Setting out clearly defined objectives, developing relevant information to assess performance, and assigning organizational responsibilities for resources and performance are central elements of effective management, and can harm mandarin and minister alike, and even a prime minister. In bringing in Treasury guidance, the threat looms particularly large for spending ministers. It is small wonder implementation has been so difficult. We pursue these points in the next subsection.

Three more Thatcher management initiatives merit discussion. The Top Management Program provides an intensive six weeks of management training to under secretaries that offers a broad view of management embracing both the public and private sectors.[11] The program probably is too brief. At the same time the program is a start toward serious management training for the upper reaches of the civil service. The Top Management Programme takes high level civil servants away from their jobs for six weeks, provides an intensive training experience, and during four of the six weeks mixes the under secretaries in equal proportions with their counterparts in the private sector. If the six-week program produces a cadre of alumni both committed to management and recognizing the value of training, it could have a big impact.

An even newer Management and Personnel Office (Cabinet Office) effort is the Senior Management Development Programme (SMDP) to be offered to principals and assistant secretaries. SMDP, which is to be linked closely to the Top Management Program, will provide five days a year of training and developmental jobs throughout their careers to eligible persons. A listing of needed knowledge and skills (based on a survey of 500 staff in the SMDP grades) includes "management of resources/organizations, management of staff, knowledge/understanding of the content of your [the staff member's] own work, information technology, and more specialized knowledge/ expertise ... representational/presentational skills, written/administrative skills, policy management, economics, accounting and finance, quantitative skills, statistics, law, and industrial relations."[12] Such an array of skills, except for the lack of emphasis on policy analysis, well describes the core of a typical U.S. public policy masters degree program. Although too new to evaluate, both the Top Management Programme and SMDP move in the right direction and offer evidence of an awakening commitment to modern management in British central government.

Surely, the most controversial Thatcher "initiative" has been her strong interest in the appointment of permanent secretaries, something earlier prime ministers had left mainly to the mandarins. Mrs Thatcher inherited a "bulge" with the retirement of several permanent secretaries as Burch has reported: "Between 1981 and 1983, 11 of the 23 most important permanent secretary posts became vacant through natural retirement."[13] Mrs Thatcher's aim was to break down the "closed, cozy society of smooth mandarins by adding a bit of grit."[14] As David Lipsey put it in looking at the new Treasury team under Peter Middleton: "By temperament, the new men are doers rather than thinkers – the quality that caught the prime minister's eye."[15] Whatever Mrs Thatcher's motives, there is no evidence that she sought permanent secretaries who followed the Conservative Party line.

These appointments highlight a critical issue. Has Mrs Thatcher found the organizational key by putting a new style mandarin in place with an action-oriented, managerial style to drive the machine? According to Lipsey, the new Treasury team under Middleton (youngish at forty-eight to make permanent secretary) is ready to take its direction from the political masters, not "agonizing over ... the strategy but welcoming the sense of direction it gives to their tactics."[16] Or, have Mrs Thatcher's intuitions not been thought through so that she missed the mark in not seeing the interrelationship between thinking *and* doing? Clearly "thinking" can be debilitating if what should be done is agonized over endlessly so that nothing happens or there is only the most minor movement. Rightly or wrongly, this procrastination seems to be Thatcher's perception of the managerial style of the smooth mandarins she inherited. But "doing" is dangerous too without in–depth strategic analysis. *Most dangerous may be talented managers who take objectives without sufficient strategic analysis and use their considerable organizational skills to push them forward; the ultimate threat can be good execution of bad policy.*

Based on my interviews in 1985 (roughly two years after the Middleton appointment), one thing is clear: the changes have not made a big difference thus far. In the first place subsequent appointments after Middleton to some extent blurred the "thinker–doer" dichotomy. A number of people were asked whether the new permanent secretaries would have been prime candidates for the positions if Thatcher had not interested herself in the appointments. There was a fair amount of disagreement but most people said the appointees would have been likely to make the short list even without Thatcher. The new permanent secretaries are somewhat younger than in the past so they may have been further down the list if things had been done as before. However, whatever the new permanent secretaries' abilities or "thinker–doer" orientation, each is a product of the mandarin system. None came from the outside. Each had travelled the normal, lengthy route leading to the top of the British civil service. It is hardly surprising that the management scene does *not* look all that different after this part of the Thatcher management revolution.[17]

The Thatcher government's concept of management

The Thatcher government has had an impoverished concept of management as revealed by several telltale signs: a mechanistic view of control, the disregard for civil servants' morale, and a "costs" mentality. For this government the most basic elements of management – people, dynamic organization, motivation, leadersip – often have been left out, replaced by costs and an archaic command and control mystique of leaders and docile followers, coupled uneasily with the belief that recalcitrant civil servants must be brought to heel. We need to consider several points more systematically.

A mechanistic view of control

In commenting on a management definition by Michael Heseltine, then Secretary of State for the Environment, William Plowden captured much of what is wrong with Thatcherism management philosophy:

The strategy has concentrated on developing sophisticated information systems, and on acquiring information about the cost and application of resources. This is fine as far as it goes. But as a "total" strategy it is simply not viable. To argue otherwise indicates an accountant's view of management, not a manager's. To misquote Oscar Wilde, it looks as though tomorrow's Whitehall manager will know the cost of everything but the value of nothing. As far as any theory of personal relationships can be detected, it is a kind of military "command" relationship, in which people all the way down the line do as they are told with no questions asked.[18]

This mechanistic view held by the Thatcher government is at the heart of its management problems and the notion will be elaborated on shortly.

Civil servant morale

Any good manager knows that staff is the most valuable organizational asset. The "bureaucrat bashing" that has come to sell so well in the period of the run up to elections and even afterward is a grave threat to effective government performance. Doing it before an election may be a costly requirement of winning. *Attacking civil servants after election is foolhardy indicating either a lack of understanding of how to manage, a disdain for managing, or both.*

The argument, as must be clear from my earlier comments, is not that the civil servants are blameless and in no need of political leadership. But a meat axe is seldom the best weapon. Lord Bancroft, former head of the Home Civil Service, surely is right when he laments: "Many will argue, and with force, that this [Civil Service] self-confidence was far too high and in any case totally ill-founded ... But something has gone far wrong with an undertaking whose staff find it necessary to be furtive, evasive or apologetic about their occupation."[19] No management error looms larger than alienating an organization's work force.

An anti-analytic, cost-fixated government

A conviction politician is likely to be anti-analytic. Doing hard analysis can show that a favored policy is not working, a proposed one is unlikely to work or that a current policy in disfavor is doing well. Deciding first (without analysis) and selectively using facts to support the case is much easier. Earlier British governments (except Heath) have hardly been high on policy analysis, but the Thatcher govern-

124

ment has reached a new level of distaste for analysis that brings uncongenial findings.

One interviewee spoke of the "cost of managing costs," arguing that the Thatcher government has gone back to "input budgeting," and claiming that administration has had an "internal balance sheet mentality as opposed to a public policy mentality." He added that thus far "FMI has been anti-management." Despite its rhetoric, FMI so often comes down to focusing mainly on input monitoring rather than on efficiency, effectiveness or even economy. The goal seems to be cheap government, not good government.[20] The argument is not to deny that a good manager should be cost-conscious, but a narrow concern with costs may be penny-wise and pound-foolish. Cutting the size of the Inland Revenue Service may reduce salaries but reduce tax yield far more. Management ultimately is about achieving objectives over time, not about spending less come what may. The good manager should not only be cost-conscious but outcome-conscious. Institutions exist to accomplish goals. More economical administration is a means, not a goal.

The gains from the Thatcher management efforts

Mrs Thatcher's long tenure and tenacity have made management a continuing concern at the top layers of the government. Being management conscious has become much more acceptable. As discussed earlier, the scrutinies force wide thinking about management. The mechanistic nature of FMI is being questioned. As a 1986 publication of the Institute of Directors has observed: "The burst of interest in how Whitehall works covers a wide range of issues."[21] Indeed, just as in the American case where PPBS failed as a system but succeeded in bringing hard analysis to government, so FMI could vanish but leave a broad management focus as heritage. The Thatcher management revolution like her economic revolution has yielded mixed, conflicting results. For example, on the one hand, her bullying of ministers and mandarins has often lowered morale or driven out talented people; on the other hand, her forcefulness when combined with longevity has made her management message hard to circumvent. Whether her government will move beyond the narrow cost focus toward some of the principles discussed later in this chapter is debatable. At best her first two governments may have established a base for gains but most of the distance remains to be covered. British government remains pre-modern.

The U.S. experience at the top offers valuable positive and negative lessons. On the one hand, the United States has done a much better job than Britain in sorting out relationships between political executives and high civil servants and in providing the former a reasonable shot at fulfilling their responsibility for agency management. On the other hand, two developments have damaged political executives' control of their agencies. First, the White House has increasingly worried about political executives being won over by their civil servants to make the agency's rather than the president's case. That fear has led to White House efforts to establish strong central control over political executives including occasional attempts at running policies from the White House. Second, recent administrations have created much animosity between political executives and higher civil servants with a consequent decline in civil servant morale and status.

The basic leadership/management structure

In 1939 the Executive Office of the President (EOP) was created by moving the budget office from the Treasury and giving institutional structure to the growing number of presidential aides under President Franklin D. Roosevelt. Over the years the EOP has expanded to include major analytic and advisory offices for economic, domestic and national security policies. Several points need to be made in contrasting the U.S. and British systems. First, the EOP is the president's office alone. Only the Office of Management and Budget (OMB) among the major policy offices has a large cadre of career civil servants. Other analytic offices such as the Council of Economic Advisers and the National Security Council staff have a total or nearly total staff turnover at a change of administration from one party to the other. Even OMB has political executives in all the key leadership positions. Second, the EOP has a much broader mandate than the No. 10 staff and Cabinet Office combined. The EOP has the budget function and a major role in economic policy. Third, the major

126

decisions at the top are made by the president and an inner circle dominated by presidential staff, not cabinet members. Fourth, the Executive Office of the President is large, numbering roughly 2,000 staff of which 1,700 or so will be permanent and the rest either detailed from executive departments or serving as temporary consultants. In sum, the president has a large staff he can call his own. The president and the EOP are at the center of the Executive Branch and stand atop executive government.

While the U.S. personnel system is complex, it can be said that with only minor exceptions the president controls *all* of the top agency positions many of which are subject to Senate confirmation but only a minute number are ever challenged. Political executives and other political appointees at the top of the government are not chosen through any kind of open, merit competition. Often appointments are to pay off loyal supporters after election. Loyalty rather than competence may be the main criterion for choice. A Cabinet secretary may be restricted severely by the White House in filling the key subcabinet positions. However, it can be said that the appointment process allows either presidents and/or agency secretaries to put in place their people at the top of the department.

The top agency civil servants today will be three or four layers down with far less status and power than civil servants in other major western nations. Nor in any of these other countries is there found the level of distrust exhibited in the United States. Britain under Mrs Thatcher has started down this misguided path too. It is a particularly grave error in light of the quality of the higher civil service and the dearth of outsiders willing and able to provide the analytic and managerial skills that are now lacking in British central government.

The Executive Office of the President: vision and reality

The vision of the EOP at its inception and the reality of today are much at odds. The EOP was to have been a relatively small, cohesive body with a careful blending of outsiders and high level generalist careerists. EOP staff were to be intelligence gatherers, analysts, strategists, coordinators, facilitators, advisers and managers of the presidential decision processes, not policymakers or operators trying to run departmental programs. Looking back nearly fifty years the earlier vision of the EOP had about it an unrealistic orderliness and separation of functions (a politics/administration dichotomy) but much of that vision remains desirable. Cohesiveness still is critical for an effective EOP. So, too, is a leanness of staff and function, and a capacity for strategic thinking. But, the most glaring weakness of all is the imbalance at the very top between outsiders and career staff.

Missing in today's EOP are generalist civil servants working directly with the president's top people and the president to provide institutional wisdom.[22] There is an extreme imbalance with no civil servants near the inner circle about the president. Heclo is so bothered by the outcome that he argues "I would rather see the Executive Office of the President bureaucratized with civil servants than by the customary layers of governmentally inexperienced short-timers ... *But we should not have to choose between a government of tyros or of mandarins.*"[23]

In the American case the distrust of civil servants has been so high in recent presidencies that arguing for civil servant generalists at the top may only be a pious hope. Britain in contrast is closer to a reasonable balance with the imbalance at this point being in favor of mandarins. The danger as in the U.S. case is the growing distrust of civil servants. *But there still appears to be a real opportunity to establish a well-balanced, lean staff of generalist-specialists at the top of the British government. The early vision for the EOP may be a much more likely reality for Britain than the United States.*

SHARED GOVERNANCE

The American shared governance experience stretches for roughly a quarter of a century from the rapid growth of President Lyndon Johnson's Great Society through President Ronald Reagan's attempts to cut back on federal grants to state and local governments. I will look at these extremely rich experiences by drawing on the emerging literature on policy implementation.[24] Much of the American implementation work has focused on shared governance where one political jurisdiction (usually the federal government) grants funds to another political entity to operate the funded programs. A central message is the need to concentrate on the point where goods or services are delivered. Here is where most policy gets made. The hard truth is that rules alone will not be sufficient guide to appropriate action in

128

complex programs. Discretion by the front-line staff is both unavoidable and desirable.

Discretion creates a basic management tension. Those at the top of programs may well be uncomfortable because discretion at lower levels threatens direct, tight, hierarchical control. At the same time effective performance in complex settings demands flexibility and discretionary judgments made on-the-spot. Front-line workers are central to successful service delivery: "The commitment and capacity of the final service delivery organization and concomitantly the individual persons who actually provide services are the central focus of the implementation perspective. Here the critical institutional investment must be made in managerial and staff capability that allows these organizations to exercise reasonable discretion in providing needed services at the point of delivery and to cope with the implementation of program changes."[25]

In the analysis that follows, the public sector experience is supplemented by recent business studies, particularly Peters and Waterman's *In Search of Excellence* that focuses on outstanding American companies.[26] What is so intriguing about the private sector studies of excellent companies is the similarity of the research techniques used to those now dominating implementation research and the basic compatibility of the findings with the implementation findings from the public sector. Putting together the public and private sector research is a useful exercise as long as the task at hand is to mine the latter for insights and for corroborating findings, not to establish immutable laws of implementation that span the public and private sectors.

At this point basic differences between the British and American central governments in their approaches to shared governance need to be considered briefly. A main British focus has been macroeconomic, concerned with total grants to local authorities and these authorities' public borrowing. The U.S. government, particularly during the Reagan administration, has interested itself to some extent with the overall level of grants to states and localities but much less so than Britain. However, the American government pays no attention to state and local government borrowing and generally speaking can be said to have little or no macroeconomic focus. Rather attention has centered on specific programs – on micro concerns – far more than in Britain. Almost all federal grants are categorical or block grants with significant federal restrictions in them rather than general revenue sharing, which is equivalent to rate support grants. The American shared governance experience is much richer in terms of micro program and policy management issues.

Autonomy and control

Autonomy is one of the two central elements of realistic delegation, control is the other. Goldsmith and Clutterbuck quote John Clothier of C. & J. Clark (Britain's international shoe company) as follows: "The core value of our business is clear lines of responsibility. Can someone say: 'I did that!'"[27] "I did that" means "I had a fair shot at success. I'm on the line for winning or losing." Granting subordinate managers the autonomy to make decisions that can lead to success or to failure is a key element in establishing clear lines of responsibility.

Control is the other side of the coin of reasonable delegation. Between the top position and the lowest management level are managers who need autonomy over their own operation and control over their subordinate managers. Nowhere is the dilemma of balance more clearly posed. Goldsmith and Clutterbuck point out: "Our successful [British] companies all maintain very tight controls on areas that matter. They seek a balance between strict controls and the flexibility that all major business must have to react to market conditions and opportunities. Each has evolved its own solution to this innate conflict."[28]

The link between autonomy and control is information. *Excellent companies are information-rich and are aggressive users of this information.* Information is a guide to action. It must be obtained quickly to support needed adjustments. Information and analysis often focus on process and explicit behavior because they are the key points of adjustment. Excellent companies fight secrecy when it blocks the aggressive use of information as a guide or as an indirect control factor. The classic bureaucratic pathology of secrecy is fought on pragmatic rather than ideological grounds.

The regulatory mentality

No one argues that there should be no rules and regulations. Rules and regulations can set out specifically what is desired and form the basis of evaluation for determining whether or not what is being done is consonant with desired means and/or goals. Rules and regulations can provide explicit federal intent. Checking on compliance can clarify federal intent by straightening out the ambiguous cases. Local choices are not inherently better than national ones.

At the same time difficulties in crafting workable rules seem to grow geometrically with complexity. The problem can be stated simply: *Rulemakers cannot anticipate the future clearly enough or calculate the interplay of factors in a complex situation so as to determine the right rules.* We are back to the need for discretion and judgment.

The worst manifestation of the regulatory mentality is the conversion of rules-as-means to rules-as-an-end in themselves. This conversion is most likely to occur over the issue of control under shared governance. Federal officials, particularly in the field offices, often have little real power. Not only does Washington (departmental headquarters) keep them on a short leash, field offices often lose at the local level on big issues where local officials can use or threaten political clout. So the relatively weak federal staffs equate control with following written procedures.

Organizational responsiveness

Unless there are strong efforts to avoid bureaucratic pathologies, both public and private organizations will develop such maladies as they grow larger and their environments become more complex. An organization needs to be "anti-bureaucratic" if it is to reap the benefits of bureaucratic organization and yet escape rigidness, ponderousness, and a regulatory mentality (pathological rulemaking).

Peters and Waterman argue that the best companies are *"learning organizations,"* their "response to complexity is fluidity."[29] Excellent companies in contrast to less successful organizations use small units and informal or ad hoc teams. They work to maintain the benefits of smallness, not obviously in overall size, but in the degree of autonomy in small units. Such companies find that economies of scale are often offset by growing rigidity and loss of flexibility. The essence of anti-bureaucratic measures is both to grant smaller units sufficient flexibility to act with discretion and to reward this discretion. Some companies will not allow a division to grow beyond some relatively small size. There is nothing like the massive production lines to make individuals feel insignificant.

131

Excessive layering is a critical pathology in a large organization. Looking up from the bottom, there appears to be an endless hierarchy peopled with managers, many of whom never see the production line. Excessive layering is usually the critical problem for "slow-moving, rigid bureaucracy."[30] The excellent companies seek simple form (a minimum of middle managers between the top and the lowest operating units) and lean staffs at the top. They push autonomy toward the bottom of the organization. Another bureaucratic pathology limiting organizational responsiveness is *oversized headquarters staffs*. Successful companies in both Britain and America have sought lean staffs at the top. The problem is not necessarily that big headquarters staffs carry out wrong-headed functions but that they undertake functions better executed elsewhere in the organization.

Specialists and generalists

What successful businesses in the U.S. and Britain have found is that neither narrow specialists or generalist-generalists are the kinds of people needed at the top. Peters and Waterman argue that "the star performers [among the excellent companies] are seldom led by accountants or lawyers ... Most of the leaders ... have come from operational backgrounds."[31] Goldsmith and Clutterbuck make the point even more dramatically:

Many unsuccessful companies are deeply suspicious of generalist managers. Promotion ... is primarily via functional channels and people are neither encouraged nor, in many cases, permitted to cross between them. On the other hand, it may be equally dangerous to populate a company with generalist managers who do not begin with a strong functional background to enable them to understand the fundamentals of the business they are in. The best of both worlds – in manufacturing industry at least – is probably to ensure that a high proportion of managers begin with a thorough technical knowledge and develop generalist skills. Our observations are that our very successful companies tend to make the transition to broader management skills early in the manager's career, while less successful companies may delay the transition until the manager's habits and way of thinking may be petrified with his narrow functional role.[32]

The Washington game

At the top the federal agencies often lose sight of the objective of helping people – of delivered policy – and become entangled in playing the Washington game. The world of federal agency management revolves around what happens in Washington, D.C. What happens in the field is also important but far more in terms of potential political repercussions that may embarrass Congress or the administration. Program performance *per se* is not likely to be a hot issue.

The Washington game – or London game – is but another manifestation of the politics/policy imbalance. Correcting it may be the biggest challenge facing managers in British central government. If the ministry head is not concerned with implementation and policy delivery, except in cases of potential political embarrassment, those near the top will not be either. A gap will exist between political leadership and executive management at the critical point where the two should merge.

Leadership

"Operations is policy" is something the top must take into account in major organizational decisions that involve the field. The greater insight is that top and bottom must be linked for success. The leader still matters. Only the top can establish and maintain organizational goals. Only the top can bring forth the guiding vision and a strategy that gives reality to that vision. The leader must combine intangible vision with the concrete organizational reality. In one of the most important statements in *In Search of Excellence*, the authors argue:

An effective leader must be the master of two ends of the spectrum: ideas at the highest level of abstraction and actions at the most mundane level of detail. The value-shaping leader is concerned, on the one hand, with soaring, lofty visions that will generate excitement and enthusiasm for tens or hundreds of thousand of people ... On the other hand, it seems the only way to instill enthusiasm is through scores of daily events, with the value-shaping manager becoming an implementer par excellence. In this role, the leader is a bug for detail, and directly instills values through deeds rather than words: no opportunity is too small. So it is at once attention to ideas and attention to detail.[33]

Strategic thinking belongs at the top. Goldsmith and Clutterbuck quote an executive of a successful British company in observing that "strategy is very centralized, tactics very decentralized."[34] Strategic planning clearly illustrates the Goldilocks Theorem. On the one hand, not planning can be fatal. It does not make much sense to avoid thinking about where one ought to go and how to get there. On the other, overplanning can be just as bad. "Staying on the drawing board" too long can stop all action. Sending "it" to the planning office can be the same as sending "it" to a committee. A further critical danger is planning beyond the available numbers so that all sorts of assumptions and proxies are used to bring elegance to a master plan that has a crumbling foundation. The planning rule in light of the kinds of uncertainty that face most public and private programs is: Make sure that the original plans get the general direction right; don't plan beyond the information; and adapt the plan to take account of new information. Planning is a continuing process, not a one-time exercise to produce a detailed, inflexible master strategy.

Both Peters and Waterman and Goldsmith and Clutterbuck stress the crucial role of long-term leadership. In the U.S. case the biggest difference between public and private sector management may be the turnover rates of managers in the former: "How well would corporations perform if their chief executive officer and a number of senior vice presidents came in and went out roughly every ... 2 years, which is the average life expectancy for federal agency political executives, and worked with a staff of corporate career personnel who were strangers to the new executives? Even if political executives concentrate on program substance, it is hard for them to take a long view, embracing goals that can be accomplished only after they have left the scene."[35] Rapid turnover of political executives may be endemic in the federal government. It also may be an overwhelming phenomenon in complex social service programs since having political executives who are knowledgeable about these programs and who will stay for a considerable period of time is most unlikely in the present political milieu. Putting civil servants higher in the chain of command as in Europe may simply not be feasible in American government.

Leaders have two overriding tasks. One is to supply the vision of long-term goals and to motivate those below to seek these goals. This task is the classic charge of the top leader. The second is to seek balance between innate conflicts. Such steering is less dramatic – less visible – than motivational leadership. Yet finding and keeping the delicate balances may be the hardest leadership trick of all.

6

THE ANALYTIC PERSPECTIVE

Previous chapters have indicated the dimensions of the pre-modern, anti-modern British central government and the needed elements of modernization – political leadership, executive management, and policy analysis. Now we turn to options for modernization. This chapter offers a conceptual framework for the analysis of specific options to reform British central government presented in Chapters 7 and 8 and for the broader treatment in the final chapter.

A FRAMEWORK FOR THE POLICY ANALYSIS

Policy analysis will offer a better base for decisionmaking, providing policymakers with both relevant information and a framework for assessing feasible options. The test is not that the analysis moves inextricably to the analyst's preferred option as, say, the mystery novel sleuth's piecing together of evidence that pinpoints the culprit. The feasible options for a complex policy issue are almost always a "mixed bag" of pluses and minuses, an uncomfortable offering of difficult tradeoffs. We are not operating in some value-free setting where optimal technical solutions can be developed but in a world where policy and politics are not separable. Different decisionmakers will bring different, but legitimate concerns and values to the policymaking process. The most useful analysis provides a sound basis for applying these differing concerns and values.

The institutional perspective

Curing the British Disease requires two great leaps – first a transformation of British central government and second a strong socioeconomic program with central government playing a pivotal role. The book treats only the first great leap. The driving *hypothesis* is that a modernized central government institutional structure and staff – defined in terms of strong analytic, strategic, leadership and managerial capacity and clearly defined lines of responsibility – must be put in place first to support formulation and implementation of policies to halt Britain's economic decline. This institutional perspective has several critical elements.

First, the principal concern is *not* structure per se in its static sense but *the organization in motion*. An organization chart showing hierarchy and clear lines of authority and responsibility, carefully drawn statements of objectives and functions, and detailed job descriptions does not *pari passu* produce effective institutional performance. People intrude. Institutional structure matters; organizational staffs matter more. Structure is formal and static and often dominated by informal relationships. More importantly, leadership at various levels is needed to make the organization move. The dynamic organizational dimension is institutional capacity. Generalized capacity defines broad categories or areas of competence; specialized capacity indicates particular skills and/or knowledge. The organization generally may need more analytic and managerial capacity; a particular unit, a higher education analyst. *Capacity connotes being good in action (dynamics), not simply looking good on paper (statics).*

Second, institutional knowledge is needed at the top about how the organization works. The organization-man leader is not necessarily knowledgeable about the specifics of much of the organization's effort. Too much concern for detail by the leader can be deleterious in seeing the trees not the forest. *What the top leader must understand is how the institutional process itself works and why the operational level is so critical to organizational policy performance (delivered policy).*

Third, politics and organization merge together at the top. Neither political nor organizational mastery alone will yield effective policy performance. The leader must have a vision (the first element of strategy) and the political mastery to sell it. He or she must also have sufficient organizational mastery to guide the policy formulation and implementation process over time so as to stay on course or to be able to correct the course in a changed environment. In the book separating the political and the organizational for discussion purposes facilitates the analysis of organizational mastery. However, if such a separation is interpreted as actually holding in practice, it is at best misleading and usually dangerous.

Fourth, effective organizations tend to be strong throughout – i.e., from top to bottom. In the private sector, for example, sales may be held back because an imaginative product conceived by a strong design department and well-made by a manufacturing unit is not well-marketed by a weak sales force. Or, a strong sales force may not be able to sell a poorly designed and manufactured product. In the private sector bureaucratic politics played by one unit may hurt overall organizational effort. The dangers are greater in the public sector where both intra- and inter-party rivalries loom large. In Britain the prime minister may see other ministers as potential political threats if made strong or the central government may want to punish local governments dominated by the opposition party. A political win may be scored, but it will be a Pyrrhic victory resulting in weak ministries and local authorities with less capacity for effective institutional and policy performance.

I want to emphasize that the notion of strong government throughout implies neither greater centralization nor more government power or effort *vis-à-vis* the private sector. A future prime minister who wants to decentralize so as to give local government more control over spending from central government funds or to shift activities from the public to the private sector needs to strengthen the center to support such dramatic institutional changes. British government as presently structured and staffed lacks the capacity to implement the changes needed for moving successfully to fulfill either goal.

The notion of strong government speaks mainly to competence not to size. And increasing size generally places a heavier and heavier burden on competence. *Central government is more likely to do what it does well if it does less rather than more.*[1] The notion of strong government throughout calls for greater competence at the center and the periphery and simply does not address directly the question of the relative sharing of effort by central government, local government, and the private sector.

Fifth, responsibility or accountability, the two terms are used interchangeably, is a key aspect of effective organizational performance. Who is to answer for a particular institutional effort? The meaningful assignment of organizational responsibility, as discussed in Chapter 5, requires two conditions. One is the clarity of accountability. The other is the availability of sufficient resources so that the person or unit held responsible has a reasonable chance of accomplishing the specified objectives. Not meeting these two prerequisites makes the notion of accountability meaningless in policy terms and ambiguous in political terms.

Sixth, effective *institutional* performance is a necessary but not sufficient condition of effective policy performance. Without strong institutional capacity (or good fortune), the organization can not deliver the desired policy performance. With strong institutional performance, however, effective policy performance is not assured. Bad luck may intervene; well implemented and executed policies may fail. It is a complex fallible world. *The most that can be claimed legitimately is that raising institutional capacity increases the probability of policy success.* But we do not know how much. The claim is about the direction of impact, not necessarily about the intensity or the time path of impact.

Finally, understanding organizations requires a systems approach in which various segments of the organization (system) are analyzed in terms of how well they fit together in an ongoing institutional process. At times, however, our limited ability in exposition will necessitate focusing on a single segment such as the new select committees or more broadly the Parliament. But conceptually we need to think of interrelationships such as between Parliament and the training of ministers to head large organizations or between the Cabinet and Parliament. One ailing segment simply may not be repairable when considered in isolation if the cause of the problem is in another segment of the organization. Or, repairs may "cure" one ailing unit but at the expense of creating grave problems for another unit.

Thinking in systems terms does not mean in depth analysis of every part because of a minor malfunctioning. An automobile that will not start does not require checking the entire vehicle before seeing if the battery is dead. Given a dead battery, however, it makes sense to ask if some other problem is the actual cause of failure. In the case of a generally well-running organization, tinkering with one unit that seems to be working poorly often does not demand great concern about the rest of the organization although it helps to ask if some other unit or factor outside of the unit in question is the causal problem or if fixing the ailing unit causes significant unintended consequences. Where the entire system is performing badly, system-wide analysis is not simply desirable, it is absolutely necessary. Partial analysis or a quick fix of one segment may do more harm than good. *At the heart of my analysis is the strong belief in an overall weakness in the British central government that demands a systems approach and concentration on the critical interrelationships in the institutional process.*

Means and Ends

The institutional process may be conceptualized in terms of two overlapping categories: means and ends (objectives), and/or intermediate and final objectives. Table 1 in the introductory chapter offers several policy options (i.e., means) that if successful are expected to fulfill the objective of efficient and effective institutional performance. For example, increasing the number of policy analysts (a means) is aimed at providing British central government greater institutional capacity (an intermediate objective) than presently to formulate, implement and manage social and economic policies. The intermediate objective in turn is expected to contribute to a desired final policy goal such as British citizens being better off in socio-economic terms relative to other advanced nations.

Increased institutional capacity also can be viewed as a means of achieving the desired final policy outcomes. Hence increased institutional capacity can be either a means or an intermediate objective. These intermediate (institutional) objectives are the results desired in a successful first great leap. At the same time this initial great leap involving institutional changes is a stage before the development and implementation of specific policies meant to treat directly the British Disease. The institutional objectives of the first great leap are the means in the second great leap to the desired final outcomes. This is another way of indicating that the first great leap is a necessary prerequisite of the second one, that greater institutional capacity must precede better policy performance.

The critical institutional objective of efficient and effective central government institutional performance is too broad, not offering a handle for assessment. Table 2 sets out three more detailed institu-

Table 2. *Institutional objectives*

---

1. Increased *policy responsibility* and *performance orientation* for major central government executives
2. *Greater capacity* of
    a. British central government to carry out the basic functions of directional leadership and strategy; policy formulation and choice (decision-making); scrutiny and challenge; and policy management[1]
    b. Local authorities to manage and operate central government funded policies in line with central government objectives
    c. Citizens and their representatives to scrutinize and challenge government policies and strategies and to offer alternatives
3. Improvements in the *quality, timeliness, and availability of policy information, analysis and advice* available to the key actors in the decisionmaking process

---

[1] The specific responsibilities of the key central government actors are: prime minister *alone* – directional leadership and strategy; Cabinet *including* the prime minister – policy formulation and choice; Parliament – scrutiny and challenge; and departments – policy formulation and choice and policy management.

tional objectives involving responsibility, capacity and information, trying to balance parsimony and generality with enough specificity to provide a tighter definition and put the broad objective in more measurable terms. The first thing to note about this table is that for purposes of discussion it is cast strictly in policy, not politics, dimensions. Efficient, effective governmental performance also has a set of politics objectives that in some respects would be similar to the institutional policy objectives. Certainly improved political information, analysis and advice are desirable. It is, as we have discussed, a basic responsibility of the top to blend policy and politics.

The three institutional objectives in Table 2 draw heavily on the American analytic and implementation experience to spell out the critical elements of a modernized central government. I have tried to be sufficiently general to elicit broad support for the objectives while maintaining a degree of specificity. For example, persons who disagree strongly about whether or not there should be a Prime Minister's Department can agree that the center needs more analytic capacity. The battle will be over the means of increasing capability, not the institutional objective itself.

Two aspects of the assigned responsibilities in Table 2 need elaboration. First is the choice to go beyond the central government to citizens and local authorities. These assigned responsibilities could be cast in normative terms as rights – citizens' right to know and communities' right of self governance. But such rights are also obligations (obligations being the obverse of rights) justified as much in pragmatic or functional terms as in normative ones. *More effective challenge and scrutiny by citizens and their representatives are expected to move governments toward better information and analysis and clearer lines of responsibility. Without strong local government capacity (and commitment too), central government policies operated through local authorities are much more likely to fail.* Hence the assigned functions of citizens and local governments positively reinforce the central government functions.

Second, the explicit assignment of responsibilities in the footnote to Table 2 indicates how I have parceled them out among the main central government actors. The most controversial assignment – the responsibilities given to the prime minister alone – is discussed in detail in a later chapter. Other than this, the responsibilities seem to accord with the conventional wisdom about who does what in central government. Overlap of responsibilities needs mentioning. The main one within the central government is policy formulation and choice shared by the Cabinet and the departments, an expected result. Also, scrutiny and challenge are (or should be) a part of policy formulation and so not solely the preserve of Parliament. Finally, the other two actors have responsibilities that overlap explicitly with those of the central government – citizens, challenge and scrutiny, local government, policy management – that may not accord with the views of particular readers.

The institutional objectives in Table 2 provide a basis for assessing the options. Will a particular option increase (i) the clarity and degree of policy responsibility and the level of policy orientation, (ii) the level of generalized and specialized capacity of the actors and their organizational units to execute specific functions, and (iii) the availability of sound, timely policy information, analysis and advice to key actors in the decisionmaking process? In a detailed analysis this question should be posed not just in directional terms but also as to intensity (how much). The analyst also should be concerned with implementation feasibility and with possible side effects or undesired consequences caused by an option (a point treated shortly).

Table 3. Options and institutional objectives

	Responsibility	Capacity	Information
House of Commons			
1. Eliminate question time	D		
2. Increase in policy analysts	I	D	
3. Committees a primary vehicle		D	
Prime minister and Cabinet			
4. Prime minister responsible for overall strategy	D	I	
5. Prime minister's policy unit		I	D
6. New analytic and strategic units in Cabinet Office	I	D	
Whitehall departments			
7. Ministers control senior appointments	D	I	
8. Ministers not in Parliament having full access to Commons	D	I	
9. Minister's strategic and analytic unit		I	D
10. Departmental management strategy	D	I	
11. Abolish single permanent secretary	D	I	
12. New civil servant promotion structure		D	
13. Elite training college for civil servants		D	
Public information			
14. Strong FOI Act		I	D
15. Increased central government funding of nongovernmental research organizations		I	D

D, Direct I, Indirect

Table 3 matches the fifteen options presented earlier in Table 1 with the three institutional objectives of responsibility, capacity and information. Each option is assessed to determine whether it is expected to have a direct (D) or indirect (I) impact on the three institutional objectives. Six options are aimed directly at increasing responsibility, five at capacity, and four at information. The capacity objective needs further discussion. While capacity has only a limited number of options aimed directly at it, the ten options intended for a direct impact on responsibility and information *all* are expected to have an indirect influence on capacity. These ten indirect impacts imply a simple causality hypothesis – for example, more policy analysts will bring forth more sound, timely information which will enhance Parliament's capacity to engage in meaningful scrutiny and challenge.[2] Assessment in this case involves two separable aspects. First, if the number of policy analysts is increased significantly (that this can be done is not certain), will an increase occur in the availability of sound, timely information, analysis and advice? Second, will that increased availability (the direct impact) raise capacity?

Two further assessment questions need to be asked. Can the proposed option be implemented in the form anticipated? Will the option cause serious unintended consequences?

Feasibility and unintended consequences

Policy analysts generally split the feasibility question into two parts – political and administrative feasibility. The former focuses on sale-ability in the political arena. Will the government of the day agree to a significant increase of the number of policy analysts in Parliament? If not, would Parliament be likely to go against the government and opt for the increase? Administrative feasibility covers a variety of issues including bureaucratic resistance (bureaucratic politics), skill or experience shortages, managerial deficiencies, and coordination and communication blockages.

What is logically consistent on paper may not be politically or administratively feasible in practice, either being impossible to execute or costing too much to put in place. Parliament simply may not choose to increase the number of analysts significantly or it may hire people who are not qualified policy analysts. The internally logical model, indicating that more analysts bring more available information which enhances capacity, can collapse in practice either because the likelihood of increasing policy analysts significantly is low or because the costs of doing so are inordinately high.

The last key assessment question asks whether or not the option will induce unintended negative consequences. Unintended consequences fall into two classes. First are those that are anticipated in the sense of perceived as a potential deleterious development. Major surgery carries the risk of dying on the operating table. Central government efforts to stimulate economic growth through deficit spending run the risk of creating strong inflationary pressures. In the case at hand, a significant increase in policy analysts clearly threatens an unacceptable level of staff influence on MPs. The second class of unintended consequences are those likely not to be thought of during the policy formulation period. Perhaps unwisely, policymakers seeking to desegregate elementary and secondary schools in major U.S. central cities by busing white and minority children did *not* anticipate massive white flight either to private schools or to surrounding suburbs, which had few if any minority families. *The policy analyst has a special responsibility to search for and highlight such unintended consequences.*

In that regard, one unintended but clearly expected consequence needs underscoring. Public sector institutions are fragile entities that do not handle change well. And no change is likely to have higher institutional consequences than those that modify the status of people currently on board or the existing customs and practices. Organizational units dislike giving up resources. People in these units do not yield personal power easily. An agency may face no more difficult kind of implementation than that of reorganizing its structure where its own bureaucracy has both inside knowledge and power, including the staying power of the career civil service. The only harder case may be ones involving *politicians* whose status and turf are at risk.

A LOOK AHEAD

The next two chapters set out and analyze various institutional options intended to increase accountability, capacity and information. Consider the strategy and tactics of this analysis. The book's primary strategic goal is a material improvement in the information and analytic base for thinking about the reform of the central government institutional structure, not the recommendation of a specific package of options. The principal tactic will be to use the analytic framework to explore competing policy options.

Policy analysts treating options may employ two different tactics – one is to compare options and make recommendations; the second is to stop at comparison. However, even where recommendations are made, the analysts' recommendations should not dominate. Policy analysis is not simply an exercise in advocacy. Far more important is the building of a base that guides decisionmakers through the development of a framework and the discussion and analysis of options. There is a second, related reason for not pushing to the recommendation stage, and certainly for not offering an explicit package of institutional options to modernize British central government. Such an approach carries the message that there is a generalizable, optimum options package that dominates competing packages on the key dimensions of logic, feasibility, and lack of unintended consequences and that it has been found or at least can be found. That surely is not the message I want to impart.

This is not to say, that were I called forth by a prime minister to indicate how to go about making central government institutional changes, I would have none to offer. I would. However, I would not claim that the recommended options were a dominant package. Moreover, later chapters will make clear how I would approach the modernization issue given a reasonable period of time to work with decisionmakers. But I have not been asked to do so and consider it counterproductive to act as if I had been – to proceed as if the decision to modernize British central government had been made.

What needs to be done in the next several chapters is to analyze further why British central government must be transformed to cope effectively with the British Disease and to show that the framework and the analysis of options are useful in the serious consideration of the means of modernization.

7

MODERNIZING THE PARLIAMENT AND THE CENTER

In the United States, the Executive and Legislative Branches are truly independent. Further, the Executive Office of the President houses the key presidential institutions, is the nerve-center of the Executive Branch, and stands atop the government. But what is the top of the British government? Even agreeing on the center raises problems. Sir Kenneth Berrill argues "the 'center' is the 'troika' of the Prime Minister, the Chancellor of the Exchequer and his ministerial team and the Foreign Secretary and his team."[1] I prefer to include only the Prime Minister's staff and Cabinet Office, and of course the Cabinet itself, as the center.

Changing Parliament is the critical first step toward central government modernization yet fundamental change in Parliament is highly dependent on leadership from the government of the day. Ultimately any discussion of fundamental parliamentary change becomes so frustrating because the likelihood that Parliament will rise up and act as a body to defy the current Executive Branch and *future* Executive Branches (that is, Cabinet members yet to be), whatever party is in power, is so small. The thrust for basic change must come from the government, or more accurately the prime minister and Cabinet. *In short, Parliament is the starting place for the problem; the prime minister and Cabinet as leaders of both the center and Parliament are the starting place for any likely solution. The catalyst almost certainly must be the prime minister as political leader.*

PARLIAMENT

The increasing independence of members (the unwillingness to give *unthinking* support to the government) and the select committee and the NAO changes signal a growing concern for scrutiny and challenge. The House of Commons today, however, still looks much like the Commons of twenty or fifty or a hundred years ago in its basic features of exclusiveness, the importance of floor debate, and the lack of technical capacity to challenge the government of the day. Parliament, the embodiment of pre-modern, anti-modern British central governance, must change dramatically for there to be significant modernization. The overriding issue is whether or not changes that do not immediately break the basic mold can make much of a difference. The issue of whether incrementalism can do the job will bedevil us in other areas but it seems to pose special difficulties with Parliament. On the one hand, it is desirable as a general rule to avoid institutional disruption by keeping changes incremental. On the other hand, the major (nonincremental) changes that are needed seem most unlikely to come about if pursued through several incremental changes over time. If a nonmember is brought into the Cabinet, he or she may suffer Frank Cousins' fate. If the chamber of the House of Commons continues to focus the parliamentary process, the old ways and mores may hold and in holding impede severely if not block effective central government modernization. There can be no omelet without breaking eggs.

The changes in Parliament that would most improve central government overall are dominated by two "do nots." Do not let the debate on the floor of the House of Commons remain the be-all and end-all of the parliamentary process. Do not select ministers only from the ranks of MPs. Do improve Parliament's capacity to scrutinize and challenge ranks only third.

Ending the central role of floor debate

At lunch one day with a person who has written widely on British government, I was discussing possible incremental changes in Parliament. My companion asked whether such marginal changes would make any difference, given the continued emphasis on debate on the floor of the Commons and then said: "*What if you never allowed*

Parliament to meet as a full body but required all business to be done in committees?" My off-the-top-of-the-head answer boiled down to saying you would in essence have reinvented the U.S. Congress where committees and subcommittees do so much of the work. Two points about this discussion need elaboration. First, no question about governmental structure looms larger than whether basic change can come throughout the government if the House of Commons continues to do its work on the floor. Second, the U.S. Congress, while not a model, offers a rich experience.

In a discussion of the West German Bundestag Renate Mayntz made this comparison with the British Parliament: "Relatively little depends on [the West German chancellor's] performance as leader in relation to parliament as a whole. This stands in obvious contrast to the case of the British Prime Minister and is related to the character of the German Bundestag, which is *more a working than a debating parliament*."[2] I cannot say whether Professor Mayntz intended to do more than set out an illustrative comparison in a volume that treats seven Western European governments. But her comparison is apt. Making the distinction between a working and a debating parliament lays bare why Bruce George as quoted in Chapter 2 puts Britain near the minimal legislatures of the Eastern bloc and other dictatorships. "Genuine legislatures," to use George's biting terminology, work mainly in committees and subcommittees supported by staff aides with floor debate often a minor factor in legislative decisionmaking.

Can Britain have a "genuine legislature" if there is not a dramatic breaking of the mold? Less draconian measures than proposed by my lunch companion – e.g., abolishing question time – might lessen the institutional shock. But they are details. The basic issue is how to stop chamber debate from being the crucial barrier that blocks modernization.

Several key differences need discussing in considering Congress' relevance to the British case. First is Congress' full constitutional independence from the Executive Branch. Congress can defy the president by defeating his legislation, by refusing to confirm his nominees to office or to ratify his treaties, by passing legislation formulated in Congress, and, when necessary, by overriding a presidential veto. At the same time Congress has extended contact with the Executive Branch including well-established relationships with agency officials. Through legislation Congress can set out information gathering and reporting by the Executive Branch agencies.

Second is Congress' structure. Woodrow Wilson wrote in 1885: "It is not far from the truth to say that Congress in session is Congress on public exhibition, whilst Congress in its committee-rooms is Congress at work."[3] What Wilson characterized as "committee government" in legislative policymaking flourished until the early 1970s. It reached its high point from 1937 to 1971 when a handful of powerful, well-entrenched committee chairmen mainly from Southern and Western states dominated both the House and the Senate. Today subcommittee government predominates.[4] In the earlier period subcommittees existed, but they were controlled tightly by the committee chairs. Now subcommittee chairs operate with considerable autonomy. Power is far more decentralized with much of the action going to the subcommittees. Almost 100 years after Wilson's statement, Asbell said of the Senate, and his statement holds even more strongly for the House of Representatives: "[T]he traditional public privilege of ... watching the full Senate from the gallery is the doodad, the window dressing ... The subcommittee markup is not merely a step in the legislative process. For most bills the markup *is* the legislative process."[5]

The dominance of committees and subcommittees in the Congressional policymaking process should not be overstated. Senators in particular still like floor debate and attendance often is high. Floor debate over great issues can be dramatic and significant. Further, of late there has been more of a tendency to rewrite legislation on the floor through amendments.[6] But subcommittee government, as distinct from committee government, predominates. Davidson points out: "To a large degree, subcommittee government is staff government. The modern Capitol Hill bureaucracy betrays the character of Congress as a decentralized, nonhierarchical institution."[7] Where once a handful of all powerful, committee chairmen were in firm control, many power centers flourish in committees and subcommittees.

Some key size differences between the Senate with 100 members and the House with 435 members are relevant to how the Parliament might operate. One is floor (chamber) debate. Senate rules facilitate floor action in allowing unlimited debate and not restricting amendments from the floor. The classic case is the one senator filibuster that

149

can tie up the entire chamber. In contrast the House restricts the number both of hours of debate and of amendments. Now part of the difference no doubt comes from quite different historical development in the two bodies. But size is a key factor too. And the House of Representatives is still only two-thirds the size of the House of Commons. Another difference is specialization. Senators are spread more thinly across policy areas often serving on several committees while House members tend much more to specialize. House members are more likely than Senators to be experts themselves on a particular subject and are less dependent on staff.

The centralization through the committee structure that worked well for so long finally went too far as heavy-handed oligarchs violated the Goldilocks Theorem by holding power too tightly. It appears decentralization now has overshot in the other direction. As former Congressman Henry S. Reuss (a liberal Democrat serving Wisconsin from 1955 to 1982) observed in the February 17, 1986 issue of *The Washington Post National Weekly Edition*: "Congress is overrun with subcommittees and staff, as a result of a revolution that went too far. There was a successful move in the 1970s to come to grips with the Neanderthal rigidity of seniority and committee chairman autocracy ... But in the House, we went overboard ... there is no focusing of responsibility."

We may be seeing Congress at another time of correction. Indeed, Congress may be in the midst of a long adjustment since the subcommittee system in its present virulent form (over 100 subcommittees in both the House and the Senate) only dates from the 1970s. But the point should not be missed that Congress today continues to be a formidable body able to challenge the president to a degree that in other countries would create a government crisis and likely force a general election.[8] As Patterson argues "Congress is semi-sovereign."[9] In this sense Congress in its broadest dimensions is not a model for parliamentary government. Yet much of how it uses power is directly relevant.[10]

The third key difference is staff size. Malbin puts the number of staff at over 23,000 and points out that the Canadian Parliament is second in the world with 3,300 legislative staff.[11] These numbers overstate the case in containing roughly 6,000 functionaries including a 1,000-strong police force. Large numbers of staff serve constituency and re-election functions (much less a burden in Britain), not those of policy analysis or advice. Further, the demands for personal help are large both because of the nature of state, local, and interest group politics and because of the openness of federal agencies to Congress members and staff. These people are not relevant to our discussion. But even with adjustments, the congressional staff available to do policy work is large.

Fourth is the fast growth in recent years of policy analysis and related activities. Congress got a late start long after the Executive Branch. Much of the impetus for analysis came from the 1974 Budget Act that established new House and Senate Budget Committees, Senate and House Budget Committee staffs, and the Congressional Budget Office (CBO). The latter, which was the first congressional policy analysis staff, merits further discussion.

CBO is labeled as an independent agency in Congress (the General Accounting Office, the Library of Congress and its Congressional Research Service, and the Office of Technology Assessment are the others) because it serves the entire Congress not a specific committee and hence is supposed to be nonpartisan. All of these offices including CBO can provide direct help on request to an individual Congress member although committees (and in the case of CBO, the two budget committees) have priority status.

The CBO staff dominated by economists and other policy and cost analysts numbers about 200. The first head Alice Rivlin, who is a left-of-center Democrat, had directed an Executive Branch policy analysis office and was serving at the Brookings Institution before taking the CBO position; the second (current) head Rudolph Penner, who is a right-of-center Republican, came directly from the American Enterprise Institute.[12] The political coloration is underscored because CBO has gained the reputation for accuracy and nonpartisanship in its cost estimates of legislative proposals and in its economic forecasts. CBO estimates are generally considered the starting point for policy discussion not just in Congress but nationally since White House estimates are expected to be "cooked" to support administration proposals.

Be clear CBO numbers do *not* drive out political concerns. Congress does still support policies that data and analysis call into question. However, analysis often bounds the debate giving it more reality. Policy analysis by the CBO and others has made Congress members more performance-oriented and much more sophisticated.

What has been written so far is not meant to refute the argument that congressional staffs are too large and have too much power – an argument captured in the title of the previously cited Malbin book *Unelected Representatives*. Rather I emphasize the positive side of staff. Competent analytic staff serving individual members directly or through a party grouping in Parliament (discussed shortly) could improve scrutiny and challenge. Alternatively, information and analysis could be nonpartisan with a CBO-type staff serving all of Parliament. Such nonpartisan information and analysis could provide a base for scrutiny and challenge by any user be it an individual MP, front-bench opposition or a select committee.

The implications of the American congressional experience are important, but should not be carried too far. That Congress today is overstaffed and too decentralized should serve as a warning to those who would start on the path of committee and subcommittee government. But such overstaffing and decentralization is not inevitable. The committee system dominated for a long period of time and collapsed because of an idiosyncratic development – the disproportionate power of conservative Southern Democrats during a period (now passed) of one party rule in the South. Further, the proliferation of staffs and subcommittees has in part been a response to the special circumstances of American Federalism, particularly the power of individual states. Yet, even if the outcome is inevitable at least in mild form, taking the route is not necessarily the wrong choice. If there is one institutional verity, it is that of change. The institutional fix of today becomes the roadblock of future years. The great danger is to view institutions in their present configuration as a final solution.

Comparative analysis can go only so far. No American evidence answers the question of whether Parliament must be changed dramatically at one time or can be modified through a number of incremental steps over time that add up to the same amount of change as the one dramatic step. Nor does the available evidence indicate the negative consequences of a nonincremental shift. To make the logical argument that a modernized Parliament could benefit Britain is not to answer either whether such modernization is feasible (i.e., will be implemented properly) or whether a modernization proposal, even if implemented as desired, will bring unintended negative consequences of such a magnitude that Britain will be worse off.

Ministers and junior ministers from the outside

The parliamentary apprenticeship prepares British ministers for the task of representing their departments in Parliament and probably inhibits development of the capacity to perform the management function. Although as discussed earlier, the available supply of outsiders is small, surely there are people out there who can manage a department better than some of the thin supply of competent MPs and the occasional Lord (e.g., political leaders in local government).

But can these outsiders survive in Parliament? Unless Parliament in all its fury decides to destroy the intruders, they should be able to survive with help from "regular" members and civil servants. A handful of ministers and junior ministers brought into the House of Commons, and perhaps expected to run for Parliament in the next election, if not already Lords, could give the House a more varied perspective and add management and substantive policy expertise.

Survivability in Parliament, however, may not be the right question. The more basic issue is why should ministers be in Parliament. This last question leads from Parliament to the Executive and will be pursued there. However, a fundamental parliamentary issue does need considering here: Can Parliament be changed so that only one minister or junior minister from a department need be on the floor of the House of Commons?

Even though American Cabinet secretaries are not (indeed, cannot be) current members of Congress, one of their most important tasks is representing the department in Congress. More broadly, a secretary often is considered the "outside" person, not just for relations with Congress but for the department's external relations with various interest groups, while the number two person in the department (also a political appointee) is the "insider" responsible for daily management. Nonmember political executives could still appear before select committees if the House of Commons chooses to restrict the chamber to members only.

More analytic capacity and clout

That the government of the day should have its current and proposed policies subjected to scrutiny and challenge is a fundamental principle of British parliamentary government. Given this watchdog function, the main issues are the source of the challenge, the capacity of the challenger, and the challenger's clout (power).

The source of the challenge is the starting point. The two main contenders are Parliament as a body and the parties. Analytic capacity could be developed through such mechanisms as the select committees and the NAO. The parliamentary opposition might gain more analytic capacity through analytic staff serving individual members, the party or parties *in* Parliament, or in research departments or other party vehicles outside of Parliament. A basic issue is who should be the watchdog. The departmental select committees may not be the right vehicle and so misdirect time and effort. George Jones proposes that "party committees of MPs should be developed as major centers for policy formulation" and would confine select committees "to investigate the administration of policy and to limit their cross-examination of witnesses to civil servants."[13] More drastically, department select committees could be done away with. But the Jones proposal sets out the clear choice between Parliament as a body and the parties recognizing that combinations, one of which Jones himself lays out, are variants on the two primary options.

The choice – party or Parliament or some combination – depends on values, on constitutional interpretation, and on one's assessment of implementation feasibility. Say the basic choice is party. The vehicle for challenge and scrutiny could be individual MPs, all major parties, or just the parties on the front benches and could come through a structure within Parliament or an extra-parliamentary vehicle such as a party research department (funding coming in both cases from the government).

The issues of capacity and clout remain. Key questions concern the numbers of staff, kinds of staff skills and experience needed, and the institutional mechanisms to be used to focus the scrutiny and challenge. As long as the numbers remain small – say a few more select committee staff – the amount of change too is likely to be small. Larger numbers of staff and much greater power to force the government to provide information, however, can bring basic change. For example, the opposition party could be given enough analytic staff and sufficient access to official information to make it a much more fair encounter between the opposition and the government backed by civil servants.

We need to step back for a moment and ask, "Analysis to do what?" The answer is different if the analytic capacity and clout are to arm Parliament as a body versus the arming of the opposition party. Accept for purposes of discussion the distinction made so clearly by George Jones that only the government and the opposition, not Parliament as a body, are concerned with policy formulation, an activity which includes considering competing objectives. The National Audit Office and the Public Accounts Committee make this same distinction in holding that the government's stated objectives are taken as given and the watchdog role is confined to the economy, efficiency, and effectiveness of existing programs and policies.

But there are watchdogs and there are watchdogs. A Pekingese can bark loudly, a German shepherd can tear off a burglar's arm or worse. A select committee or the NAO staffed with evaluation specialists could conduct well-designed evaluations asking how efficiently or effectively a policy is working or contract with outside policy research organizations to execute such a study. The select committees could have the authority to require departments to conduct such evaluations and report the results just as the U.S. Congress has done. Although this approach would not strengthen the opposition party directly, both the information from the analyses and the added staffs of the select committees could aid in making the evaluative results understandable for the nonspecialist MPs. Further, with the availability of policy-relevant data, the hiring of a small number of competent policy analysts by the opposition party to put the numbers in partisan terms could have a big payoff for a limited outlay of funds.

If the arming was of the party so that policy objectives were *not* off limits, the impact on governance would likely be even larger. There could be more of a fair fight between the government supported by legions of civil servants and the party with money for staff and studies. Moreover, *if* the staff serving the opposition had strong analytic skills, ministers and mandarins well may find it necessary, if not pleasant, to think in analytic terms.

A host of questions remain of which the most obvious, and frustrating, is why would the government of the day adopt such a course of action. But there are others of great importance if we assume that such a course of action would be adopted. Would MPs including those on the opposition front benches think in performance terms if better analytic information was available? Where would competent staff and organizational capacity be found to carry out the analysis? Would such staff increases and added clout make Parliament like the U.S. Congress with all its alleged faults?

Wanted: *An organization-man (or woman) prime minister to modernize the British government.* The prime minister, first and foremost, must be a competent political/policy leader. Organizational knowledge alone will not do; neither will political mastery alone. Assume for purposes of analysis that a prime minister has political mastery. For the kinds of changes being discussed, he or she will need such mastery. How should the organization-man prime minister operate in terms of institutional processes and structure? The prime minister must recognize the need for strength both at the center and in the departments and move boldly to develop such strength. Everything that follows is detail – albeit important detail. The critical first choice is ministers. Harris observed that "Attlee ... thought that choosing ministers was one of a prime minister's most exacting tasks."[14] No early organizational decision is more important. The prime minister must see that his or her performance depends on the performance of strong ministers. Policy performance is not a zero–sum game.

The "ideal" prime minister would appreciate the need for analytic and strategic capacity at the center generally and the special need for strategic thinking at the top of the government. He or she also would recognize the prime minister's special role as catalyst for change. Finally, this "ideal" prime minister would have the vision to see the need to modernize British central government overall (including Parliament) and a strategic sense of how to modernize the key institutions. Modernization demands the highest order of leadership combining political mastery, broad vision and organizational mastery.

Barriers to modernizing the center

Suppose that a future prime minister appreciated the need for modernization and the institutional dimensions and demands of that modernization, he or she would face three main barriers to modernizing the center. First is the concern about a presidential prime minister which crystallizes in the issue of a Prime Minister's Department.

Second is the fear of large-sized staff. Third is the limited supply of capable people, an issue to be discussed in a later chapter.

Does being a catalyst for change and keeper of the government's strategy make that prime minister presidential? Not necessarily. Either the direct or the facilitator style is appropriate generally although the former seems more likely in the current setting. Attlee in his particular way was both catalyst and keeper of the "vision."

If "presidential" is being used pejoratively as a kind of shorthand for not wanting a leader who seeks domination of ministers, I would concur not only for Britain but for the United States. If "presidential" is employed more specifically as a shorthand for not liking Mrs Thatcher's policies including her management style, I would reiterate my pragmatic problems with that style whoever pursues it.[15] For example, both John Kennedy and Richard Nixon's management styles were just as suspect as Mrs Thatcher's in trying to dominate cabinet ministers. This point needs emphasizing because creating a Prime Minister's Department does not *pari passu* bring a presidential prime minister (although surely it points in that direction) nor does building up the Cabinet Office and keeping a Prime Minister's Office deter a prime minister bent on being presidential. Hence, my approach involves mainly pragmatic rather than constitutional issues.

Those debating the need for a Prime Minister's Department start from broad agreement that the British center needs greater analytic and strategic capacity. The main issue is where to locate that capacity. Lurking beneath the surface, however, is the British fear of big staffs. How much that fear is of size alone and how much it is entangled in a big staff being associated with a prime minister's putsch to gain Cabinet dominance – to be presidential in the pejorative way British critics often use that term – is unclear.

A Prime Minister's Department

The case against a Prime Minister's Department has been offered by Professor George Jones: "The logic of the British Constitution is that prime ministers do not intervene in the policy responsibilities of specific ministers in order to advance personal prime ministerial objectives. Their intervention makes constitutional sense if it is to enhance collective cabinet government."[16] Jones' list of those serving the prime minister includes only personal, political and public relations staffs and a private office of civil servants. No policy unit and no policy advisers drawn from the outside are to be found. It is the barest of offices, stripped of all policy concerns except for (i) the political presentation of policy, (ii) the possible impact of policy on the party, and (iii) the linking of the prime minister to the departments and the processes of government through the private office civil servants. Jones closes his long article as follows: "For policy advice she should turn ... to a unit available to all cabinet ministers ... Such a central office will serve not only the prime minister but her colleagues too and be a force to strengthen not weaken collective decisionmaking processes. Any augmentation of the center of government should seek to enhance the analytical and evaluative capacity of this Cabinet Office, serving all ministers, and not to create a Prime Minister's Department."[17]

A major option lies between the Jones proposal and a full-fledged Prime Minister's Department. This "mixed option" has the following features: a policy unit in the Prime Minister's Office (but not necessarily housed entirely in No. 10), a separate strategy unit in the Cabinet Office, and greater analytic capacity within the Cabinet Office. A mixed option allows a new prime minister, seeking greater analytic capacity in support of his or her exercise of political control, to avoid the battle over creating a new Prime Minister's Department with all its ideological baggage. A prime minister seeking domination is not blocked by the lack of a Prime Minister's Department and may even be hindered by one. A large department with a permanent staff can develop over time a number of bureaucratic pathologies while the Cabinet Office has a history of flexibility (discussed below). Whatever the constitutional facade, a strong prime minister can make an analytic unit within a Cabinet Office structure his or her own. The battle for a department would not be worth it to a new prime minister.

If a Prime Minister's Department had been established and hence the bureaucratic battle already fought by an earlier prime minister, it might be unwise for a new prime minister to dismantle the department if the issue had been played out and dismantling would reopen old battles. However, a new prime minister should be alerted to the dangers of increasing bureaucratization. A full-scale Prime Minister's Department can be an immediate roadblock either because it will try to retain hard won independent power or because it will find difficulty in adjusting to a new prime minister's goals and style. The main argument against a Prime Minister's Department is pragmatic, flowing from well-known bureaucratic pathologies.

A prime minister needs a critical mass of people he can call his own. Most likely such people will be exclusively or primarily from outside the government. It is a fiction that the policy interests of particular Cabinet ministers and those of the prime minister are always the same. Both interests are legitimate. Even in Jones' restricted Prime Minister's Office, there is a separate political staff the minister can call his or her own. The same should be true on the policy side. This policy analysis unit's main job would be to keep the prime minister informed through intelligence gathering and analysis and to see that the prime minister's policy concerns were being taken into account. The unit would not be the main source of analytic and strategic capacity at the center. Such capacity would be in the Cabinet Office.

Structuring the prime minister's policy analysis unit presents a number of problems. One is the need to have sufficient institutional knowledge to work with other government analysts. Another is to establish linkages with the groups with which it needs to work. Finally, keeping the size of the staff (especially the outsiders) down will not be easy.

Two suggestions are in order. The first is that everyone in that unit *does not* need to be physically housed at No. 10 Downing Street. The U.S. case is instructive. The West Wing of the White House in being near the president is the most prestigious of locations. Heads of major units such as the domestic and foreign policy staffs are located in the West Wing, but their staffs will be in other buildings. The key people in the Policy Unit should be in No. 10, but outstationing other staff in the Cabinet Office has advantages beyond simply reducing crowding. Interaction among Policy Unit analytic staff physically located in the Cabinet Office and members of the Cabinet Office's augmented staff should enhance the competition of policy ideas. Additionally, the prime minister is more likely to be in the various bureaucratic and analytic networks if his or her people are in the Cabinet Office. Call the effort intelligence gathering, label it spying if you will, there is no substitute for being on the ground, as any diplomat will tell you, be the country in question friendly or unfriendly.

A prime minister should *not* rule out seconding civil servants as CPRS did. As long as the leadership of the policy analysis unit is dominated by outsiders, secondment makes sense. The argument is not that secondment definitely ought to be done. A prime minister already having key civil servants in his private office and relying heavily upon the Cabinet Secretariat may want a unit exclusively of outsiders. An in-between position that seems desirable is to use former civil servants whom I would label as outsiders. If the former civil servant would still be loyal to the career civil service or his or her department then that person should not be hired for loyalty and experience but only the latter. Seconded or former civil servants bring an institutional knowledge other outsiders often (indeed, nearly always) lack. Given the shortage of competent analysts, such a source of help should not be ignored.

A major problem at the top is that the short run tends to drive out the long run. A strategic unit, therefore, is hard to develop and maintain. Thinking strategically is an exceedingly difficult task in the crisis world of No. 10 (or the White House). This mixed option would put the strategic unit in the Cabinet Office to provide some insulation. But that leaves a problem inherent in strategic efforts. On the one hand, the strategic unit does not want to be so detached from ongoing policy that it appears out of the mainstream of policy thinking. On the other, the unit can suffer from being so caught up in today's policy issues that its staff lacks the time needed for strategic thinking. No obvious tactic ensures the needed balance. One possibility would be to have the unit physically located in the Cabinet Office but with its director (the government's chief staff strategist) housed in No. 10.

The Cabinet Office is appealing as a location for much of the added analytic and strategic capacity. There are two reasons. First, any prime minister (even one with dreams of being "presidential") needs Cabinet support to exercise effective political control. That Cabinet (or civil service) bashing is a poor tactic should be clear to a performance-oriented prime minister. Second, the Cabinet Office has a history of being a good place to locate all sorts of units. Moreover, since the Cabinet Secretariat has no permanent higher civil servant staff, save the Cabinet Secretary himself, getting rid of a unit seems more likely if a future prime minister wants to abolish it.

Staff size

The issue of staff size merits separate discussion. In few areas are the Unites States and Britain so far apart. At the same time current U.S.

thinking, based on experience with oversized policy staff, holds that "lean and mean" is a desirable characteristic for analytic and strategic units. The quality of "lean and mean" is intended to produce a rapid response. The trick is to avoid bureaucratic unwieldiness. One tactic is to use temporary people either from the outside or on secondment. Another tactic, perhaps used in conjunction with the first one, is to keep down the size of the total staff. Lord Rothschild wanted all the CPRS professional staff to fit around his conference table.

There is, however, no magic number – certainly no absolute right number unless perhaps defined in terms of invariant physical space. Even here, one has to be careful. The lament that not one more person can be put in the assigned area in No. 10 is not necessarily a valid argument if space is available in the Cabinet Office. No general right answer exists. Further, it is tautological to define lean and mean as "relatively small" – relative to what? The "just right" size is entwined with the related issues of competence and function.

As to the former, take CPRS which struck me as generally being understaffed. However, it was almost always only lean, not mean in the sense of effective. Was that because CPRS had too few hard-edged policy analysts? Would a twenty person unit, balancing policy analysts and others, have been large enough? If not, would a unit with 21 or 25 or 30 persons have been? Would the higher numbers still be lean and mean?

One key dimension of size is function. "Lean and mean," at least in part, depends on what levels of effort are required by a given set of functions. For example, the Office of Economic Opportunity (OEO) analytic office in the late 1960s had roughly forty high level staff members and seemed spare considering the number of functions if performed. But just as there is no magic number for competent staff given a specified set of functions, there is no magic set of functions to recommend. The problem does not arise from a static consideration of functions but from the dynamic demands of operating a complex office. After laying out functions appropriate for an agency analytic office based on the 1960s experience, I pointed out:

In considering the problems of organizing and administering an analytic office, it is important to recognize that the difficulties do not arise from an illogical blending of incompatible functions. The converse is true: the weight of logic and evidence indicates the need both for performance of the various functions ... and for the compatibility (the supportive nature) of these

161

functions. However, one can do all the right things in a *static* sense, putting on paper a brilliant organization scheme that links everyone together, and still find that setting the office in motion – the dynamics of a complex bureaucratic entity – remains extremely difficult ... [The] dilemma is that there are real problems in handling many functions, and there are real problems in *not* putting reasonable functions in [the] office.[18]

Unfortunately, determining that *each* stated function is appropriate does not guard against an unwieldy office if there are more functions than can be well-managed. That is, the summing of staff across functions can create an office that is too big to be highly responsive. Here is a classic tradeoff problem between responsiveness on the one hand and adequacy of functional coverage on the other. What is critical at the start is to look realistically at functions to determine the minimum required for adequate coverage. Reducing either the number of functions or of staff assigned to functions to increase responsiveness can have a real cost but the benefits may be worth it. These considerations push us into implementation analysis where an actual situation and the particular cast of characters need to be in place before determining specific answers. Such an analysis is beyond the book's scope.

One final point on staff size: my estimate on the maximum size for lean and mean (the tipping point toward "fat and slipshod," or at least unwieldiness) would probably be higher than that of the typical British critic. Certainly my interviews support this supposition. At the same time I believe that the estimates would not be so far apart if needed functions and competence are analyzed carefully. Going back to CPRS again, my impression of the operation prior to Robin Ibbs was that of amorphous global functions combined with staffs usually lacking in specialized competence. With Ibbs, functions were slashed deeply and competence in the key area of economic (industrial) development appeared adequate. For once CPRS may have been close to the right size given its functions. At the same time the Ibbs' CPRS was quite narrowly focused for a policy office serving the top of the government. However, CPRS apparently performed as its main client – Mrs Thatcher – wanted.

Prime minister and cabinet

After observing that the somewhat updated "1916-model Cabinet machine" will not do the job in today's complex world, Peter

Hennessy argues: "The area to go for as a priority ... [is] the capability of ministers in Cabinet and Cabinet Committee, the activities at which they perform least well and which, in consumer terms, matter most. Two changes are desparately needed: a reduced ministerial workload to make space for better analysis and thought ... and an enhanced supply of both raw and processed food for thought."[19] He goes on to say that how to accomplish this is a matter of taste but his prescriptive preference "would be for ministerial *cabinets* linked with a revived CPRS serving the Cabinet as a collective entity."[20] Several comments on Hennessy's diagnosis and prescription are warranted.

First, there is a basic assumption that Cabinet ministers should be the central government's primary *overall* policymakers, thereby choosing Cabinet government over presidential government. It is not clear whether that assumption rests on an even more basic one that collective decisionmaking at the top is an end in itself or whether Hennessy believes Cabinet government is a more effective means than presidential government. I suspect it is a bit of both and prefer myself to cast Cabinet government as one means (option) in seeking more responsible, effective British central government (the objective). Cabinet government as it now exists is part of the pre-modern, anti-modern fabric that must be redone. The biggest problem is incompetence combined with complacency as Hennessy concluded: "If the fairy godmother of reform were to grant me one long-term change, it would be to improve the pool of talent from which prime ministers can draw the twenty-two men and women on whom we so crucially depend. For, at the moment, very few Cabinet ministers or potential Cabinet ministers perceive a serious problem with the system. In failing to do so, they are part of the problem, not part of the solution."[21] Cabinet government is better viewed as a means to the end of effective, responsible British central government and thus is on trial to see how it contributes to or detracts from this basic goal.

Second, while ministerial competence is central for both Hennessy and me, it is not clear that performance in Cabinet and Cabinet committee is carried out as poorly as the other key ministerial function of managing the department. And it is certainly not clear which of these two functions is more important. Hennessy's call both for more ministerial time to analyze and an enhanced supply of supporting analysis and for a ministerial *cabinet* tied to a resurrected CPRS is broadly compatible with both the collective cabinet responsibility and

163

departmental management functions. But it still leaves the relatively important question – overall policymaker versus ministry manager (leader) – unanswered. This kind of tradeoff issue helps make more clear why a systems approach is needed and also why it may be useful to treat Cabinet government as means rather than an objective (questions returned to in this and later chapters).

Third, Hennessy does not elaborate on the mechanics of how a ministerial *cabinet* and the revived CPRS are to work together to enhance the minister's Cabinet role. Leaving aside the larger issue of the Cabinet's role and hence whether such a ministerial unit is desirable, I can attest from my own direct experience that a policy unit in an agency could combine analysis to support both ministry and overall government issues. The Office of Economic Opportunity when established in 1964 was charged both with operating a number of anti-poverty programs and coordinating the overall federal government anti-poverty effort. The OEO policy unit focused on both OEO's own programs and those of other agencies and the division I headed had a major role in the analysis of external (to OEO) programs. What Hennessy proposes seems practicable at least in the sense that a ministerial analytic unit can serve the minister in both the ministry management and the Cabinet roles.[22]

Let us now turn to the leadership role of the prime minister and Cabinet where the central question is the source of the political leadership which could provide substance and shape to major governmental reform. Effective political leadership at the center demands coherent strategy that gives direction to the government of the day. Here it is worth quoting at some length Lord Hunt, Secretary of the Cabinet from 1973 to 1979:

My own belief is that in the circumstances of a modern industrialized state a Prime Minister – as Head of the Government ... as the person with unique overview of all Government activities and as the leader of his or her party – has no option but to exercise a special responsibility as guardian for the Government's strategy as a whole to ensure that its constituent parts are consistent and coherent ... [T]he Prime Minister must steer, though in a direction which the Cabinet as a whole supports ... Nor do I believe, given the pressures on the center ... that the problem [of the Prime Minister developing a clear strategy] can be evaded by giving greater delegation to departments – although I feel strongly that if a clear strategy is laid down and monitored by the center that in itself would do more than anything else to facilitate greater delegation to departments ...

[T]o acknowledge that an important part of the role of the Prime Minister is to act ... as the keeper or monitor of the Cabinet's strategy would certainly not mean the end of Cabinet Government. It does however raise the important question of how the Prime Minister is to be serviced, because strategic oversight necessarily involves information so that the Prime Minister is properly and fully briefed, and early warning so the Prime Minister can intervene in time.[23]

In Lord Hunt's long statement, the premiership emerges as a complex activity. The prime minister is not simply first among equals but also not a figure so dominant that cabinet members are pushed aside (that is, not dominated as is a U.S. Cabinet, at least as interpreted in Britain). The prime minister's first duty is itself a modernizing act in developing and keeping the government's strategy. The prime minister must be the government's strategist for two reasons. First, he or she alone among the key Cabinet members has no spending remit (or antispending one as in the case of the Chancellor). Second, and relatedly, *leading* a ministry should be the main responsibility of the Cabinet member and that task properly performed is an all consuming job.

The prime minister as strategist also has the responsibility for insuring that needed information and analysis are available to the government. Here too the prime minister must be a modernizing force. If not the prime minister, then who is going to take leadership in building up necessary staff strategic and analytic capacity?

Lord Hunt sets out both the guardian of strategy and steering functions. The former is a unique role for prime ministers necessary both because they are party leaders and because they bring (or should bring) a balanced overview that department ministers are unlikely to have. The steering function also is particular to the prime minister but tied explicitly to Cabinet determination of the direction of steering. The second role clearly casts the prime minister as implementer of Cabinet policy. The guardian role seems more independent, a combined formulator/implementer. At the same time both functions single out the prime minister for taking *responsibility*. Guardianship of overall government strategy and policy steering demand prime minister leadership and acceptance of responsibility.

OPENNESS

The discussion of secrecy might fit in either this or the next chapter since it permeates all of British central government. But it seems appropriate to put the issue of greater openness near the treatment of the prime minister and Cabinet because only leadership from the top is going to loosen the deadening hand of secrecy.

The discussion of secrecy in Chapter 2 can be summarized as follows. First, if significantly more openness is desired in British central government, a strong Freedom of Information Act is needed. Second, such legislation while necessary is not as important as an attitude toward openness. Such an attitude flows from seeing openness both as an end in itself (a key goal of democracy) and as a means to more effective government performance. David Steel quite succinctly catches the essence of openness as an end and some flavor of it as a means in this statement from his foreword to *The Secrets File*: "A genuine democracy extends far beyond the right of citizens to have the occasional vote for their Member of Parliament or local councillor. The real test is whether people can influence decisions as they are taken, can know exactly what is happening and why, and, ideally, find it possible to support decisions and policies on the basis of access to the facts."[24] Finally, even where a positive attitude toward openness exists, the bureaucratic drive is toward secrecy so that vigilance is required if a reasonable degree of openness is to be maintained.

Des Wilson, an advocate of strong FOI legislation, has set forth the following objectives and machinery of administration for a sound act:

It should institutionalize a presumption that all administration should be open, except where there are clearly-defined overriding reasons for secrecy.

It should firmly commit politicians and civil servants to implement the principles in practice.

It should remove all unjustified barriers to the implementation of the spirit of the legislation.

It should set up the mechanisms whereby this can be achieved.

The machinery of administration should also meet a number of requirements:

It should ensure publicity of what information exists.

It should establish a way whereby the public can obtain that
information easily and quickly.

It should create an opportunity for appeal where the information is
denied.

It should enable the monitoring and reviewing of the legislation.

It should define the exemptions and guarantee that information is
properly protected.[25]

Details must be debated including necessary exemptions such as for
some national security information.[26] The tendency is to exempt far
too much information rather than making too much available. Recall
in the U.S. case the 1966 Act had to be tightened significantly in 1974
and required Congress to override a presidential veto.

As already discussed, openness can go too far and seems to have
done so in some cases in the U.S. But Britain is far from that danger
point and seems most likely to opt for much more secrecy than is
needed on pragmatic grounds. The real danger, which the mid-1987
Iran-Contra congressional hearings made so vivid, is to continue with
a level of secrecy that blocks both internal and external challenge. The
big implementation problem is to overcome the opposition of both the
politicians and top civil servants who so benefit from secrecy. Moving
toward openness is more difficult in Britain than in the United States
both because of the long-standing positive American attitude toward
openness and because of the interconnectedness of British institutions. There is no independent legislature to force a FOI Act on the
Executive Branch. Only a determined prime minister can push
openness legislation through Parliament and in so doing force his or
her own Executive Branch to be more accountable. It will require a
tour de force performance.

8

MODERNIZING THE MINISTRIES

A main theme of Chapter 7 was that the prime minister must be the government's first source of strength as strategist, catalyst, and direction setter if British central government is to be made more effective. The other two legs of the stool – the ministerial political leadership and the higher civil servants – too must be strong if the government is to be well-managed. Moreover, there needs to be a balanced strength between "outsider" (ministers, junior ministers and special advisers) and career officials. Such a balance can combine the energy, vitality, competence, and commitment of the former with the accumulated experience and expertise of the latter. This notion of balanced strength in the departments is one of the two central themes of the current chapter. The other is that ministers should have sufficient resources and discretionary control so they can *legitimately* be charged with basic responsibility for managing their departments.

The themes of this and the previous chapter are interrelated. The prime minister, not the ministers themselves, has the power to make the fundamental choice to create an institutional environment conducive to departmental capacity. This initial choice – the first critical option for the departments – puts the ball in the prime minister's court. And no question is more critical for effective central governance because the answer determines the fundamental relationships among the prime minister, ministers, other political appointees, and the higher civil servants. The answer also is critical as to whether the structure of British Central government is likely to foster (or block) the realistic determination of ministerial strategy and delegation of responsibilities and the development of a more committed, competent civil service over time. To opt for the status quo or for limited changes that do little to alter the institutional environment means that ministers generally will not have the resources and discretion needed for exercising responsibility.

THE FIRST CRITICAL CHOICE

At no other point does the desirability of an organization-man prime minister loom so large as in the decision about ministry management. Most fundamentally, that decision implicitly or explicitly determines the primary focus of the domestic ministries, and particularly that of the ministry political executives and the mandarins. Is that primary focus to be up toward Cabinet and the chamber of the House or down toward the field where central government funded goods and services are delivered? What is a proper power balance among the prime minister, the ministers (with their three hats of departmental role, Cabinet member, and member of Parliament), and the higher civil servants? No problem requires such a delicate blending of political and organizational skills as the search for a balance that adequately accommodates the intertwined demands of both politics and management.

A recent report by the National Academy of Public Administration (NAPA) underscores the balance issue. That report emphasizes the vitality and energy that outsiders can bring to government, claims that the "uniquely American in-and-outer system of leadership selection" has been beneficial on the whole, and yet argues that the system has gone too far so that the number of political executives should be reduced.[1] What is so important is that this sound notion of bringing in outsiders to staff the top executive positions has been carried too far. One critical cost of the American imbalance between political executives and senior career officials is isolating the latter from the centers of top level decisionmaking, thereby depriving the government of their accumulated experience and expertise. Even more basically, the wedge of distrust has warped the appointment process by making loyalty to the president and his agenda a far more important criterion than competence.

The most important recommendation of the NAPA report is that "*substantive policy knowledge and administrative experience are not incompatible with political qualifications and should be the primary criteria in the selection and confirmation of presidential appointees.*"[2] In specifying competence as the main criteria for appointment, the report comes down strongly for the centrality of a departmental performance orientation. But is this orientation possible in the highly charged political world of Washington or London? Here the report is worth quoting:

The argument that the appointment process is heavily and inalterably political is one that we have heard often in our research. We share this perception. But what does that mean? That good politics and good management are mutually exclusive? That the president's political objectives can be accomplished only by filling some positions with political hacks or single-minded ideologues who lack executive qualifications?

We think not. In a country as rich as ours in talent and resources, it ought to be entirely possible to find and recruit individuals who possess both the training and skills necessary to perform effectively as presidential appointees and the political credentials and sensitivities necessary to operate successfully in the Washington environment. Good politics and good management are not mutually exclusive. Indeed, they are complementary. Good management is very often the essence of good politics. If one reads the roll of the very finest presidential appointees of the postwar years, it is remarkable how many of them combined managerial ability, substantive policy knowledge, and political sensitivity.[3]

The American case is instructive because bringing in outsiders has gone too far while Britain now errs clearly in the opposite direction. But before the balance issue comes that of control – who shall manage the ministries? An institutional structure must be developed to provide the chosen party sufficient resources and discretion to be charged legitimately with responsibility for ministry performance. If ministers are *not* to have the resources and discretion needed for exercising realistic responsibility, the other candidates are the prime minister and the civil servants.

For the prime minister to be responsible for the departments – to be presidential in its most virulent form – would require (i) tight control over ministerial political appointees and the top civil servant appointments and (ii) a strong staff at the center to analyze and perhaps direct departmental actions. It boils down mainly to weak ministers who can be dominated, extremely loyal ones who will follow the prime minister, or more likely to a mixture of both kinds. The main features

170

of this option fit well with the general configuration of the Thatcher government, at least in its post-Falklands days. The difference is either that Mrs Thatcher has *not* fully worked through the managerial demands of a strong prime minister dominated government or that she has felt unable politically to move all the way.

It seems most unlikely that a prime minister or Cabinet would opt for giving civil servants *full* responsibility for managing departments since the choice would relegate ministers and junior ministers to being "fronts" or "mouthpieces" for the departments and the mandarins in external relationships – fighting in Cabinet for the department's share of resources, defending it in Parliament, and interacting with the party and interest groups. Even though a goodly number of ministers may have been little more than the public relations person for their departments, it hardly seems an acceptable or a realistic role since it either posits the discredited politics/administration dichotomy or makes the mandarins the masters.

While civil service rule is politically unfeasible, two comments are useful. First, Britain, at least in its pre-Thatcher days, often came close to civil service rule in part because of a misguided belief in a politics/administration dichotomy and in part because ministers either fled managerial responsibility or else had no notion of how to exert it.[4] However, this structure has not yielded accountability because the facade of ministerial responsibility for everything has allowed everyone to escape answering for responsibility. Second, in placing the permanent secretaries at such a high level in the departments and giving them authority over the key high level civil servant appointments, *Britain in effect established the kind of strong control by the central government over critical high level staff resources that is needed to have a reasonable chance of exercising responsibility.* The full option would go the next step and make such responsibility by the civil servants *explicit*.

Clearly, I do not advocate such an option, believing strongly in control by politically accountable executives. However, the discussion has been useful in two ways. First, it indicates how close Britain was to this option and that such a level of control is possible. Second, the discussion suggests why the single dominant permanent secretary is incompatible with the strong minister model, a point treated in more detail later in the chapter.

MAKING MINISTERS RESPONSIBLE MANAGERS

This section considers the kind of institutional environment needed to provide ministers with sufficient resources and discretion to charge them legitimately with full responsibility for departmental management. The starting requirement is to "clear the air" by burying two notions that now clearly are obsolete and may never have been viable and substituting notions consistent with the dictates of modern management. First, the concept of ministerial responsibility for every department action should be replaced by the concept of ministerial responsibility for overall department performance and for the realistic delegation of responsibility to subordinates. Second, the notion of the complete congruity of concerns and objectives between the minister and other political appointees and civil servants should be replaced by the concept of legitimate differences that require the development of a working relationship between ministers and mandarins consonant with these differences. The two obsolete notions together have led to an unrealistic view from the top that ministers can establish the political control needed for fulfilling their responsibilities without any significant staffing changes.

To be held accountable ministers must have the authority to select subordinates whose commitment and competence they trust. Ministers need individuals who are their people, not in being "yes men," but in being loyal enough so that their actions are likely to reflect ministers' interests. If ministers do not have a team of people they trust both as to commitment and competence, ministers by definition do not have a reasonable chance to fulfill their managerial responsibilities. That is fundamental.

Legitimately charging a manager with the responsibility does not demand that the manager have no restrictions from above. Be the manager in the public or the private sector, he or she can expect funding and personnel constraints as well as various rules and regulations. The question is when are the restrictions so great that the manager has little or no chance to meet performance objectives.

In this section we first consider the roles to be played by "outsiders" – persons *not* either current MPs or peers or permanent civil servants – looking at special advisers, top managers, and line managers. After that, the issue of controlling the civil service is treated by focusing on the permanent secretary because that position as presently structured creates basic conflicts for ministerial management.

Special advisers

Special advisers fall into two categories: political and policy. The former seem relatively unobjectionable in performing tasks (e.g., party liaison) that civil servants prefer to avoid. Problems arise when political advisers stray into policy and line functions. The main complaint has been that in practice political advisers have been inexperienced and have often not understood or at least honored staff and line distinctions.[5]

Policy advisers are a different case in that they may engage in direct competition with civil servants. The practice so far has been to bring in no more than three such people per department and usually less. In small quantities competent policy advisers may even be considered valuable by civil servants in helping ministers to rid themselves of nonsense and to understand the framework and arguments used by the civil servants. A single policy adviser (or two) who is a competent expert will be acceptable to civil servants.

Potential problems come when larger numbers are envisioned such as a policy analysis and strategic unit serving the minister directly. These staffs might and probably should combine outsiders and civil servants, some possibly on secondment from other departments. Generally the unit should be headed by an outsider so that the minister has his person in charge. The clear model in structure, if not capabilities, is CPRS. This staff would have the charge to do policy analysis in support of top-level decisionmaking. Such a staff would draw on departmental units for data and might have coordinating responsibilities for information and analysis.

The beast being described is not an exact duplicate of a French *cabinet* as Klein and Lewis point out: "[M]ost French government departments do not have the precise equivalent of a Permanent Under-Secretary and one of the main roles of the *cabinet's* director is therefore to co-ordinate the work of the department: a redundant role in the [current] British context."[6] The policy analysis office option is a staff advisory, not a line function. If a minister wants managers, he should look elsewhere as discussed below.

A policy analysis unit, headed by an outsider with a staff that combines commitment and competence, can increase both ministerial control (knowledge is power) and improve the base of decisionmaking in providing a challenge to the career civil servants. However, the head of the unit in reporting directly to the minister, and perhaps junior ministers (as discussed below, the head could be a junior minister), raises basic problems of relations with the mandarins generally and the permanent secretary in particular. If the head policy analyst is not a junior minister, a key issue is the status the person should have – permanent secretary, deputy secretary, or what – to facilitate effectiveness in the rank-conscious British departmental structure. It is a question to be addressed after more basic choices about managers are made.

Managers

Even more jarring than a strong advisory group is bringing in managers from the outside. Two main options are worth considering. First would be to bring in outsiders in place of or in addition to junior ministers. If current junior ministers lack either commitment as asserted by Klein and Lewis or managerial competence, there are limitations on the minister's capacity to manage. In appointing outsiders, parliamentary sensitivity might be eased if these persons were added to the "traditional" junior minister positions or even made subordinate to them. Such an arrangement comes close to the next main option so we move to it before further discussion.

The second alternative would be to put the top civil service positions – say under or deputy secretary and above – under political control. The FDA's Environment and Transport Branch Committee has spelled out an option in which "all senior civil service posts would be on contract, say for five years, *appointments to be made by open competition* ... [If] they [ministers] wanted a deputy secretary responsible for higher education, applicants could come forward from the existing civil service, from the rest of the public sector, from the universities, and from commerce and industry."[7] This recommendation for open competition, so basic to a professional career civil service, simply is not consonant with the appointing of political executives that ministers can trust. Even if the civil service is viewed as competent, its singular commitment to ministers is suspect. Open competition makes little sense in light of this demand.

Open competition goes too far in specifying that the highest civil service positions be on contract. British civil servants have usually given their loyalty to ministers to a degree sufficient to warrant their trust. Hence a new manager needs to determine which civil servants have a *deep* commitment as professionals to serve their political masters whatever their party. The best rule is that trust should *not* be given unreservedly nor denied simply because the person served the previous administration. Hugh Heclo argues for "conditional cooperation [which] rejects any final choice between suspicion and trust, between trying to force obedience and passively hoping for compliance."[8] The Heclo recommendation is for managerial activism in testing out loyalty (and competence) over time. My own experience, as well as that of American political executives I have interviewed, is that such testing will *not* require long periods of time. A good political appointee can vet a career official rather quickly through direct experience and inquiry to determine if there is a strong commitment to serving the chosen government of the day whatever the party. After that, relatively unreserved trust is merited – the career civil servant is on the team, not in the sense of singular commitment but of professional trust.

Competence raises another issue: the shortage not only of higher civil servants with management and analytic skills but of outsiders who are both willing and competent to serve. All too often ministers have considered only loyalty and brought in people with little or no understanding of how large organizations work. The choice is not between massive talent waiting to be tapped on the outside and a disloyal, pre-modern civil service. The search will be difficult. Political executives are well advised to draw on civil servants as much as possible.

Controlling the civil service

An alternative to the current single permanent secretary position would be a managerial layer at the top made up *solely* of political appointees to whom the top civil servants would report individually. Permanent secretary status in the sense of one top civil servant would be abolished. The highest civil servant grade, however, still might bear the title of permanent secretary. This arrangement has two advantages in structural relations. First, a designated political executive team at the top would be charged with management responsibility including working out the delegated responsibility structure. This first advantage may be lost, however, if there is no marked change in how junior ministers are chosen so that the minister can call them his own. Second, the funneling of all civil servant activities through a single source will have been stopped. Once distrust sets in, the single permanent secretary crystallizes a kind of "us/them" mentality. The political executives must work with higher civil servants if the department is to be well-managed but the new structure implies a different set of relationships where top civil servants serve different masters depending on their specific functions.

A variant on this option would be to use one or more civil servants in the top management layer but without making a single civil servant the funnel for the entire department. If there were four political executives and a civil servant in the top layer, the civil servants in the next layer would answer to their political executives except for those the civil servant (or servants since the numbers are purely illustrative) in the top layer was charged with managing. The disadvantage of this variant is that it lacks the clarity of the first option – it muddies the water when new political executive–civil servant structural relationships are being developed. However, this variant could be a distinct advantage in keeping a degree of continuity. It also provides more flexibility by making eligible for appointment able higher civil servants, no small benefit given the supply shortages of qualified people. Finally, this variant could make the career service more attractive since career officials can still hope to rise to the top of the management layer even if the single, powerful permanent secretary position is no more.

Going back to the option where only political executives are in the top layer, a danger based on the American experience is that another political layer will be installed between the top one and the higher civil servants. In the American case layering is symptom rather than cause. Distrust came first and political executives begin to feel safer with their own people. The American experience can be misread. Although the level of distrust of American civil servants in the past was far lower and their rank in the hierarchy much higher than today, civil servants have not had the status within or the high prestige outside that British civil servants have had. The U.S. has had much more of a history of people coming into the government in political positions.

The issue is whether distrust can be bounded and pushed back. Partly this will depend on civil service competence and on the capacity of the mandarins to understand the new mood, including why ministers want their own people. But the ball is also in the ministers' court. If they will not or cannot practice "conditional cooperation," the civil service may be able to do little to foster cooperation.

Civil service control raises an even larger issue: who is to make the basic personnel decisions (e.g., promotion, organizational assignment) about the higher levels of the civil service including potential high flyers? Such career decisions could be made by the prime minister and his or her staff, the civil service structure as embodied in a departmental permanent secretary or in a separate (from the department) organization or in both, department line managers who will usually be career civil servants, departmental ministers, or some combination of these four. There are two principal control issues: (i) who chooses the handful of civil servants at the top; and (ii) who makes the career decisions for others. The first control issue is fundamental to the strong department model since primary control by either the prime minister or the civil service materially weakens it. A strong department model, however, does not rule out a civil service organization devoted to career development in the general sense or specific education and training (e.g., an elite civil service college). Nor does that model bar negotiations between ministers or their delegates and either a civil service organization or the prime minister as long as the minister in the main has final control over the top personnel choices.

The second control issue manifests itself at lower levels of departments. Here the issue is one of fundamental management approach. In Britain there is a basic difference in the way staffing is approached in the private sector and in the central government. As a publication of the Management and Personnel Office has pointed out: "Perhaps the most significant difference between the Civil Service and ... [private sector] organizations ... is the much greater emphasis in the latter on the *primary role of line management in personnel decisions.* Personnel management is seen as an integral and essential part of the manager's responsibilities and his performance in this area forms an important part of the assessment made of him ... *The role of personnel staff is*

177

principally to provide specialist support, advice, training, and some central services ... and *to monitor and ensure compliance with company-wide personnel policies and procedures.*"[9] Here the issue is not simply who will control the civil servant today but who will guide his career over time. That question takes us to the issue of managing the civil service.

MANAGING THE CIVIL SERVICE

In managing a resource, be it human or nonhuman, the good manager is concerned both with efficient and effective use today (the short term) and over time, recognizing that current and future use at times can be in conflict. A professional soccer team may decide to use a young player expected to be a future star even though a veteran player near the end of his career is likely to perform better that season. Part of the rationale for using the young player is to give him experience but another reason is to keep him from becoming disgruntled sitting on the sidelines. Human resources have the dimension of needing to be motivated, hardly a pathbreaking insight, but ministers may either expect civil servants like coal to extract themselves and leap into the furnace with no managerial effort or think civil servants must be driven by brute force because they are tainted by past service to a different government or totally corrupted by bureaucratic pathologies.

Today

If higher civil servants lack competence in the areas of analysis and management, three main options are available for addressing that deficiency in the short run: bringing in outsiders, brief training, and the modification of incentives. The first is not popular because it takes jobs that civil servants believe can be filled as well or better by career officials. There also is the concern that the entry is a disguised political appointment. An alternative is to bring in people on contracts (say for two years as was the case in CPRS) that can be renewed and possibly converted to career status after some probationary period such as at the end of the first contract. Given the lack of a particular skill in the civil service, the advantage of the outsider is that the skill in question is available immediately. There is a necessary learning period if the outside entry lacks government experience. For analytic and strategic

178

skills, that learning period may be brief especially if an analytic unit combines career officials and outsiders.

From the overall departmental perspective the immediate tradeoff is between short-term skill availability and both a general loss of morale and a diminishing of career incentives. Hence it is necessary to separate the short run, where "instant skills" may require outsiders, from the longer run, where special efforts may be made to upgrade career staff.

Training is better treated as a longer-term issue and even better thought of as a range of related choices of differing time dimensions integrated with a pattern of positions so that training and experience may complement each other. Training is likely to pay off only if it is built on. For example, the Top Management Programme may be a clear signal that a new and different emphasis is to be placed on management. If so, what kind of management – Mrs Thatcher's impoverished concept or "positive" management? Then, there is the question of incentives. Will more pay or faster promotion or praise be forthcoming for graduates from the current higher mandarins who, it should be emphasized, have not taken the course?

Incentives such as rapid promotion, choice assignments, high personnel ratings, and awards can help. The lack of a positive incentive – e.g., no award, no early promotion – is a powerful negative force. Where incentives become tricky is the issue of incentives for what purpose. If analytic and managerial performance are to be high priorities, the reward structure must show it. Rhetoric, even from the prime minister and the top civil servants, will not help much if nothing else happens – if there is exhortation but business goes on as usual. If at the top where Westminster and Whitehall meet what ministers desire most from mandarins is help in the parliamentary joust, little change will take place.

The longer term

If we step back and look to the future over a period of time sufficient for extended career development, all sorts of possibilities emerge. Consider the Oxbridge high flyers at entry. I have argued that they are extremely bright and that a general education has helped to prepare them to be sound generalists but that more is needed. One possibility is that the new entrants would go to a special college for a training program that concentrates on modern management and analytic techniques. Whether the course should be six months or a year or even two years and whether it should be offered immediately or in a year or two after some screening out depends on a number of factors including what needs to be imparted and on the supply of competent people to provide instruction. There also are questions about whether the training should be provided internally in the civil service or at universities or other nongovernmental organizations. One point, however, is clear: Potential high flyers need to have formal training before they become too valuable to "educate."

Elite colleges

The nature and purpose of elite training colleges – what they prepare elites to do – can be pivotal in the development of modern generalists. The issue is not elite colleges per se since Oxford and Cambridge rank in the elite universities of the world but the skills and the orientation (gestalt might be the better term) to be imparted. Such elite institutions as the grandes ecoles seek to lay the foundation for generalist-specialists. The French institutions, just as the British, stress the generalist label as they should because each of their graduates is a generalist first and foremost. Even the grandes ecoles play down specialization (except when it suits their purpose). No graduate wants to be labeled a technocrat. What distinguishes these colleges is that their students receive a solid base of technical training including an emphasis on modern management. Moreover, these colleges' basic orientation contrasts sharply with the university (general, theoretical) and the technical college.[10] The Fulton Report erred, Ezra Suleiman argues, in characterizing the top French civil servants as a "technical, specialized elite ... familiar with the slide rule and the computer, accustomed to applying strictly rational criteria to the solution of problems, and unencumbered by an education in Greek and Latin."[11] But Suleiman himself errs in underplaying the importance of the special training the grandes ecoles graduates receive: "Specialization and technical expertise ... are important only insofar as they provide a justification for the elite's monopoly on important posts in the society. While the elite rationalizes its power and privilege on the basis of its training and competence, it must also deny that it is a specialized elite that it may maintain and extend its position. Hence the innovation of the importance of being a generalist."[12]

The crucial point not to be missed, however, is that the grandes ecoles graduates receive a sufficient dose of specialized training to form the base for being a modern generalist. They are trained to be good users of specialists, not specialists themselves. Suleiman himself observed: "As a recent entering class of the Ecole Polytechnique was informed: 'The scientific training you receive will not give you the knowledge in any branch that the specialists have, but it will give you the aptitudes and the methods such as to allow you to be on top of everything.'"[13]

At issue is not purpose (turning out generalist managers) but the adequacy of the technical base provided to the students for coping with complexity in light of the fact that the technical demands of being a generalist-specialist have risen. The broad question is that of finding the balance between the general and the special in training the modern generalist.

Britain should be able to develop such an elite college or colleges. Some of the most prestigious ones have emerged in the postwar period. For example, the Ecole Nationale d'Administration (ENA) was started in 1945. There are plenty of examples of successful elite training programs around to provide a useful base on which to proceed. Take the key questions of when a student should enter the elite program and what will be the mix of classroom and on-the-job work. Elite American graduate business schools such as the Harvard Business School require two or more years of job experience after the bachelors' degree for most of their students and then offer two years of course work.[14] ENA starts with a first year in an embassy or a prefecture (the *stage*) followed by a year and a half of course work.[15]

Those who enter the grandes ecoles are products of other elite schools – the cream of the cream. If I were establishing an elite college for modern generalists expected to serve in the public sector, the Oxbridge graduates would be prime candidates both because of their brightness and because their already established elite status would enhance the new college. The main issue is not so much whether elite colleges can be established in Britain but whether the need for such colleges will be perceived by the "right" people (e.g., Oxbridge ministers and mandarins). Britain excels at creating and maintaining elite institutions. What is problematic is the will and the understanding to see and accept a new approach to central governance.

In focusing on an elite college, I do not mean to downplay job patterns and incentives that reinforce the direction of the formal training. If being posted to a top analytic unit or a management position including ones outside London are viewed as a key step on the ladder to the top, and if promotions and awards come to those who do well in such positions, real changes in behaviour are likely. This pattern does not mean politics-mongering positions should be in disfavor. The sound generalist-specialist must be able to integrate policy and politics. The issue is one of balance.

Longer-term changes

Three interrelated long-run changes are needed to establish a more competent, committed civil service and maintain it over time. First are changes aimed at building competence and involve training, career patterns, and incentives tied to specific kinds of performance. Second are efforts to restore the trust of ministers for civil servants and *vice versa*. Third is the development of a base for effective institutional management of the civil service over time. Management changes now loom as the pivotal factor as political executives intrude more and more on what was until recently almost exclusively a civil service preserve. Comments from the March 1985 *FDA News* are illuminating:

Another cause for concern [besides low pay] is the way the civil service is managed. In the past ministers left management of departments to the civil service. Now they are much more deeply involved in management, as is their right. Civil servants are entitled to expect good management from ministers if they decide to take on the burden; but in fact they do not have the time. What has developed with honorable exceptions is an autocratic style of ministerial management, exercised only occasionally, often in relation to a particular post or staff reduction exercise, which pays little heed to the need in very large organizations for stable and far-sighted management, and in particular for succession planning to provide staff with the prospect of reasonable career development. This is not surprising given that ministerial horizons rarely extend beyond the next reshuffle or election ...

Ministers should have one main objective in dealing with the problem [of civil service discontent]. They should seek to create a civil service they trust and which they and the public respect.[16]

Several points need to be made about this statement. First, the ministers' right to manage is given rather grudgingly, seemingly with the same clenched teeth style as used by the Thatcher government when praising the civil service. Nevertheless, ministers have not only a right but a duty to manage the civil service or to make a realistic

182

delegation of such responsibility. It is a responsibility that comes with the office. Second, civil service *entitlement* to good management, if there is such entitlement, misses the far more important point that the nation needs sound management of the civil service over time. The lack of stable and far-sighted management creates current and future problems, not just for the civil servants. Third, the statement of the ministers' main objective is not as self-serving as it appears on cursory reading. Trust and respect are key elements in a sound minister-civil servant relationship. The big question is how to move toward them, recognizing that the minister and the civil servants have different concerns and objectives. At issue is not just what must the minister do to establish trust and respect of the civil servants but what higher civil servants must do to merit trust and respect. That question embraces both the issue of the civil servants' appreciation of the legitimate differences between ministers and career officials and that of civil servant competence.

DOMESTIC DEPARTMENTAL MANAGEMENT STRATEGY

What are domestic ministries responsible for? Is their main function *vis-à-vis* local government to be check writing, sending out the rate support grants, and taking a hands-off stance? Or, do national objectives call for a more active central government effort? Local government is not necessarily wiser than central government nor should local autonomy always override national concerns. For example, the weaknesses of Britain's locally dominated education system in preparing students to cope with the demands of modern society combined with Britain's economic woes raise basic questions about local autonomy.[17] Technical education may be too important to leave to the decisions of local authorities. The question posed in Chapter 2 remains unanswered: *To what extent should central government become involved in formulating national policies for local efforts funded by central government and in managing and evaluating these activities to see that the programs achieve national objectives?*

The central government has three main programmatic (as opposed to macro-spending) options. First, the central government can concern itself primarily or exclusively with funds being legally spent and accounted for (fiscal responsibility in the narrow sense). Second, the Whitehall ministries can have an active managerial role sharing responsibilities with local government for determining both means and objectives and for evaluating the efficiency and effectiveness of local government efforts. Third, domestic ministries can center their efforts on increasing local government commitment to central government objectives and its capacity to deliver services to local beneficiaries. The second and third options place relatively heavy demands on central government staff.

The strongest message in the last twenty years of American domestic policy experience is that of the severe limits on government generally and on central government particularly. This evidence on shared governance has led me to reject the uneasy partnership of option two for a more restrained agency strategy concentrating on local commitment and capacity. The rejection of the more active federal role is not ideological but pragmatic. Concentrating on local delivery capacity makes more sense in light of the available American implementation experience.

My much less detailed consideration of British ministry management leads me to agree with Jones and Stewart that "the machine at the [British] center is already over-burdened by the problems of localities. The unnecessary handling of these problems by national government may prevent it from dealing adequately with those problems which can be dealt with only at the center."[18] *What central government ought and can do needs to be subjected to an intense implementation analysis by persons familiar with and involved in the programs and organizations at issue, not educated guesses by an American, or Briton, for that matter.*

The importance of the last point about the need for implementation analysis by those involved in the programs, not educated guesses by outsiders, requires underscoring and the case at hand is its most dramatic illustration. Being considered are complex institutional changes that stretch from the top of the ministry into the field and may alter the personal and institutional status of significant numbers of persons at various levels of government. An example from my own research may prove helpful.

In a study of two major U.S. federal grant programs to localities, extensive interviews were conducted at all levels of the two agencies managing the programs. Even with such detailed information, I was only willing to argue generally that a federal agency charged with administering federal grants to states and/or localities should develop an agency management strategy with a key objective of strengthening local commitment and capacity. The specific recommendation was that a federal agency should undertake an in-depth implementation analysis prior to making proposed structural changes to determine if the agency itself had the capacity to pursue the proposed strategic objective; and if so, how to go about it. My recommendation stopped short of calling for the two agencies under study to adopt the proposed agency management strategy because the implementation analysis needed to determine the feasibility of the strategy being put in place had *not* been carried out. Nor was the needed implementation analysis attempted. My role was that of an independent researcher, operating neither at the request of the two federal agencies nor in close cooperation with top headquarters officials. For me to have done the analysis on my own, relatively independent of the agencies, would have violated the most basic aspects of an in-depth implementation analysis:

Such an analysis if carried out without working directly with the staff of a particular agency would be inappropriate because of the lack of details [inside information] and the need for the organization itself to be heavily involved ... [T]he available evidence indicates both that new decisionmaking systems cannot be imposed effectively from above the agency and that internal organization changes of which the shift to an agency management strategy would be a major one cannot be put in place successfully without careful analysis and the involvement of key organizational units in the change ... [T]he only sensible suggestion is to do the analysis.[19]

9

BREAKING THE PATTERN

Today Britain requires an unusual great leap in that most such transformations are mainly or exclusively programmatic in nature, as exemplified by the New Deal and the Attlee years. Even though the Great Reform Act, which so vividly illustrates the nature of political leadership, was structurally oriented, the setting today differs drama tically. In 1832 parliamentary reform was an end in itself – the goal being sought. In the case at hand modernizing central government is a means for improving British political, social and economic status. The current central government structure is deemed undesirable, not on intrinsic political grounds as with the unrepresentative Parliament of the first part of the nineteenth century, but because the current central government institutional structure blocks the development and execution of major institutional changes that will support the second (programmatic) great leap to attack Britain's socioeconomic problems.

No recent experience is nearly so relevant for British central government modernization as that of the 1958–62 transformation of French central government from the strong parliament/weak president structure of the Fourth Republic to the Fifth Republic's strong presidency model. Here is a classic case mirroring Britain's current malady where an obsolete government structure blocked the development and execution of needed policy strategy. The French experience offers the chance to see the dynamics of a structural great leap. It is an opportunity much like that offered to military strategists studying past great battles for insights on future strategies. We turn then to the French experience before looking directly again at the British problem.

186

POLITICAL LEADERSHIP AND OBSOLETE GOVERNMENT STRUCTURE:
THE FRENCH CASE[1]

The French structural transformation had two dramatic steps – the 1958 Constitution establishing the Fifth Republic and the 1962 amendment to that Constitution mandating the election of the president by popular vote. France had experienced rapid economic modernization, urbanization, and growing affluence after World War II. But its government structure remained mired in the nineteenth century. William Andrews observed: "The fragmented and ideological political party system of the Third and Fourth Republics no longer reflected social reality. Neither did the fractionated omnipotent Parliament nor the weak unstable Executive."[2] France of the Fourth Republic (1946–1958) had an average of *two* governments a year over its twelve year life. Those governments were dominated by an unstable parliament where the main strength was in blocking action. This government structure was pre-modern, anti-modern governance with a vengeance.

By 1958, the gap between government structure and the complexity facing French government had become painfully clear. General Charles de Gaulle was called to serve as prime minister and charged with writing a new constitution. He warned that the dangers threatened the Republic itself: "This 'last chance of the Republic' will determine whether 'the French nation will flourish again or will perish';" with "Algeria plunged into a tempest of trials and emotions ... France ... finds herself menaced by ... possible civil war."[3] Here is the kind of explosive crisis that can overwhelm entrenched forces even when the structural changes wrench power and status from their hands.

The 1958 Constitution brought France a more modern parliamentary system and a stronger presidency, but with the president as an arbiter, not a chief executive, and certainly not presidential in the American sense.[4] If the first president of the Fifth Republic had not been the Olympian Charles de Gaulle, the presidential role under the 1958 Constitution would not have been dominant. As Brown has argued: "It is unlikely that the Fifth Republic in its original [1958] form could have survived General de Gaulle's departure from public life."[5]

By 1962 de Gaulle firmly believed that only a strong presidency, an

American-like chief executive, could provide a "lesser" figure than himself with the institutional power base needed to lead France. Without this institutional base, France would slip back to a strong parliamentary system. De Gaulle's vision of French greatness would not be fulfilled. An unsuccessful assassination attempt on President de Gaulle's life on August 22, 1962 brought immediate action by de Gaulle, pushing through the critical 1962 amendment into law in less than three months with a tour de force effort in political leadership.

Once it became known shortly after the August 22 assassination attempt that President de Gaulle wanted a popularly elected president, most of the leaders of the traditional parties attacked the idea claiming it would establish a dictatorship.[6] Finding himself blocked in parliament if he used procedures clearly prescribed by the 1958 Constitution, de Gaulle chose to use a constitutionally questionable national referendum that bypassed parliament. The President of the Senate Gaston Monnerville labeled de Gaulle's approach a "deliberate, intentional, premeditated and outrageous violation of the Constitution."[7]

De Gaulle pulled out all his weapons, going to the nation three times on national radio and television. He argued that his opponents wanted to subvert the republic by reestablishing the old parliamentary regime and turned the national referendum into a plebiscite on de Gaulle as leader, above the politicians and seemingly above the law. The referendum won with a 62 percent yes vote as compared to 80 percent approval rate for the 1958 Constitution; de Gaulle continued on until April 1969; France prospered.

France's economic success

France experienced not one but two great leaps in the Gaullist years. As Cohen has written in a volume reviewing the Fifth Republic at age twenty: "The Gaullists set out to modernize the French economy and succeeded. Almost no aspect of French life escaped improvement ... The French economy has not simply grown; *it has been transformed*."[8] France became the fastest growing economy in Europe. After trailing West Germany in the rate of real economic growth in the five years prior to de Gaulle (1953–8), the French real growth rate both exceeded that of West Germany in each of the next three five year periods and topped all European Economic Community countries for the period 1958–73.[9]

Several points need to be made about the French economic miracle. First, the central government had an active role: "In its strategic conceptualization and day-to-day realization, the transformation of the French economy was very much in the hands of the *Grand Commiss de l'Etat*, certainly far more than in any other Western state."[10] Suzanne Berger speaks of "the high moments of Fifth Republic dirigisme."[11] Second, de Gaulle was fortunate to inherit a strong economy and to have France helped along by the worldwide boom. But the fact remains France outperformed all the other European economies that also were benefiting from the great postwar boom. Third, strong central government leadership did not raise central government expenditures, rather there were complaints that economic modernization had gone too far sacrificing social needs and public investments in noneconomic factors such as beauty of the landscape.[12]

France under de Gaulle made the two great leaps; one, in central government structure and the other, in socioeconomic changes. Here, broadly speaking, is a classic example of what Britain must do if it is to avoid social and political instability. Can it be claimed from the French experience that central government structure was a necessary condition for the phenomenal economic growth or that the changed structure was a major causal factor of superior economic performance? Does France provide a model for Britain? The answer to all questions is no. Part of the problem of generalization in this instance is that one example does not make a case.[13] Far more important, implementation research warns of the difficulties of putting much more simple policies in place successfully even when the model that has worked is in the same country (or state in the U.S. case) and in the same general time period. The French central government structure, now nearly thirty years old, appears inappropriate for France itself today, much less for Britain. France by 1987 found itself with what appears to be critical structural problems (co-habitation) and a slow growing economy.[14]

There are, however, several tantalizing leads to draw from the French experience in thinking about modernizing British central government. First, France, during the period of de Gaulle's leadership of the provisional government, had created ENA in 1945 in a clear attempt to raise government staff capacity and provide managerial leadership. Second, de Gaulle sought to fix clear responsibility in this case in a powerful president. Third, the government was strategically oriented with strong planning efforts. Fourth, there was dominance by a strong political leader with a vision that gave direction to the strategic thinking. Finally, de Gaulle, while not an organization-man par excellence in a class with Attlee and Eisenhower, had both organizational experience and skill sufficient to master critical institutional issues.

De Gaulle as political and organizational leader

In his way Charles de Gaulle answered the political and organizational demands made on him. De Gaulle is almost too perfect as political leader, symbolizing France itself, the only man who could save the nation. In political leadership style there is a strong parallel to General Dwight Eisenhower coming to the presidency with extensive organizational and political experience but also as a military man without extended political service. Each man as president, whenever possible, cast himself as above politics and parties. There also is a likeness to Churchill of the war years. But the ultimate comparison is French: "[H]e must ... remain as pure as Joan of Arc ... [F]or Charles de Gaulle it is a matter of simple historical necessity to become the State."[15] De Gaulle embodied the French nation, and that makes for great political power. In 1962 de Gaulle's political leadership was put to the extreme test. Here we saw the leader ready to fight and fight hard for his vision, to use questionable tactics to save the nation.

"[D]e Gaulle's eyes," as Cook points out, "were on the horizons and not the sidewalks ... [His] interest in ... the actual running of his country was limited to say the least."[16] At the same time de Gaulle possessed a professional military officer's appreciation of delegation. First, he had the good sense (or luck) to choose the able Michel Debre for the most critical assignments demanding strong organizational and management skills. Not only did Debre manage the development of the 1958 Constitution and serve as de Gaulle's first premier in the Fifth Republic, he became the Ecole Nationale d'Administration's first director after the school was started in 1945 when de Gaulle headed the provisional government of 1944–6. Second, de Gaulle understood the role of subordinates and had an inner security that did not make it necessary to bully subordinates as say Mrs Thatcher or Lyndon Johnson.[17] Third, again from his military experience, de Gaulle appreciated professionalism – the well-prepared subordinate who has the training and experience to do the job with limited supervision. Here is the importance of the *enarques* who moved into key positions in the Gaullist government. Cook captures this critical point: "Under the General, the prime minister functioned as an efficient chief of staff to a commanding officer, and below the civil servants were the subordinate unit commanders .... Behind the ministers was the powerful and efficient civil service – the real instrument of Gaullist power in running France."[18]

De Gaulle was not an organizational genius like Attlee and Eisenhower, nor did he revel as they did in organizational strategy. De Gaulle, however, recognized what he did not know about organizations, what he did not like to do within the organizational structure, and how to correct for these deficiencies and preferences through staff and structural means. Organizational mastery does not require the skills of organization-man par excellence, but demands at least the kind of understanding de Gaulle had.

Some final comments

I have emphasized de Gaulle's role and tactics because that effort, especially in 1962, illustrates so vividly the dynamics of major structural reform. De Gaulle was bold throughout and boldest at the most crucial point in 1962 when entrenched forces chose to stand and fight. In that encounter de Gaulle engaged in demagoguery and skated over the edge of constitutionality in order to win. It was a great leap in central government structural reform unparalleled in France, Britain, and the United States during the last half century. At the center was the political leader pushing changes to the outer limits of stable democracy.

De Gaulle considered his actions conservative. In 1958 France was at a crucial point where it could either flourish again or perish, become a powerful democracy or a dictatorship if Algeria exploded. The threat was to the essential substance of the French nation. Nineteen sixty-two is more questionable. De Gaulle, however, saw the strong presidency – which had come about because of his unique stature, not because of the 1958 Constitution – as central to France's continuation

191

as a powerful democracy. The 1962 amendment was the logical, if not the planned, extension of the 1958 constitution-making – the finishing of that job.

Even though the 1962 amendment did not have to be unconstitutional in the legal sense since Article 11 set out a clear amendment procedure, *political reality dictated otherwise*. Moreover, any structural great leap is likely to raise fundamental constitutional challenges unless a crisis is sufficiently explosive to overwhelm the entrenched elites whose status and power are at risk.

I do not want the reader to think I hold constitutionality lightly, to be cast aside with impunity by a strong leader like de Gaulle. No people venerate their Constitution as do the Americans. So it is fitting to quote an American president, as towering in our history as de Gaulle, on violation of the American Constitution. President Abraham Lincoln wrote in a letter dated April 4, 1864, to the editor of a Kentucky newspaper on his decision to free the slaves:

[M]y oath to preserve the Constitution to the best of my ability imposed upon me the duty of preserving, by every indispensable means, that government – that nation, of which the Constitution was the organic law. Was it possible to lose the nation and yet preserve the Constitution? By general law, life and limb must be protected, yet often a limb must be amputated to save a life; but a life is never wisely given to save a limb. I felt that measures otherwise unconstitutional might become lawful by becoming indispensable to the preservation of the Constitution through the preservation of the nation. Right or wrong, I assume this ground and now avow it. I could not feel that, to the best of my ability, I had even tried to preserve the Constitution, if to save slavery ... I should permit the wreck of government, country and Constitution all together.[19]

The Lincoln statement argues that in a nation-threatening emergency, the Constitution may be set aside to preserve the nation. Written a few days before the third anniversary of that bloody, yet unfinished civil war, Lincoln's argument rings true. The same might be said of 1958 when France was in turmoil if de Gaulle had had to act unconstitutionally. The argument does not hold for 1962. The country was not facing a visible, immediate threat. However much de Gaulle may have come to symbolize France of the postwar years regaining its national glory, the failed assassination attempt can hardly be likened to the American South at war with the Union or looming civil war in France over Algeria.

De Gaulle did, however, take action based on larger concerns. He believed France's reemergence as a great nation was in jeopardy when he stepped down as president. In his last writings published after his death, de Gaulle made his grand, driving vision clear: "It is my task to demand that the common interest rise above the routines and claims of particular social categories and to show that the object of our striving for prosperity is not so much to make life easier for certain Frenchmen but, rather, to build the security, the power, and the grandeur of France."[20] Yet, even with acceptance that he acted on highest principle with no thought of personal or political gain (he did not need to strengthen the presidency to support his rule), disquiet remains.

At least in the French and U.S. cases, there was both a written constitution and a time-bounded problem – a civil war in progress that could destroy the nation, a president of advanced age whose retirement or death in office could stop France in its march toward regained grandeur. In contrast no one can say with any certainty when the British Disease will bring significant instability (or that it won't). And, if as I suggest shortly, national apathy not revolution is the likely outcome, dating the start of such apathy will not be easy, especially if Southeast England continues to flourish.

The British constitutional issue is even more vexing. I sometimes think that any modification in the status quo, especially when it affects central government structure, will be labeled unconstitutional by opponents. Admittedly, the same tactics are used in the United States but there is a resolving mechanism in the Supreme Court. At the same time many of the changes being discussed are significant and likely unconstitutional by almost any standards. The issue boils down ultimately to various assessments of dangers (those of not acting and of acting) and to values, an issue returned to again shortly.

BRITAIN TODAY

Thatcher's effort in her first two governments is the latest act in Britain's long running battle to stem Britain's economic decline. Mrs Thatcher saw the flawed industrial structure and the obsolete central government as the two most critical elements of the British Disease, and at least sensed the interrelationship of the two. But she has not achieved the needed institutional and economic great leaps. Mrs

Thatcher's institutional changes have not had the impacts on central government structure needed to modernize that government so it can cope with the British Disease. Here she has clearly failed so far and seems almost certain not to make a new effort at bringing dramatic changes. Her success or failure on the economic front thus far is legitimately debatable. However, I find the available, and admittedly conflicting, evidence adds up to failure. Further, while there is a reasonable probability of future success, I predict failure here too.

To argue that Mrs Thatcher has produced neither the necessary structural great leap nor the one required in the economic sphere is not to contend that the various impacts, both positive and negative, do not sum up to a great leap in that the total differences flowing from Thatcher policies make period A markedly different from period B. Is Ronald Butt correct in claiming that "if 1945 represented a constitutionally achieved revolution in political structure, 1979 began a constitutionally achieved counter-revolution"? Consider these large changes starting with the intended ones: privatization of state-owned industries, sale of council houses, modification of trade union rules and regulations, monetarism, lower tax rates, gains in industrial productivity, a decline in inflation, increased stock buying, cutbacks in the number of central government employees, and more central government control over local authorities. The unintended, negative changes associated with Thatcher policies also are large: the worst recession and the highest unemployment since the Great Depression, a decline in manufacturing that can be characterized as deindustrialization, lower central government civil servant morale, and the emergence of two nations, one rich and the other poor. Whether Mrs Thatcher's policies have restored the entrepreneurial spirit is a critical unanswered question. The evidence to date is so mixed that any claim of a large, positive change is questionable. However, the change thus far is in the desired direction, although the revival of the entrepreneurial spirit has a goodly distance to go if the British Disease is to be cured. Perhaps no socioeconomic issue looms larger in the third and possibly fourth Thatcher governments than whether she can go significantly further in this area.

The intended and unintended changes flowing at least in part from Thatcher policies sum up to a great leap. Whether the great leap is more positive than negative depends on so many value judgments (how is the emerging two nations to be weighted *vis-à-vis* say

194

increased productivity) that it seems fruitless to speculate. But two clear statements can be made. The first is methodological: the Thatcher great leap as compared to earlier ones in the last 50 years in Great Britain and the United States is distinctly different in not coming about from dramatic policy changes made in a relatively brief period of time, generally at the start of a new government. Second, the Thatcher great leap clearly does not achieve the needed changes in central government structure. Even if future Thatcher governments move ahead much further in economic improvement than I anticipate, future *ordinary* prime ministers still will be blocked by pre-modern British government and hence be incapable of coping successfully with future economic threats.

The assessments of past and future failure by the Thatcher governments to achieve the needed institutional and economic great leaps mean that *the specter of economic decline remains. British stability is still threatened.*

Stability can be conceived of as part of a line bounded by instability at either end. At one of the extremes, instability generates a revolution although not necessarily a violent one. There can be a bloodless Glorious Revolution or one as traumatic as the American Civil War with an even greater stability emerging once the malignancy is removed. The other direction of the stability-instability line moves toward national apathy. Nowhere have I found such apathy so vividly captured as in William Leuchtenburg's description of America in the winter of 1932–3 just before Roosevelt came to the presidency (note the striking contrast to Britain of that time):

Both American and European observers were astonished by the strangely phlegmatic response of Americans to the depression. In England, thousands of British workers marched on Buckingham Palace and Downing Street ... but in the Unites States, a country thought of as the land of lawlessness, most of the unemployed meekly accepted their lot. After a trip through New England mill towns in 1931, one commentator noted of the workers: "There was something dead in them, as from exhaustion or perhaps too much idleness, without any personal winsomeness or any power of demand ... The situation is infinitely pathetic, not to say appalling."[21]

Half a century later what now is so astonishing about Britain is the docility of the population in the face of unemployment that has reached a level as high as the 1930s. Not all is peaceful. The major strike by coal miners, soccer violence, and the racially mixed mini-riots (still remarkably tame by American standards) may have been triggered by the high unemployment. Yet, the apathy stands out, perhaps best captured by an American Paul Theroux in *The Kingdom by the Sea* describing his walk around the coast of Britain: "Sunderland was not a lively nightmare of poverty. It was dark brown and depressed and enfeebled. It was threadbare, but it was surviving in a marginal way. The real horror of it took a while to sink in. It had stopped believing there would be any end to this emptiness. Its hellish aspect was the hardest to see and describe, because it had a sick imprisoned atmosphere: there was simply nothing to do there."[22] Nothing was more striking in the June 1987 election than the extraordinary polarization on class and geographic lines. Apathy still grips the north of Britain. Restoring confidence will be a future British political leader's first great challenge as it was to Roosevelt in 1933.

The biggest difference between the two economic climates that produced the shattered confidence of America in 1932 and much of Britain today is the perceived explosiveness of the underlying situation. The Great Depression had a defined starting point in 1929 and in March 1932 at Roosevelt's inaugural the American banking system was at the point of collapse. Today the British are still debating if a crisis exists. Several different views have come to dominate thinking about how serious the British Disease is and what should be done about it.

One view sees recovery as already underway evidenced by such factors as several years of growth in gross domestic product and the vitality of London and much of the Southeast. The big institutional and behavioral changes, such as privatization, a weakening of the trade unions, and a more profit-oriented business sector, have been made. The extended double-digit unemployment in this view masked the Thatcher turnaround that has not yet moved through all the adjustments needed to overcome the many years of inept, often wrong headed policies of earlier governments. Even more general and also "optimistic" is the view that holds that Britain will somehow muddle through her problems as she has done in the past using the current governmental structure. The two views both envision little or no additional structural change except possibly further reducing government constraint, in direct contrast to the "Britain Is Dying" theme that calls for bold action now including dramatic structural changes. Despite the differences, it should be underscored that the three views

196

have a common element in that the prescribed paths are expected to improve Britain's overall economic performance and to enhance political and social stability.

Another more submerged view combines much of the pessimism of the "Britain Is Dying" theme with the prescriptions of the optimistic first theme. This hidden view, as Sir John Hoskyns has argued, is held by many of those whose ideas count: "[T]here is an *intellectual* civil war ... within the establishment, between those who know that time is running out and who feel the impulse to go back to first principles and think the problem through; and those who prefer the *status quo* or are simply too tired to go on thinking at all. To an alarming extent, those who are prepared to make the effort are outside Whitehall and Westminster."[23] A strong sense of fatalism dominates this third view. As Porter argued: "Britain was the only country in the world to have run nearly the whole course of normal industrial development ... [It] was no longer capitalist enough to survive, in a world where her competitors had become more capitalist than she."[24] Not much can be done but soldier on to the end. The script is a Greek tragedy leading inevitably to a terribly diminished Britain. Given such inevitability the fatalist elites counsel doing nothing to the underlying government structure. Enjoy it while it lasts.

The argument is not an evil conspiracy by those who want to stay in power. If there is a conspiratorial element, it is one of silence. The word is not said. The tired pessimism of the last paragraph dominates, or else the risks of adjustment are judged as too high. And the risks could be high for the elites who continue to thrive. One of them told me that the British prefer an evening with guests at home enjoying stimulating conversation to an expensive evening in a good German restaurant. But we should not conjure up stiff upper lip near poverty. There are expensive meals out, a seemingly endless number of junkets for academics, and Porsches and BMWs for business. And most of all there is an admirable level of civility. These elites are exceedingly and justifiably fond of the pattern.

THE PATH TOWARD CHANGE

Strong political leadership is the first demand for breaking the pattern that keeps British central government pre-modern. The political leader has to be both the architect and the director of change. Two immediate tasks loom large in Britain's current crisis: Making the crisis of pre-modern government urgent and developing a strategy to guide the process of change. The first task demands political mastery. Organizational mastery begins to come to the fore in the second one.

The demands on the political leader are to convince Parliament and the people that there is a crisis needing extraordinary measures and to instill a belief that something can be done. Here is the consummate political challenge for the leader. Some have met it. Churchill rallied the British people in Britain's darkest days during the summer of 1940. Speaking before the House of Commons on June 4 after Dunkirk, Churchill stood firm and defiant: "We shall not flag or fail ... [W]e shall fight in the fields and in the streets, and we shall fight in the hills; we shall never surrender." We can only speculate how much this individual political leadership contributed to the winning of the Battle of Britain as the nation stood alone in that grim summer.

A modernized, strategically oriented government is the precondition for mounting the second great leap. What should the road map for this first great leap look like? The fifteen options and the institutional objectives discussed earlier can be a starting point – a direction setter. And I cannot overemphasize the importance of a good starting point that sets basic direction. Not getting the direction right would probably be a fatal error.

A good guide will balance sufficient detail to provide some destination points and conceivably a few roadmarks along the way with enough flexibility to accommodate corrections and adjustments. But it will be a very imperfect plan needing a good guide. Here organizational mastery can be critical. It first comes to the fore in designing a road plan that can give dimension to the bold political vision and drive the great leap. Even more important is sufficient organizational mastery to make the right decisions at key points of political and organizational interaction. For example, the parts of the institutional configuration that might be abandoned or modified to meet political demands without undercutting fundamental aspects of the intended great leap need to be determined. No reasonable answer can emerge until the particular configuration is seen. That choice is more art than science. But at the margin organizational understanding may be the crucial input.

While I stop short of specifying a detailed guide, one path is clear: *The overriding task of the central government must be to build institu-*

tional capacity. That is a big job. Recall that in Table 3 *all* fifteen options are intended to increase institutional capacity directly or indirectly. A strong organization can make capacity building an ordinary, ongoing activity, integrated with other efforts. *When overall organizational structure is a critical problem, capacity building must itself become an extraordinary task preparatory to the pursuit of major program goals.*

The options and institutional objectives discussed in the last three chapters are meant as guides to further analysis and debate, not as recommendations written in stone. The discussion of the options and objectives is aimed *both* at providing the organizational dimensions and depth needed to support my argument that institutional capacity building is the first critical step if Britain is to save itself from social and political instability and at supplying the basis for further critical analysis by others. To go further than I have – to cast the total package of options as the one that should be adopted – runs the risk of obscuring the basic organizational need for critical institutional choices to be worked out in a process that includes the key organizational actors whose individual status and institutional turf are at risk. It is to commit the top-down fallacy that strong organizational leadership involves imposing institutional changes from on high without consultation with those below. Such an approach fits too well with the secrecy and command and control mentality that permeates British central government. The issue is not *whether* the top of the central government should lead but rather *how* it is to lead significant institutional change within the central government itself.

The options and objectives are aimed at two different audiences. One is concerned citizens; the other is central government policymakers, or more likely future, yet undetermined policymakers. The basic goals are similar in both cases: (i) to convince that immediate action is demanded and that major institutional changes of the type indicated in Chapters 7 and 8 are a necessary step toward coping with the British Disease and (ii) to stimulate further analysis and debate, and in the case of policymakers (or potential policymakers) to facilitate the making of policy choices.

We can go one more step in counselling the usefulness in this search of such tools as implementation analysis and strategic planning and of organizational lessons discussed earlier such as involving in the planning those whose status and power are at stake. *Going further is pure hubris.* Beyond us is the political art of groping toward a viable solution that balances the retention of what is essential with necessary changes responding to environmental pressures. Britain's big problem is to find a person with the skill and courage of Earl Grey in sticking to the decision to eliminate rotten boroughs. No task of the top leader demands more political leadership skill than that of guiding the groping process and finally making the critical choice of where to stop. *The unique leadership task is to keep the focus on structural change amid the swirl of policy demands – staying on course is the leader's great challenge.*

<h2 style="text-align:center">A FINAL NOTE</h2>

Great leaps that transform structure are inherently dangerous. The modifier "great" after all describes distance, not quality of outcome. A great leap may be in the wrong direction tearing a nation apart. But even when the great leap moves in the right direction, it usually opens a Pandora's box full of risks. There are no guarantees the great leap started right will not go terribly wrong. Even success may be far from satisfying, not just to those who lose power and status but to the winners too. Earl Grey wrote in Septermber 1837: "If I had thought that the result of the Reform Bill was to be the raising of a new [Cola di] Rienzi ... I would have died before I proposed it."[25]

Consider a successful great leap providing a modern British central government a structure to cope with the British Disease. To begin with the adjustment period needed to grope toward a new, healthy stability will likely be a disconcerting, often tumultuous time much like the fifteen months of the passage of the Great Reform Act. The leader may not be as difficult a person as de Gaulle (Attlee and Grey were not). Still the structural reforms needed by Britain are certain to elicit sharp opposition and demand great strength and boldness in leadership and probably a goodly amount of meanness to boot. I do not mean to conjure up an unrecognizable Britain of Prussian precision and American gaucheness. But it would be sheer sophistry not to warn of wrenching structural changes and underscore that a more viable Britain like the rest of the West will still have a host of problems.

An historical perspective is needed. Serious structural crises usually are confronted only after the problem has existed for a lengthy period

200

of time. The Fourth Republic with its weak president caused instablility for a dozen years before the threat of war forced action. De Gaulle's unconstitutional act seemingly set no dangerous precedent. Indeed, lancing the boil was sufficiently traumatic to serve as a warning rather than as an invitation to attack the Constitution. A similar case could be made for the Great Reform Act.

My concern at this point is less with constitutionality than the unpalatability of the options available, since my analysis uncovers no course of action without grave risks. Stand pat, apathy looms large and revolution is not ruled out. Try major changes, face both difficult implementation hurdles and significant unintended consequences with no guarantee of success. Yet there too is cause for optimism.

Start with the solidness of British stability. It is the foundation that can protect the basic core of what is so attractive about British life. Britain, even in the two decades or so of the virulent form of the British Disease, appears to have held up better than the pure economics of the situation would suggest. So arresting the decline, but with no big relative economic gains, holds promise. Second is the potential power of positive political leadership combined with the near dictatorial powers of prime minister and Cabinet that afford Britain, more than the other large Western nations, the means both to mobilize central government and to have a major domestic policy impact. Third, as a "late comer" to central government modernization Britain has much useful information and experience available to it. The wheel really does not need to be re-invented anew. Indeed, I argue immodestly that the present work offers a useful starting point. Fourth, British Cabinet government and, to some extent, the French strong president/premier structure make the combination of a political leader with some organizational understanding and an organization-man par excellence more likely than in America. Cabinet government offers much more of a precedent. In the 1945–51 Labour governments political dynamism came less from Attlee than the stars in the Big Five with Attlee being the organizational impresario. In the period of the Great Reform Act Earl Grey's political leadership was tied to Althorp's leadership in the Commons. De Gaulle had enough organizational understanding to appoint Debre as prime minister. Finally, increasing staff is easier than decreasing it. The U.S. faces a far more difficult problem in correcting excessive staffing than Britain does in adding staff. Moreover, a different ethos makes it unlikely that Britain

201

will overshoot in staff size. The big problem rather is to break the "no staff" mentality and to find the needed skills in the short term.

My optimism must be tempered by the ever present concern that the British – more pointedly, the Westminster and Whitehall elites – like their Venetian counterparts will be unwilling to make significant structural changes. The usual question asked of me by other Americans who know and admire the British is "do you really think they will make big changes?" I can hardly say candidly that I am confident that Britain will respond to the call for bold action.

As time passes, the distance for a truly conservative great leap becomes longer and more dangerous. Stability eroding into apathy offers a smaller and smaller base. The great danger is standing pat. The biggest barrier is not the technical economic base but the lack of political will. Undershooting not overshooting is the big danger. Enough of the cries of unconstitutionality, of the sanctity of obsolete institutions. I am angered generally at Britain's failure to see the basic threat to its stability and specifically at the political and bureaucratic elites for not being more concerned and more aggressive, for being fatalistic, for arguing over much less basic questions, and for often denying the crisis. Are ministers, MPs, mandarins and other elites in the relatively prosperous Southeast too comfortable, too afraid that change will affect them adversely? Why can't they see that Lord Snow's lament should be the current battle cry. In today's peacetime Battle of Britain, the crisis is nearly as grave, the threat almost as fundamental, the need for extraordinary political leadership *and* followship perhaps even more demanding than that Churchill and the nation faced so bravely. To save Britain, the pattern must be broken.

NOTES

PREFACE

1 Walter Williams, *Social Policy Research and Analysis*, Elsevier, 1971, p. 11.

INTRODUCTION

1 King set out the case succinctly in observing that "Britain is universally regarded as the [economic] sick man of Europe." Anthony King, "Politics, economics and the future of Britain," a paper proposed for the Aspen Institute Seminars, Bath, England, October 17–24, 1982, p. 1. Studlar offers a long list of books on what he calls "'the state of Britain' literature," most of which have come out in the last decade or so and bear such grim titles as "Alas, alas for England," "Why has Britain failed?," and "Is Britain dying?" Donley T. Studlar, "Introduction: dilemmas of change in British politics," in Studlar and Jerold L. Waltman (eds.), *Dilemmas of Change in British Politics*, University Press of Mississippi, 1984, pp. 2, 16–17. As will be made clear shortly, the Thatcher governments (the first two ending in mid-1987) have made the "Britain is dying" theme debatable.

2 There have been earlier calls for modernization and efficiency in Britain, particularly for industry but also for government. The first Wilson government "emphasized the importance of science and technology and held out the prospect of a new Britain 'that is going to be forged in the white heat ... of revolution.'" Dennis Kavanagh, "From gentlemen to players: changes in political leadership," in William B. Gwyn and Richard Rose (eds.), *Britain: Progress and Decline*, Tulane University, 1980, p. 84. The Heath government was committed specifically to central government reform and will be discussed in a later chapter. Kavanagh offers a good

brief summary of the modernization theme in *ibid*, pp. 83–7. Also see Andrew Gamble, *Britain in Decline*, Macmillan, 1981, pp. 122–31. The Thatcher modernization efforts are treated extensively in this and later chapters. Also worth noting is Christopher Pollitt's recent work on changes in the machinery of government, *Manipulating the Machine*, Allen & Unwin, 1984. But Pollitt does not see such changes as all that important citing Michael Stewart that "changes in the machinery of government ... are largely for Westminster-Whitehall consumption; *nobody else takes much notice.*" *The Jekyll and Hyde Years*, J. M. Dent & Sons, 1977, p. 120, emphasis added. I have much more drastic changes in mind.

3 A former permanent secretary of the Ministry of Defense, Sir Frank Cooper, makes a similar point: "[Cabinet Ministers] failed to cope ... in the post-war years with things which are highly complex ... We've got a very unhealthy and ... largely obsolescent political system." Quoted in Peter Hennessy, *Cabinet*, Basil Blackwell, 1986, p. 166. John Garrett, a Labour MP and also a management consultant, has stated: "The British civil service, for all its strengths, is not organized or managed in a way which enabled it to cope with the problems of modern Britain and our machinery for Parliamentary and public scrutiny is clearly inadequate to meet the requirements of an alert and informed democracy." John Garrett, *Managing the Civil Service*, Heinemann, 1980, p. 192.

4 Bruce Headey in a still useful book observed: "Making due allowance for the multiple factors involved ... it still seems reasonable to suggest that the fact that Treasury ministers by and large lacked more than a layman's understanding of economics and Defense ministers lacked managerial experience and skills, is one significant and neglected explanation for the post-war record." *British Cabinet Ministers*, Allen & Unwin, 1974, pp. 277–8.

5 Walter Williams, "Implementation and Social Policy," a paper presented at the Western Political Science Association meeting, Sacramento, California, April 13, 1984.

6 Stephen Wilks, "Has the state abandoned British industry?," *Parliamentary Affairs*, January 1986, pp. 45–6.

7 Quoted in "Re-skilling government," Institute of Directors, 1986, Paragraph 34 (no page numbers).

8 The sociocultural argument is presented most fully in Martin J. Wiener, *English Culture and the Decline of the Industrial Spirit, 1850–1980*, Cambridge University Press, 1981. Edmund Dell also has made a similar argument about the relative importance of basic factors and of government. Edmund Dell, "Collective responsibility: fact or facade?" in *Policy and Practice*, Royal Institute of Public Administration, 1980, p. 28.

9 Ralf Dahrendörf, *On Britain*, British Broadcasting Corporation, 1982, p. 161.

10 C. P. (Lord) Snow, *The Two Cultures and the Scientific Revolution*, 1959, Cambridge University Press, p. 42.
11 *The Tower Commission Report* (full text of the President's Special Review Board), Times Books, 1987.
12 For a good treatment of the causality issue using the Treasury as example, see Colin Thain, "The Treasury and British decline," *Political Studies*, December 1984, pp. 581–95.
13 Constitutional change requires approval by extraordinary votes in both houses of Congress and in fifty state legislatures. As Sundquist has observed: "Not only may [a constitutional] amendment be blocked by 34 percent of the voting members of one house of Congress but, if it passes that hurdle, it can still be defeated by the adverse vote, or simple inaction, of as few as thirteen of the ninety-nine legislative houses, or fewer than 14 percent. No other country has a mechanism for constitutional amendment that requires so high a degree of national consensus." James L. Sundquist, *Constitutional Reform and Effective Government*, Brookings, 1986, p. 242. The Sundquist book presents a thoughtful, detailed argument that reform of the basic constitutional structure is most unlikely.
14 Geoffrey K. Fry, *The Changing Civil Service*, Allen & Unwin, 1985, p. 21. Sir John Hoskyns has observed that "being a professional politician turns out to mean being an *amateur* minister." Sir John Hoskyns, "Conservation is not enough," Institute of Directors Annual Lecture, 1983, p. 9, emphasis in the original.
15 Philip Norton points out "that there is no legal impediment to the appointment of a minister who is not a member of either House of Parliament." Philip Norton, *The Commons in Perspective*, Martin Robinson, 1981, p. 50.
16 Philip Giddings, "What has been achieved?", in Gavin Drewry (ed.), *The New Select Committees: A Study of the 1979 Reform*, Clarendon Press, 1985, p. 376.
17 William Plowden, "Whate'er is best administered," *New Society*, April 9, 1981, p. 53. Despite Prime Minister Thatcher's emphasis on management, Plowden observes four years later that "in many respects the civil service has not changed greatly in the past ten, twenty or indeed fifty years." William Plowden, "What prospects for the civil service?" a Lecture to the Royal Society of Arts, February 6, 1985, p. 2.
18 Dell, "Collective responsibility: fact or facade," p. 39.
19 Walter Williams, "British policy analysis: some preliminary observations from the U.S.," in Andrew Gray and Bill Jenkins (eds.), *Policy Analysis and Evaluation in British Government*, Royal Institute of Public Administration, 1983, pp. 20, 23–4.
20 William Plowden observed in discussing the conservatism of the civil service: "This [conservatism] is at least partly due to the sincerely held belief that there is little wrong with existing practices, and that critics do

not understand the constraints with which the service has to work."
William Plowden, "The higher civil service of Britain." in Bruce L. R.
Smith (ed.), *The Higher Civil Service in Europe and Canada: Lessons for
the United States*, Brookings, 1984, p. 35.

21 Quoted in *The Washington Post National Weekly Edition*, April 15, 1985.

22 S. E. Finer, "Thatcherism and British political history" in Kenneth
Minogue and Michael Biddiss (eds.), *Thatcherism: Personality and
Politics*, Macmillan, 1987, p. 140.

23 John Cole, *The Thatcher Years: A Decade of Revolution in British Politics*,
BBC Books, 1987, p. 206.

24 C. F. Pratten, "Mrs Thatcher's economic legacy" in Minogue and Biddiss
(eds.), *Thatcherism*, pp. 93–4.

25 Les Metcalfe and Sue Richards, "The impact of the efficiency strategy:
political clout or cultural change," *Public Administration*, Winter, 1983,
p. 441.

26 George Jones and John Stewart, *The Case for Local Government*, Allen &
Unwin, 1983, p. 4.

27 For my extended comments, see Walter Williams, *Government by Agency*,
Academic Press, 1980, especially pp. 127–47.

28 Quoted in Wiener, *English Culture and the Decline of the Industrial Spirit
1850–1980*, p. 162.

29 Quoted in "The National Audit Office," *Public Finance and Accountancy*,
June 1984, p. 25.

30 Bernard Asbell, *The Senate Nobody Knows*, Doubleday, 1978, p. 452.

31 Michael Brock, *The Great Reform Act*, Hutchinson University Library,
1973, p. 150.

32 *Ibid.*, p. 151. Butler described the period as "The most vigorous agitation
ever known in the country." J. R. M. Butler, *The Passing of the Great
Reform Bill*, Longmans, Green, 1914, p. 257.

33 Webb has observed: "The government was overwhelmingly aristocratic
more so than any government since the eighteenth century; only four of
the fourteen members of the cabinet sat in the Commons, all but one were
great landlords." R. K. Webb, *Modern England*, 2nd Edition, Harper &
Row, 1980, p. 195.

34 G. M. Trevelyan, *Lord Grey of the Reform Bill*, Longmans, Green, 1920,
pp. 268, 272. Trevelyan, Brock and Briggs quote favorably John Bright's
statement from an 1864 speech at Birmingham: "It was not a good Bill,
but it was a great Bill when it passed." *Ibid.*, p. 272; Brock, *The Great
Reform Act*, p. 332, Asa Briggs, *The Age of Improvement: 1783–1867*,
Harper and Row, 1965, p. 260.

35 Brock, *The General Reform Act*, p. 336.

36 G. Bingham Powell, Jr., "Incremental democratization: the British
Reform Act of 1832," in Gabriel A. Almond and others (eds.), *Crisis
Choice and Change*, Little, Brown, 1973, pp. 145–6. This piece is good

on coalition building, an important area my brief account cannot do justice to.

37 Robert Blake, *Disraeli*, St. Marin's Press, 1967, p. 248, emphasis added.
38 Anthony King, "Margaret Thatcher: the style of a prime minister," in Anthony King, *The British Prime Minister*, Second Edition, 1985, pp. 137–8.
39 *Ibid.*, p. 122.

1 THE GOVERNANCE PROBLEM IN BROAD PERSPECTIVE

1 Quoted in Bruce Headey, *British Cabinet Ministers*, Allen & Unwin, 1974, p. 226.
2 Sir Frank Cooper, "Freedom to manage in government," Royal Institute of Public Administration Winter Lecture Series – 1982/3, London, March 19, 1983, p. 1.
3 Thomas J. Peters and Robert H. Waterman, Jr., *In Search of Excellence: Lessons from America's Best Run Companies*, Harper & Row, 1982, p. 41.
4 Phyllis Ellickson, Joan Petersilia, and others, "Implementing new ideas in criminal justice," R-2929NIJ, The Rand Corporation, April 1983, pp. 74–5, emphasis in the original.
5 Ben Heineman, Jr., "Managing politics and policy," in Lester M. Salamon and Michael S. Lund (eds.), *The Reagan Presidency and the Governing of America*, Urban Institute, 1984, p. 169.
6 Ralf Dahrendorf, *On Britain*, British Broadcasting Corporation, 1982, p. 20.
7 Andrew Gamble, *Britain in Decline*, Macmillan, 1981, p. 21.
8 Meghnad Desai, "Economic alternatives for Labour, 1984–9," in *Socialism in a Cold Climate*, Unwin Paperbacks, 1983, p. 39.
9 Gamble, *Britain in Decline*, pp. 140, 202.
10 John Eatwell, *Whatever Happened to Britain?*, Oxford University Press, 1984, p. 42.
11 Gamble, *Britain in Decline*, p. 21.
12 After discussing that Britain's economic problems go back to the 1870s, Desai observed: "[W]hat needs to be explained is the miraculously easy period of 1948–63." Desai, "Economic alternatives for Labour, 1984–9," p. 39. As discussed below, real GDP in 1960–1973 grew at three times the rate of 1979–1985 and two and one-half times the 1973–79 rate. C. F. Pratten, "Mrs Thatcher's Economic Legacy" in Kenneth Minogue and Michael Biddiss (eds.) *Thatcherism: Personality and Politics*, Macmillan, 1987, pp. 76–77.
13 Cited in John Newhouse, "Profiles: the gamefish, " *New Yorker*, February 10, 1986, pp. 99–100.
14 Eatwell, *Whatever Happened to Britain?*, pp. 10–11, 128.
15 Gamble, *Britain in Decline*, p. 21.

16 *Ibid.*
17 Eatwell, *Whatever Happened to Britain?*, pp. 12–13, emphasis in the original.
18 Dahrendorf, *On Britain*, p. 20.
19 Quoted in Geoffrey Smith and Nelson W. Polsby, *British Government and Its Discontents*, Basic Books, 1981, p. 6.
20 *The Economist*, May 31, 1986, p. 78.
21 *The Economist*, December 21, 1985, p. 86.
22 *The Economist*, June 7, 1986, p. 65.
23 *The New York Times*, November 11, 1985.
24 Alan Walters, *Britain's Economic Renaissance: Margaret Thatcher's Reforms 1979–1984*, Oxford University Press, 1986, pp. 171–2, emphasis added.
25 *Ibid.*, p. 177. Professor Walters is quite cautious in his treatment of the years 1979–84 observing toward the end of the book: "To conclude this review with a judgment of the success of the Thatcher reform would be premature, not to say presumptuous, considering my involvement in the process itself." *Ibid.*, p. 184.
26 *The Economist*, October 5, 1985, p. 62.
27 Pratten, "Mrs Thatcher's Economic Legacy," pp. 76–7.
28 *United Kingdom*, OECD Surveys, January 1986, p. 18, emphasis added.
29 *The Economist*, July 26, 1986, p. 53; *The Economist*, May 31, 1986, p. 62.
30 *The Economist*, February 14, 1987, p. 50; *The Economist*, February 8, 1986, p. 56. The "fiddles" were mainly government job creation or training programs that had relatively short durations.
31 *The Economist*, July 26, 1986, p. 53.
32 Pratten, "Mrs Thatcher's Economic Legacy," pp. 87–8.
33 *Ibid.*
34 *United Kingdom*, p. 50.
35 *The New York Times*, January 9, 1987.
36 Ian Jack, "Liverpool v. Turin: more than just football," *Sunday Times Magazine*, August 25, 1986, p. 20.
37 *The Economist*, January 24, 1987, p. 51.
38 David Marquand, "The opposition under Thatcher: or the irresistible force meets the movable object" in Minogue and Biddiss (eds.), *Thatcherism*, p. 112.
39 S. E. Finer, "Thatcherism and British political history" in Minogue and Biddiss (eds), pp. 131, 135–7. The quote is from page 135. Pratten stated: "A principal objective of the Conservative party is to protect and further the interests of the groups or classes in British society which support it ... [T]he managerial and professional class and skilled workers have had a good recession." Pratten, "Mrs Thatcher's Economic Legacy," pp. 89, 92.
40 Joel Krieger, *Reagan, Thatcher and the Politics of Decline*, Polity, 1986,

pp. 196, 213. The quote is from page 213.
41 Pratten, "Mrs Thatcher's Economic Legacy," p. 79.
42 Eatwell, *Whatever Happened to Britain?*, p. ix. Britain in the Thatcher years, mainly because of the North Sea oil became a major creditor nation again. See *The Economist*, December 13, 1986, pp. 61–2; and *The New York Times*, January 12, 1987.
43 *The New York Times*, October 9, 1985.
44 *The Times* (of London), March 2, 1982.
45 Dahrendorf, *On Britain*, p. 160.
46 Martin J. Wiener, *English Culture and the Decline of the Industrial Spirit, 1850–1980*, Cambridge University Press, 1981.
47 *Seattle Times*, June 16, 1987.
48 *The Economist*, May 31, 1986, p. 75.
49 Eatwell, *Whatever Happened to Britain?*," p. 15.
50 Gamble, *Britain in Decline*, p. 31.
51 It is ironic that both Thatcher and Ronald Reagan who are so anti-statist in rhetoric have been so statist in practice. See Krieger, *Reagan, Thatcher, and the Decline of Politics*.
52 OECD, *Long Term Trends in Tax Revenues of OECD Member Countries, 1955–1980*, OECD Studies in Taxation, 1981, p. 11.
53 Douglas E. Ashford, *Policy and Politics in Britain: The Limits of Consensus*, Basil Blackwell, 1981, p. 24.
54 Stephen Wilks, "Has the State Abandoned British Industry?," *Parliamentary Affairs*, January 1986, p. 45.

2 AN AMERICAN'S VIEW OF BRITISH GOVERNMENT

1 Mayntz has made a similar point in discussing German central government: "A strong chancellor does not employ ministers who are weak in their own sphere." Renate Mayntz, "Executive leadership in Germany: dispersion of power or 'Kanzlerdemokratie'?" in Richard Rose and Ezra Suleiman (eds.), *Presidents and Prime Ministers*, American Enterprise Institute, 1980, p. 169.
2 *Hansard*, January 28, 1983, p. 1219. Nelson Polsby has made a similar distinction in contrasting transformative versus arena legislatures with the U.S. being the best example of the former and Britain being the prototypical arena legislature. Polsby observed that "I find it useful to contemplate the two classic cases as tendency toward the ends of a continuum." Nelson W. Polsby, "Legislatures," in, Fred I. Greenstein and Nelson W. Polsby (eds.), *Governmental and Institutional Processes*, Volume 5, Handbook of Political Science Series, Addison-Wesley, 1975, pp. 280–1.
3 Philip Norton, *The Commons in Perspective*, Martin Robinson, 1981, p. 43.
4 An American academic, Jorgen Rasmussen, argues that "a sensible

government is likely to find that it needs to make policy concessions to the Commons about as frequently as does the President to the Congress." Jorgen Rasmussen, "Executive and legislative roles," in Richard Hodder-Williams and James Ceaser (eds.), *Politics in Britain and America*, Duke University Press, 1986, p. 27.

5 Norton, *The Commons in Perspective*, p. 177, emphasis added. For a short discussion of the legislative record of governments since 1974 including actual defeats of government bills, see Max Beloff and Gillian Peele, *The Government of the UK*, Second Edition, Weidenfeld and Nicolson, 1985, pp. 122–3.

6 *Ibid.*, p. 75.

7 Geoffrey Smith and Nelson W. Polsby, *British Government and Its Discontents*, Basic Books, 1981, p. 126.

8 Mayntz, "Executive leadership in Germany", p. 148.

9 Philip Giddings, "What has been achieved?", in Gavin Drewry (ed.), *The New Select Committees: A Study of the 1979 Reform*, Clarendon Press, 1985, p. 367.

10 Lock shows a total of seventy-six staff members for all committees as of January 1981 and 171 outside specialist advisers appointed in the 1979–83 Parliament. My sixty to seventy figure is for a single point in time and comes from interviews. Geoffrey Lock, "Resources and operations of select committees – a survey of the statistics", in Drewry (ed.), *The New Select Committees*, pp. 333–41. Lock's chapter (pp. 319–47) provides much basic data on the committees.

11 Giddings, "What has been achieved?", pp. 376–7.

12 Gavin Drewry, "The 1979 reforms – new labels on old bottles," in Drewry (ed.), *The New Select Committees*, p. 319.

13 Lock, "Resources and operations of select committees," pp. 345–6.

14 *Ibid.*, pp. 331–2.

15 *Ibid.*, p. 334. The failure to use the NAO comes out strongly in my interviews.

16 Ann Robinson, "The financial work of the new select committees," in Drewry (ed.), *The New Select Committees*, pp. 317–18.

17 Lock, "Resources and operations of select committees," pp. 323, 325.

18 Beloff and Peele, *The Government of the UK*, pp. 148–9.

19 Drewry, "The 1979 reforms," p. 386; Giddings, "What has been achieved?", p. 376, emphasis added. See also *ibid.*, pp. 368, 371, 379.

20 Gavin Drewry, "Scenes from committee life – the new committees in action," in Drewry (ed.), *The New Select Committees*, p. 353.

21 Since Cabinet and Parliament are inseparably linked, it could be claimed that Cabinet is an extension of Parliament. One reader of a draft of this chapter suggested this was the case and that Cabinet committees can be viewed as an extension of Parliament. Such a formulation misses an issue critical for the book – information availability. One of the main functions

of congressional committees is to inform the House and Senate. In contrast, Cabinet committees are a key element in the minister-mandarin information monopoly.

22 Priscilla Baines, "History and rationale of the 1979 reforms," in Drewry (ed.), *The New Select Committees*, p. 16.

23 The second and third arguments against select committees are presented (not necessarily supported) in *ibid.*, pp. 16–17. The third claim seems to be saying there is virtue in equal ignorance among backbenchers.

24 George W. Jones, "The House of Commons – a threat to good government," *London Review of Public Administration*, Issue 16, 1984, p. 25.

25 For a very broad scale attack on the select committees, see M. H. Tallbogs, "Has increased, is increasing – and ought to be diminished: a plea for fewer burdens on members of Parliament," *London Review of Public Administration*, Issue 15, 1983, pp. 1–11.

26 "The National Audit Office," *Public Finance and Accountancy*," June 1984, p. 21.

27 *Ibid.*, pp. 21, 23.

28 Roughly the same charge is made in the U.S. concerning the General Accounting Office (GAO) serving Congress. GAO, sensitive to the charge, has added social scientists to its staff but still is accountant dominated. The point is not that the accountant's orientation is inferior but rather that it is different from the policy analyst's.

29 "National Audit Office: the first 12 Reports," *Public Money*, September 1984, p. 69.

30 Edmund Dell, "Should ministers manage?" a paper presented to the Central Government Sector Conference organized by the Royal Institute of Public Administration, CIPFA Conference on Management of the Public Sector, Eastbourne, June 7–9, 1983, p. 13.

31 Richard Rose, *Do Parties Make a Difference?*, Macmillan, Expanded Second Edition, 1984, p. 89. Also, see Richard Rose, "British MPs: more bark than bite?", in Ezra N. Suleiman (ed.), *Parliaments and Parliamentarians in Democratic Politics*," Holmes & Meier, 1986, pp. 8–39.

32 *Ibid.*, p. 91.

33 *Ibid.*, pp. 100–1, emphasis in the original.

34 Anthony Lester, "Fundamental rights: the United Kingdom isolated?", *Public Law*, Spring 1984, pp. 46–7. The quote from Dicey is found in A. V. Dicey, *Introduction to the Study of the Law of the Constitution*, Tenth Edition, Macmillan, 1965, p. 145.

35 Richard E. Neustadt, *Presidential Power: The Politics of Leadership from FDR to Carter*, Wiley, 1980, p. 26, emphasis in the original.

36 Such a statement does not imply that a prime minister, even with a strong majority, is invincible and can ignore political pressures with impunity. Thatcher so dominant in 1984 appeared to be much more vulnerable to Parliament two years later.

37 Harold (Lord) Wilson, *The Governance of Britain*, Weidenfeld and Nicholson, 1976, p. 1, emphasis added.
38 *Ibid.*, p. 4. One must admire how adroitly Lord Wilson turns Crossman's own career against the Crossman thesis and at the same time puts down Crossman's Cabinet activity during the 1964–70 period.
39 *Ibid.*, p. 5.
40 Peter Hennessy, *Cabinet*, Basil Blackwell, 1986, p. 4.
41 Ezra N. Suleiman, "Presidential government in France," in Rose and Suleiman (eds.), *Presidents and Prime Ministers*, p. 103.
42 Donald Shell, "The British constitution in 1984," *Parliamentary Affairs*, Spring 1985, p. 148, emphasis added. Shell's reference to a naturally sensitive issue concerns the Conservative backbench uproar over proposed parental contributions for university living costs and tuition of students. Again, it is worth noting the Thatcher decline by 1986.
43 Hennessy, *Cabinet*, p. 194.
44 Michael Cockerell, Peter Hennessy, and David Walker, *Sources Close to the Prime Minister*, Macmillan, 1984, p. 248.
45 Walter Williams, a book review, *Journal of Policy Analysis and Management*, Fall 1986, p. 122.
46 I recognize the dangers of an active press but think the risks are worth it.
47 Cockerell, Hennessy and Walker, *Sources Close to the Prime Minister*, p. 15.
48 Des Wilson, *The Secrets File*, Heinemann, 1984, pp. 136–9, 146; Beloff and Peele, *The Government of the UK*, p. 36.
49 Clive Ponting, *The Right to Know*, Sphere Books, 1985, p. 208.
50 Quoted in Peter Hennessy, Susan Morrison, and Richard Townsend, *Routine Punctuated by Orgies: The Central Policy Review Staff 1970–83*, Strathclyde Papers on Government and Politics No. 31, Politics Department, University of Strathclyde, 1985, p. 27. The quote is from an interview with Sir Frank Cooper on October 31, 1983.
51 *The New York Times*, February 17, 1987.
52 Dell, "Should ministers manage?", p. 14.
53 Barbara Castle, *The Castle Diaries 1974–76*, Weidenfeld and Nicolson, 1980, p. 124, emphasis added.
54 See Bruce Headey, *British Cabinet Ministers*, Allen & Unwin, 1974. Among past ministers Headey found few good managers and few who thought they should be managers. He offers some case examples as exceptions of which Denis Healey is the most interesting. See also Bruce Read and Geoffrey Williams, *Denis Healey and the Politics of Power*, Sidgwick & Jackson, 1971.
55 Hugo Young and Anne Sloman, *No, Minister: An Inquiry into the Civil Service*, British Broadcasting Corporation, 1982, p. 94.
56 Rudolph Klein and Janet Lewis, "Advice and dissent in British government: the case of the special advisers," *Policy and Politics*, September

1977, p. 20. See also Kevin Theakston, *Junior Ministers in British Government*, Basil Blackwell, 1987.

57 Peter Kellner and Lord Crowther-Hunt, *The Civil Servants: An Inquiry into Britain's Ruling Class*, MacDonald General Books, London, 1980. This is not to argue that civil servants do not try to steer ministers toward their way of thinking. See Beloff and Peele, *The Government of the UK*, pp. 117–18.

58 John Garrett, *Managing the Civil Service*, Heinemann, 1980, p. 33.

59 For an interesting account of difference between the public and private sectors from the perspective of a career civil servant, see David Howells, "Marks and Spencer and the civil service," *Public Administration*, Autumn 1981, pp. 337–52.

60 See Richard Rose, "The political status of higher civil servants in Britain," in Ezra N. Suleiman (ed.), *Bureaucrats and Policy Making*, Holmes & Meier, 1984, p. 154.

61 William Plowden, "The higher civil servant in Britain," in Bruce L. R. Smith (ed.), *The Higher Civil Service in Europe and Canada*, Brookings, 1984, p. 27, emphasis added.

62 Geoffrey K. Fry, *The Changing Civil Service*, Allen & Unwin, 1985, p. 56.

63 *Ibid.*, p. 69, emphasis added.

64 Fry argues that the home civil service selection system is not biased in favor of Oxbridge graduates. *Ibid.*, p. 61.

65 William Plowden, "Whate'er is best administered," *New Society*, April 9, 1981, p. 53.

66 Heclo makes this recommendation in his penetrating book on the U.S. civil service, and I believe it applies also to the British case: "Conditional cooperation emerges between ... extremes. It implies a kind of cooperation that is conditional on the mutual performance of the political appointees and the civil servants. It emphasized the need of executives and bureaucrats to work at relationships that depend on the contingencies of one another's actions, not on preconceived ideas of strict supervision or harmonious goodwill. *Conditional cooperation rejects any final choice between suspicion and trust, between trying to force obedience and passively hoping for compliance.*" Hugh Heclo, *A Government of Strangers: Executive Politics in Washington*, Brookings, 1977, p. 193, emphasis added.

67 Beloff and Peele, *The Government of the UK*, pp. 39–45. For a summary of recent central-local relations, see *ibid.*, pp. 309–24.

68 George W. Jones and John Stewart, *The Case for Local Government*, Allen & Unwin, 1983, p. 30.

69 Rose, "The political status of higher civil servants," p. 164.

3 EXPERT INFORMATION AND ANALYSIS

1 Richard R. Nelson, *The Moon and the Ghetto: An Essay on Public Policy Analysis*, W. W. Norton, 1977, p. 23.

2 Walter Williams, *Social Policy Research and Analysis: The Experience in the Federal Social Agencies*, Elsevier, 1971, p. xi. Both this book and the Nelson book cited in Note 1 give details about the development of policy analysis generally and in the federal government.

3 *The Reorganization of Central Government*, Cmnd 4506, October 1970, p. 6. For a good discussion of the Heath approach, see Christopher Pollitt, *Manipulating the Machine*, Allen & Unwin, 1984, pp. 82–106.

4 *The Reorganization of Central Government*, pp. 4, 6.

5 *Ibid.*, p. 13.

6 The sad tale of PAR is told by Andrew Gray and Bill Jenkins, "Policy analysis in British central government: the experience of PAR," *Public Administration*, Winter 1982, pp. 429–50. CPRS is chronicled in Peter Hennessy, Susan Morrison and Richard Townsend, *Routine Punctuated by Orgies: The Central Policy Review Staff, 1970–83*, Strathclyde Papers on Government and Politics, No. 31, Politics Department, University of Strathclyde, 1985.

7 In the American case I am relying on my own study based on both direct experience in and subsequent research on the Johnson administration years when PPBS was initiated (it died not too long afterward early in the Nixon administration). See Williams, *Social Policy Research and Analysis*, expecially pp. 17–35, 169–93.

8 See D. Lee Bawden and John L. Palmer, "Social policy: challenging the welfare state," in John L. Palmer and Isabel V. Sawhill (eds.), *The Reagan Record*, Ballinger, 1984, p. 201. The most notable program, the Job Corps which was part of the original War on Poverty legislation, was protected by Congress from the Reagan cuts because of strong positive evaluative data.

9 Gray and Jenkins, "Policy analysis in British central government," p. 442.

10 Christopher Pollitt, "The Central Policy Review Staff 1970–1974," *Public Administration*, Winter 1974, pp. 376–7.

11 William Plowden, "The British Central Policy Review Staff," in Peter R. Baehr and Bjorn Wittrock (eds.), *Policy Analysis and Policy Innovation*, Sage, 1981, p. 65.

12 Hennessy and others, *Routine Punctuated by Orgies*, p. 79.

13 Quoted in *ibid.*, p. 85.

14 *Ibid.*, p. 91. Note the two quoted paragraphs are statements from separate people.

15 The entire letter is found in *ibid.*, pp. 105–8. The quote is from page 105.

16 *Ibid.*, p. 98.

17 For treatments of the Policy Unit under Donoughue and in the Thatcher governments, see Bernard Donoughue, "The conduct of British economic

policy 1974–79" in Richard Hodder-Williams and James Ceaser (eds.), *Politics in Britain and the United States*, Duke University Press, 1986, pp. 119–41; and Peter Hennessy, *Cabinet*, Basil Blackwell, pp. 194, 221 (Note 40).

18 Quoted in Hugh Young and Anne Sloman, *But, Chancellor: An Inquiry into the Treasury*, British Broadcasting System, 1984, p. 24.

19 Quoted in *ibid.*, p. 108.

20 John Maynard (Lord) Keynes, *New Statesman*, January 28, 1939, p. 122.

21 William Plowden, "What prospects for the civil service?" a lecture to the Royal Society of Arts, February 6, 1985, p. 12.

22 Sir Frank Cooper, "Freedom to manage in government," An address to the Royal Institute of Public Administration, March 19, 1983, pp. 20–1, emphasis added. I was on sabbatical in London at the time, although out of the city when Sir Frank spoke. I asked people how mandarins reacted to such a pointed comment by one of their own. The answer was, "Oh, Frank's just letting off some steam after retirement."

23 J. M. Lee, "The Cabinet Office of the United Kingdom," Franco-British Seminar: L'Organization Du Travail Gouvernemental Conseil D'Etat, Paris, March 23, 1985, p. 17.

24 The two are not to be equated as a Department of Health and Social Security undersecretary once tried to do: "I have concluded ... that for administrative civil servants policy analysis is nothing more-or-less than what prose was to M. Jourdain." Robin Birch, "Policy analysis in DHSS: some reflections," *Public Administration Bulletin*, December 1983, pp. 33–4. A more realistic view is offered by Brian Hogwood but he emphasizes the lack of an agreed job description for policy analysts. Brian W. Hogwood, "Policy analysis: the dangers of oversophistication," *Public Administration Bulletin*, April 1984, pp. 19–28.

25 Martin Trow, "Notes and impressions based on a visit to England," December 1984, January 31, 1985, pp. 15, 17.

26 Williams, *Social Policy Research and Analysis*, pp. 9–10.

27 See *ibid.*, pp. 169–88.

28 The Reagan administration has been anti-analytic so the cutbacks in executive branch analytic staffs have not been to make staffs "lean and mean" but to eliminate or downgrade analytic efforts.

29 Alice M. Rivlin, "A public policy paradox," *Journal of Policy Analysis and Management*, Volume 4, Number 1, 1984, p. 20.

30 Lester C. Thurow, *Dangerous Currents*, Random House, 1983, p. xvi.

31 Williams, *Social Policy Research and Analysis*, p. 60.

32 Quoted in the August 29, 1985 issue of *The New York Times*. This article reports that all but one of the eight departments had success rates above 70 percent. The Department of State was the culprit at 29.1 percent. But Defense had a success rate of 92.4 percent (second highest after the Health and Human Services rate of 98.9 percent).

4 TOP LEADERSHIP

1 Stephen E. Ambrose, *Eisenhower: The President*, Simon and Schuster, 1984; Fred I. Greenstein, *The Hidden Hand Presidency: Eisenhower as Leader*, Basic Books, 1982; and Robert A. Divine, *Eisenhower and the Cold War*, Oxford University Press, 1981. For a brief, but useful critique of the Eisenhower literature starting with the early books that denigrated his presidency, see Anthony J. Joes, "Eisenhower revisionism: the tide comes in," *Presidential Studies Quarterly*, Summer 1985, pp. 561–71.
2 Ambrose, *Eisenhower*, p. 627.
3 *Ibid.*
4 Peter Hennessy and Andrew Arends, "Mr Attlee's engine room: Cabinet committee structure and the Labour government, 1945–51," Strathclyde Papers on Government and Politics No. 26, Politics Department, University of Strathclyde, 1983, p. 1.
5 Kenneth Harris, *Attlee*, W. W. Norton, 1983, p. 567.
6 Of the recent books, see Alan Bullock, *Ernest Bevin: Foreign Policy Secretary, 1945–51*, Heinemann, 1983; Kenneth O. Morgan, *Labour in Power, 1945–51*, Oxford University Press, 1984; Henry Pelling, *The Labour Governments, 1945–51*, Macmillan, 1984; and Ben Pimlott, *Hugh Dalton*, Jonathan Cape, 1985. Bullock treats Attlee the most favorably of the four authors, in part no doubt because the Attlee–Bevin relationship was so close, critical, and fruitful.
7 This assertion needs to be qualified to some extent for Attlee in that he did at times dither over major decisions (a point discussed later).
8 Ambrose, *Eisenhower*, p. 20.
9 Quoted in Hennessy and Arends, "Mr Attlee's engine room," p. 12.
10 Quoted in *ibid.*, p. 31.
11 Harris, *Attlee*, p. 268.
12 Greenstein, *The Hidden Hand Presidency*, p. 136.
13 *Ibid.*, p. 87.
14 Ambrose, *Eisenhower*, p. 10, 510, emphasis added.
15 Harris, *Attlee*, pp. 401, 404, 408.
16 Quoted in ibid., p. 254.
17 Greenstein, *The Hidden Hand Presidency*, p. 50.
18 For accounts of this kind of behavior, see Pimlott, *Hugh Dalton*, pp. 483–4, 509–10; and Bernard Donoughue and G. W. Jones, *Herbert Morrison: Portrait of a Politician*, Weidenfeld and Nicolson, 1973, pp. 409, 437. In their account of the 1949 sterling devaluation crisis, the latter authors, in describing a meeting of the Economic Planning Committee on June 15, 1949, to discuss that crisis, observed that "Attlee showed signs of panic." *Ibid.*, p. 437.
19 For the definitive treatment of Morrison's organizational talents, see *ibid.* It is worth commenting briefly on the fact that the Labour government had two strong organization men in Attlee and Morrison. That is

probably two more than any other recent British government. Yet Morrison could not have substituted for Attlee, not because Attlee was necessarily more skilled (I know of no one who has made such a comparison, or could at this point), but because of the great animosity between Morrison and Bevin.

20 I have drawn heavily in this subsection on extended discussion on Attlee with Kenneth Harris, Peter Hennessy, George W. Jones, Kenneth O. Morgan, and Ben Pimlott. However, I am solely responsible for the judgments.

21 Greenstein, *The Hidden Hand Presidency*, p. 245.

22 Peter Riddell, *The Thatcher Government*, Martin Robinson, 1983, p. 6.

23 Dennis Kavanagh, "Whatever happened to consensus politics?," *Political Studies*, December 1985, p. 542. For a useful discussion of "the emergence of Selsdon Man" showing that Heath's views were quite similar to those of Thatcher, see Michael Stewart, *The Jekyll and Hyde Years*, J. M. Dent & Sons, 1977, pp. 109–12.

24 For a good statement on the view of the civil service in the year Mrs Thatcher was elected, see Neville Nagler, "The image of the civil service in Britain," *Public Administration*, Summer 1979, pp. 127–42, especially pp. 127–30. Nagler at the time was a principal in the Home Office.

25 Hugh Stephenson, *Mrs Thatcher's First Year*, Jill Norman, 1980, p. 25.

26 Anthony King, "Margaret Thatcher: the style of a prime minister", in Anthony King (ed.), *The British Prime Minister*, second edition, Macmillan, 1985, p. 117.

27 See James B. Christoph, "Rubbing up or rubbing down? Dilemmas of civil service reform in Britain," in Donley T. Studlar and Jerold L. Waltman (eds.), *Dilemmas of Change in British Politics*, University Press of Mississippi, 1984, pp. 60–1. Another American Hugh Heclo notes that "Mrs Thatcher is said to work very effectively through individual civil servants who have acquired her trust .... But the civil service as such is apparently anathema." Hugh Heclo, "Whitehall and Washington revisited: an essay in constitutional lore," in Richard Hodder-Williams and James Ceaser (eds.), *Politics in Britain and the United States*, Duke University Press, 1986, pp. 112–13.

28 *The Economist* reported that (i) no assistant secretary or senior principal resigned in 1981–3 while forty-three of the former and sixty-two of the latter left in 1984–85 and (ii) roughly twice as many principals resigned in 1985 as in 1981 (67 to 34). *The Economist*, July 12, 1986, p. 52.

29 Most striking was the fall in quality of the National Security Council staff and a direct line can be traced to the Iran-Contra scandal. More will be said about that affair shortly.

30 In an off-the-record interview with a White House reporter, who was sympathetic to President Reagan and had covered his governorship in California, I was told Mr Reagan knew nothing about how California

government worked when he became a governor in 1966 and knew next to nothing when he stepped down in 1974.

31 Jorgen Rasmussen, "Executive and legislative roles," in Hodder-Williams and Ceaser (eds.), *Politics in Britain and the United States*, p. 16.

32 King, "Margaret Thatcher: the style of a prime minister," p. 125.

33 Peter Hennessy, *Cabinet*, Basil Blackwell, 1986, p. 99.

34 The similarities in decisionmaking approach are so great and so basic that President Reagan will not be considered separately in this subsection but instead treated more broadly in the next one.

35 Riddell, *The Thatcher Government*, p. 7.

36 See John Newhouse, "Profiles: the gamefish", *New Yorker*, February 10, 1986, p. 80.

37 King, "Margaret Thatcher", p. 98.

38 Newhouse, "Profiles,", p. 77.

39 *Ibid.*, p. 79.

40 For a treatment of the "Reagan-as-America-myth" theme, see Gary Wills, *Reagan's America: Innocents at Home*, Doubleday, 1986. For a more balanced biographical view, see Lou Cannon, *Reagan*, G. P. Putnam's Sons, 1982.

41 *The New York Times*, March 11, 1987, emphasis added. For reserved, but most revealing discussion of President Reagan's ineptitude, see *The Tower Commission Report*, Times and Bantam Books, 1987.

42 Richard E. Neustadt, "Presidents, politics, and analysis," B. C. Denny Lecture Series, Graduate School of Public Affairs, University of Washington, Seattle, Washington, May 13, 1986, p. 19.

43 Niccolo Machiavelli, *The Prince*, Norton, 1977, p. 71.

44 Harris, *Attlee*, p. 566. Attlee was one of the few survivors of the 1931 Labour Party election debacle (both Herbert Morrison and Hugh Dalton losing their seats) and was seen by many as a "temporary" leader practically to the moment he became prime minister in July 1945. See *ibid.*; Morgan, *Labour in Power 1945–1951*; Donoughue and Jones, *Morrison*; and Pimlott, *Dalton*.

45 Bevin's biographer, Alan Bullock, cites favorably Michael Foot's remark that "often enough Bevin *was* Attlee. It would be folly to overlook the powerful authority of this composite figure." Alan Bullock, *Ernest Bevin: Foreign Secretary 1945–1951*, Heinemann, 1983, p. 56, emphasis in the original.

46 See Walter Williams, "The Carter domestic policy staff," in Stuart Nagel (ed.), *Public Policy Analysis and Management*, JAI Press, 1986, pp. 23–67.

47 *Seattle Times*, January 21, 1985.

48 G. W. Jones, "The Attlee governments," a review of several books, *Government and Opposition*, Winter 1985, p. 126. Kenneth O. Morgan in one of the reviewed books observed: "The Attlee government ... was a landmark in the history of modern Britain ... It was without doubt the

most effective of all Labour governments, perhaps amongst the most effective of any British government since the passage of the 1832 Reform Act." Morgan, *Labour in Power, 1945–1951*, pp. 500, 503.

49 The rest of this section relies heavily on recent works that benefit from the opening of the public records for 1945–1951: Morgan, *Labour in Power, 1945–1951*; Pelling, *The Labour Governments, 1945–51*; Harris, *Attlee*; Bullock, *Ernest Bevin: Foreign Secretary, 1945–1951*; and Pimlott, *Hugh Dalton*. The Harris book also benefits from the author's extended discussions between 1958 and 1967 with Lord Attlee. The Bullock book is the last of three distinguished volumes on Bevin by this author but the only one drawing on the newly available public records.

50 Fred I. Greenstein, "Eisenhower's presidential leadership," in Marc Landy (editor), *Modern Presidents and the Presidency*, Lexington, 1985, p. 131.

51 Bullock, *Ernest Bevin*, p. 844. Britain was at war fifty-two months in World War I and seventy-one months in World War II compared to twenty and forty-four months for the U.S.

52 Pelling, *The Labour Governments, 1945–51*, p. 261.

53 Morgan, *Labour in Power, 1945–51*, p. 151. Also see Pimlott, *Dalton*, pp. 439–40.

54 Morgan, *Labour in Power, 1945–51*, pp. 326–7.

55 See particularly Paul Addison, *The Road to 1945*, Quartet Books, 1977. This book is useful both for the immediate prewar years and the war years. Pimlott's treatment of Hugh Dalton's role in the prewar years also is excellent. See Pimlott, *Hugh Dalton*, especially pp. 203–24.

56 Morgan is excellent on this point. Morgan, *Labour in Power, 1945–1951*, pp. 500–3.

57 Pelling, *The Labour Governments, 1945–1951*, pp. 265, 268; Pimlott, *Hugh Dalton*, pp. 465–6.

58 Bullock, *Ernest Bevin*, p. 854.

59 Addison, *The Road to 1945*, p. 118.

60 For a discussion of the role of "outsiders" in Treasury, see Pimlott, *Hugh Dalton*, pp. 468–70 and Peter Hennessy and Sir Douglas Hague, *How Adolph Hitler Reformed Whitehall*, Strathclyde Papers on Government and Politics, No. 41, Politics Department, University of Strathclyde, 1986.

61 See Addison, *The Road to 1945*, pp. 18–19.

62 Pimlott, *Hugh Dalton*, p. 368.

63 Morgan, *Labour in Power, 1945–51*, p. 496.

64 Bullock, *Ernest Bevin*, p. 856.

65 Bullock quoted Attlee on Bevin from *The Observer*: "Ernest looked, and indeed was the embodiment of common sense. Yet I have never met a man in politics with as much imagination as he has, with the exception of Winston." Alan Bullock, *The Life and Times of Ernest Bevin*, Volume 2,

Heineman, 1967, p. 102. As Bullock himself wrote: "[Bevin] was never troubled by indecisiveness, was a determined man at any time and in a crisis showed a strength and self-confidence which calmed other people's fears. Far from being worried by responsibility, he did not so much enjoy power as embrace it." Bullock, *Ernest Bevin*, p. 95.

66 *Ibid.*, p. 87.

67 Not exactly an unbiased observer, Dalton wrote in his notes of Cripps: "The man has the political judgment of a flea." Quoted in Pimlott, *Dalton*, p. 262. A more balanced view, still indicating Cripps' lack of political understanding, is that of Dalton's and Morrison's biographers in discussing the 1947 effort of Cripps and others to push out Attlee. See *ibid.*, p. 512 and Donoughue and Jones, *Herbert Morrison: Portrait of a Politician*, pp. 416–19.

68 Pimlott, *Hugh Dalton*, pp. 500–1. Harris observed that "Cripps was not [1947] the epic figure on the domestic scene." Harris, *Attlee*, p. 354.

69 See Pimlott, *Hugh Dalton*, pp. 152, 171, 191, 444–6, 470.

70 Donoguhue and Jones, *Herbert Morrison*, p. 364.

71 Bullock, *Ernest Bevin*, p. 55.

72 A perceptive reader questioned Attlee's stamina because he seemed "to fold up with psychosomatic illnesses at critical moments." Again, it is necessary to distinguish between ordinary and extraordinary circumstances. During the far more numerous ordinary situations, Attlee displayed great stamina. That he may have folded in crisis is important but not an aspect of physical stamina per se.

73 Harris, *Attlee*, pp. 403–4.

74 *Ibid.*, p. 566.

75 *Ibid.*, p. 569, emphasis added.

76 Like Attlee, Morrison was a superb chairman but a more dominant one. The consummate skills he exhibited on The London County Council simply may not have worked with the Labour prima donnas even if Bevin had been at least neutral toward Morrison.

77 Donoughue and Jones, *Herbert Morrison*, p. 178.

78 Quoted in Bullock, *The Life and Times of Ernest Bevin*, volume 2, pp. 100–1. The quotation is from the March 6 and 13, 1960, issues of *The Observer*. We might also note Lord Attlee's own deep understanding of power demonstrated by his statement.

5 PUBLIC MANAGEMENT

1 *The Economist*, November 2, 1985, a special section on winter books, p. 7. The two books being reviewed are Walter Goldsmith and David Clutterbuck, *The Winning Streak Workout Book*, Weidenfeld and Nicholson, 1985; and Tom Peters and Nancy Austin, *A Passion for Excellence*, Collins, 1985. Each is a follow-up to earlier works about which more will

be said. *The Economist's* warning about the study of management, fads and gurus is well-taken. But management itself remains a serious topic.

2 Henry Mintzberg, *The Nature of Managerial Work*, Harper & Row, 1973, p. 96, emphasis in the original. The ten roles are defined at pages 92–3.

3 *Ibid.*, p. 4.

4 Fred I. Greenstein, "Eisenhower's presidential leadership," in Marc Landy (ed.), *Modern Presidents and the Presidency*, Lexington, 1985, p. 131, emphasis in the original.

5 Bill Jenkins and Andrew Gray, "Policy evaluation in British government: the search for efficiency," a paper prepared for a workshop on "Policy effects: theories, methods and applications in evaluation research," European Consortium for Political Research, Barcelona, Spain, March 25–30, 1985, p. 13.

6 For an extended treatment of scrutiny, see Norman Warner, "Raynerism in practice: anatomy of a Rayner scrutiny," *Public Administration* Spring 1984, pp. 7–22.

7 Nevil Johnson, "Change in the civil service: retrospect and prospects," *Public Administration*, Winter 1985, p. 424.

8 Andrew Gray and William I. Jenkins, "Public management and accountability in British central government," a paper prepared for the ECPR Planning Session on "Problems and prospects of public management," Barcelona, March 26–30, 1985, p. 7. This paper provides a good brief description and discussion of both Rayner scrutinies and FMI, see pp. 3–9.

9 *Ibid.*, pp. 6–7, emphasis in the original.

10 For a much more favorable view of FMI casting it as a flexible system, see Johnson, "Change in the civil service," p. 424.

11 See *ibid.*, p. 425.

12 "Senior management development program," Cabinet Office (Management and Personnel Office), no date, p. 3.

13 Martin Burch, "Mrs Thatcher's approach to leadership in government: 1979–June 1983," *Parliamentary Affairs*, Autumn 1983, p. 410.

14 The quote is from a civil servant commenting from the audience at a seminar "Politicizing the British civil service," Royal Institute of Public Administration, May 10, 1983.

15 *Sunday Times*, March 27, 1983. See also *Top Jobs in Whitehall*, Royal Institute of Public Administration, January 1987.

16 *Sunday Times*, March 27, 1983.

17 Two problems were brought up by interviewees that are not germane to our discussion but could be important. First, since the new permanent secretaries are younger, will they burn out in these demanding positions? Second, if Labour wins, will it throw out these permanent secretaries as "tainted" by Thatcher and perhaps politicize the top levels of the civil service?

18 William Plowden, "What prospects for the civil service?", *Public Administration*, Winter 1985, p. 408.
19 Lord Bancroft, "Whitehall: some personal reflections," a Suntory-Toyota Lecture, London School of Economics, London, December 1, 1983, p. 3.
20 Gray and Jenkins, "Public management and accountability in British central government," p. 21; Plowden, "What prospects for the civil service?", p. 412.
21 "Re-skilling government," Institute of Directors, 1986, paragraph 12.
22 Hugh Heclo reminds us of efforts to establish a careerist secretariat during the mid-1940s. "Most noteworthy was General (later Secretary of State) George C. Marshall's quiet lobbying for a permanent White House secretariat modeled on British lines. Had Marshall's scheme succeeded, Ambassador Averell Harriman would have returned from Russia in 1945 to be cabinet secretary." Hugh Heclo, "The Executive Office of the President," in Marc Landy (ed.) *Modern Presidents and the Presidency*, Lexington, 1985, p. 72.
23 *Ibid.*, p. 79, emphasis added.
24 For a brief discussion of the development of the policy implementation area, see the chapter entitled "The intellectual baggage" in Walter Williams *The Implementation Perspective*, University of California Press, 1980, pp. 10–21.
25 *Ibid.*, p. 17.
26 Thomas J. Peters and Robert H. Waterman, Jr., *In Search of Excellence*, Harper & Row, 1982. I also use the Goldsmith and Clutterbuck book on strong British companies that in the words of its authors "unashamedly draws for its basic approach on the U.S. book *In Search of Excellence*." Walter Goldsmith and David Clutterbuck, *The Winning Streak*, Penguin, 1984, p. 1. As mentioned in note 1, these authors have just published follow-ups that led *The Economist* to draw analogies between the study of management as it is emerging and pop-sociology and to label its proponents as would-be gurus. Sad to say, *The Economist* hit the mark – Thomas J. Peters in *In Search of Excellence* now is "just plain" Tom Peters in *A Passion for Excellence*. I do not, nor necessarily does *The Economist*, believe that the new misguided phase undoes the validity of the earlier work.
27 Goldsmith and Clutterbuck, *The Winning Streak*, p. 24.
28 *Ibid.*, p. 8.
29 Peters and Waterman, *In Search of Excellence*, pp. 50, 110, emphasis in the original.
30 *Ibid.*, p. 270.
31 *Ibid.*, pp. 84, 288.
32 Goldsmith and Clutterbuck, *The Winning Streak*, p. 145.
33 Peters and Waterman, *In Search of Excellence*, p. 287.

34 Goldsmith and Clutterbuck, *The Winning Streak*, p. 41.
35 Walter Williams, *Government by Agency*, Academic Press, 1980, p. 18.

6 THE ANALYTIC PERSPECTIVE

1 Books can be written on this issue so it is easy to be misleading. In particular, in speaking of more or less effort by the central government, it is critical to distinguish between the level of expenditures and the degree of difficulty of the tasks attached to these expenditures. Thus, transfer payments are generally a less demanding task than education so one could argue for greater central government outlays for transfers while also arguing for less central government involvement in education and be consistent. Such an issue need not concern us here.

2 If this simple causality model holds, one would expect a causal chain so that greater capacity to engage in meaningful scrutiny and challenge could generate the demand for still more policy analysts. Over time too many analysts or too many analytic functions may threaten effectiveness.

7 MODERNIZING THE PARLIAMENT AND THE CENTER

1 Sir Kenneth Berrill, "Strength at the center – the case for a Prime Minister's Department," Stamp Memorial Lecture, University of London, December 4, 1980, p. 5.
2 Renate Mayntz, "Executive leadership in Germany: dispersion of power or 'Kanzlerdemokratie'?," in Richard Rose and Ezra N. Suleiman (eds.), *Presidents and Prime Ministers*, American Enterprise Institute, 1980, p. 147, emphasis added.
3 Woodrow Wilson, *Congressional Government*, Mentor Books, 1954, p. 79.
4 Roger H. Davidson, "Subcommittee government: new channels for policy making," in Thomas E. Mann and Norman J. Ornstein (eds.), *The New Congress*, American Enterprise Institute, 1981, pp. 99–106.
5 Bernard Asbell, *The Senate Nobody Knows*, Doubleday, 1978, p. 11, emphasis in original.
6 See Davidson, "Subcommittee government," pp. 127–8; and Barbara Sinclair, "Coping with uncertainty: building coalitions in the House and Senate," in Mann and Ornstein (eds.), *The New Congress*, p. 220.
7 Davidson, "Subcommittee government," p. 114. Ornstein has observed in the same vein: "The result [of the rise of subcommittee power] is the greatest degree of decentralization Congress has ever experienced and far broader dispersal of power than is found in any other legislative body on earth." Norman J. Ornstein, "The House and the Senate in a new Congress," in Mann and Ornstein (eds.), *The New Congress*, p. 379.
8 Samuel C. Patterson, "The semi-sovereign Congress," in Anthony King

(ed.), *The New American Political System*, American Enterprise Institute, 1978, p. 171.

9 *Ibid.*, p. 177.

10 The several articles cited in *The New Congress* and *The New American Political System* provide useful analyses of Congress before and after the critical change period of the 1970s. The Asbell book offers a journalist's detailed look at how subcommittees and committees work in a specific case. Another excellent journalistic treatment of this type is T. R. Reid, *Congressional Odyssey: The Saga of a Senate Bill*, Freeman and Company, 1980.

11 Michael J. Malbin, *Unelected Representatives*, Basic Books, 1980, p. 10. The numbers are higher today but Malbin provides useful breakdowns of the numbers, and I rely on *ibid.*, pp. 9–27, 252 (Table A-1).

12 Both Brookings and AEI are private nonprofit policy research and analysis organizations that house a large number of government in and outers. Dr Rivlin has returned to Brookings.

13 George W. Jones, "The House of Commons – a threat to good government," *London Review of Public Administration*, Issue 16, 1984, pp. 23, 25.

14 Kenneth Harris, *Attlee*, Norton, 1982, p. 405.

15 Hennessy offers the judgment that "[Prime Minister Thatcher's] style is not collegiate. But to call it 'presidential' is both to go too far and to dignify it." Peter Hennessy, *Cabinet*, Basil Blackwell, 1986, p. 111.

16 George W. Jones, "Helping the prime minister: the British experience, 1868–1984," pp. 45–6.

17 *Ibid.*, p. 48.

18 Walter Williams, *Social Policy Research and Analysis*, Elsevier, 1971, p. 186, emphasis in original. The OEO analytic office and the size issue are treated in *ibid.*, pp. 169–88.

19 Hennessy, *Cabinet*, pp. 194–5.

20 *Ibid.*, p. 195.

21 *Ibid.*, pp. 195–6.

22 Williams, *Social Policy Research and Analysis*.

23 John (Lord) Hunt, "Cabinet strategy and management," mimeo paper, no date, pp. 10–11.

24 David Steel, in the Foreword of Des Wilson, *The Secrets File*, Heinemann, 1984, p. x.

25 Des Wilson, "Freedom of information by law: an alternative to secrecy," in Wilson, *The Secrets File*, pp. 156–7.

26 Wilson offers a list of exemptions in *ibid.*, p 149.

8 MODERNIZING THE MINISTRIES

1 *Leadership in Jeopardy: The Fraying of the Presidential Appointments System*, The Final Report of the Presidential Appointee Project, National

224

Academy of Public Administration, November 1985, p. 3. On the same page the report points out that "no other nation relies so heavily on noncareer personnel in the management of its [central] government."

2 *Ibid.*, p. 7, emphasis in the original.

3 *Ibid.*, p. 8.

4 The politics/administration dichotomy is still alive and well and being debated as witnessed by two 1985 *Public Administration* articles, one by Nevil Johnson advocating "a sharper distinction [in the ministries] between officials specialising in policy advice and political support function, and those ... with managerial functions," and a second by William Plowden warning of the belief "gaining currency in the [Thatcher] government" that ministry management problems "can be avoided if the proper distinctions are made between policy and administration (or implementation): the former ... reserved for elected politicians and political advisers, and the latter left to civil servants." Nevil Johnson, "Change in the civil service: retrospect and prospects," *Public Administration*, Winter 1985, p. 430; and William Plowden, "What prospects the civil service?," *Public Administration*, Winter 1985, p. 404.

5 For a general discussion of how political advisers have fared, see Christopher Pollitt, *Manipulating the Machine*, Allen & Unwin, 1984, pp. 109–11.

6 Rudolf Klein and Janet Lewis, "Advice and dissent in British government: the case of special advisers," *Policy and Politics*, September 1977, p. 21. The authors also note most members of the *cabinet* are civil servants since they can take political positions in the French system. But this issue need not concern us here.

7 "Future organization of the senior civil service," *FDA News*, March 1985, p. 5, emphasis added. It should be noted that neither the entire FDA nor the branch writing the piece are recommending such a change. Rather options are being discussed.

8 Hugh Heclo, *A Government of Strangers: Executive Politics in Washington*, Brookings, 1977, p. 193.

9 J. S. Cassells, *Review of Personnel Work in the Civil Service*, Report to the Prime Minister, Management and Personnel Office, Her Majesty's Stationery Office, July 1983, p. 64, emphasis in the original. The Cassels report goes on to observe that "a further important difference is that *it is the individual employee who has the primary role in developing his career.*" *Ibid.*, emphasis in the original. This second point will not be pursued now, but I note it to underscore how different is the private sector approach.

10 For an extended treatment of the grandes ecoles, see Ezra N. Suleiman, *Elites in French Society*, Princeton University Press, 1978. Suleiman titles a chapter "The basis of elite formulation: the universities vs. the grandes ecoles." *Ibid.*, p. 31.

11 *Ibid.*, p. 163.

12 *Ibid.*, pp. 174–5.

13 *Ibid.*, p. 166.

14 The Harvard Business School restricts all of its first year students to a common core of management/analytically oriented courses before permitting some specialization in areas such as investment banking in the second year.

15 See *ibid.*, p. 164. Suleiman points out: "The work done at the school revolves around the study of administrative and judicial matters, economics, international affairs, and social problems." *Ibid.*

16 "Future organization of the senior civil service," pp. 4–5.

17 For a discussion tying school training directly to economic performance, see S. J. Prais and Karen Wagner, "Schooling standards in England and Germany: some summary comparisons bearing on economic performance," *National Institute Economic Review*, May 1985, pp. 53–76.

18 George Jones and John Stewart, *The Case for Local Government*, Allen & Unwin, 1983, p. 4.

19 Walter Williams, *Government by Agency*, Academic Press, 1980, pp. 234, 265. The need for internal analysis also applies to other institutional recommendations made earlier in this and the previous chapter (a point considered in the final chapter).

9 BREAKING THE PATTERN

1 I am indebted to John Keeler for helping me develop this section.

2 William G. Andrews, *Presidential Government in Gaullist France*, State University of New York Press, 1982, pp. 208–9.

3 *Ibid.*, p. 1. Andrews translation.

4 See *ibid.*, pp. 5–33, for an extended treatment of the perceived relationship between parliament and the president as the 1958 Constitution was being enacted.

5 Bernard E. Brown, "The decision to elect the president by popular vote," in James B. Christoph and Bernard E. Brown (eds.), *Cases in Comparative Politics*, Third Edition, Little, Brown, 1976, p. 167.

6 See *ibid.*, pp. 175–6.

7 Translated and quoted in *ibid.*, p. 178.

8 Stephen S. Cohen, "Twenty years of the Gaullist economy," in William G. Andrews and Stanley Hoffman (eds.), *The Fifth Republic at Twenty*, State University of New York Press, 1981, pp. 240–1, emphasis added. This edited volume has a number of useful chapters on the French economy. See *ibid.*, pp. 204–310. For a French–British comparison, see John Zysman, *Government, Markets and Growth*, Cornell University Press, 1983, pp. 99–232 and the appendix showing growth rates for 1954–1981.

9 Bela Balassa, "The French economy under the Fifth Republic, 1958–

1978," in Andrews and Hoffman (eds.), p. 209.

10 Cohen, "Twenty years of the Gaullist economy," p. 244.

11 Suzanne Berger, "Lame ducks and national champions," in Andrews and Hoffman (eds.), p. 293.

12 Volkmar Lauber, "The Gaullist model of economic modernization," in Andrews and Hoffman (eds.), pp. 232–5.

13 For a broader comparison of Britain, France, the U.S., West Germany and Japan, see Zysman, *Governments, Markets, and Growth*. Such evidence, however, does not support strong generalization from one country to another.

14 For a discussion of France's economic problems, see *France*, OECD Surveys 1986/1987, January 1987.

15 Don Cook, *Charles de Gaulle*, Perigee, 1983, pp. 16, 299. Cook twice cites cases where de Gaulle likens his actions to Joan of Arc and quotes Roosevelt's derisive remark that "sometimes he thinks he's Joan of Arc." *Ibid.*, pp. 16 (Roosevelt), 257, and 294. Also, see Brown, "The decision to elect the president by popular vote," p. 173.

16 Cook, *De Gaulle*, pp. 374, 376.

17 *Ibid.*, p. 18.

18 *Ibid.*, pp. 376–7.

19 Abraham Lincoln, "The prerogative theory of the presidency," in Harry A. Bailey, Jr. (ed.), *Classics of the American Presidency*, Moore, 1980, p. 34.

20 Quoted in Berger, "Lame ducks and national champions," p. 292. I have used this translation rather than the English translation of Charles de Gaulle, *Memoirs of Hope*, Simon and Schuster, 1971, p. 160.

21 William E. Leuchtenburg, *Franklin D. Roosevelt and the New Deal*, Harper Torchbooks, 1963, pp. 26–7.

22 Paul Theroux, *The Kingdom by the Sea: A Journey around Great Britain*, Washington Square Press, 1984, p. 376. See also Theroux's description of his visit to a holiday camp where large numbers of the men were unemployed but able to pay for a week or two on their dole. *Ibid.*, pp. 159–65. I am well aware that the Theroux description of Sunderland could fit some American towns too. In Washington State, for example, a depression in the timber industry has left some small logging or mill towns in a status much like Sunderland.

23 Sir John Hoskyns, "An agenda for change," Institute of Directors, 1985, p. 8, emphasis in the original.

24 Bernard Porter, *Britain, Europe and the World 1850–1982*, Allen & Unwin, 1983, pp. 140, 144. Overall Porter appears to hold a sweeping fatalistic view of Britain's decline in economic and geopolitical status and power.

25 Quoted in Michael Brock, *The Great Reform Act*, Hutchinson University Library, 1973, p. 331.

INDEX

Italy, 30, 31, 34–5

Jack, Ian, 34
Japan, 30, 33
Johnson, Lyndon, 101, 107, 112, 191
  administration, 81–2, 128
  see also Office of Economic
    Opportunity
Johnson, Samuel, 111

Keynes, J. M., 77, 109

Labour, 10, 24, 31, 35, 37, 65–6, 201
  see also Attlee
Laski, Harold, 96
Layfield Report, 66
leadership, 133–4, 136
  approaches, 106–8
  competence and confidence, 108–14
  dominance, 106–8
  political, 20, 146, 168, 190, 197,
    200–2
  see also Attlee, Eisenhower, Thatcher
Lincoln, Abraham, 192
Liverpool, 33–4
Lloyd George, David, 55, 100
Lobby, 17, 56
local government, 65–6, 137, 183–5, 194
London County Council, 111
London School of Economics and
  Political Science, 36, 75

management, 6, 11–12, 58, 89, 136
  defined, 115–17
  delegating responsibility, 118–19
  functions, 59
  "Thatcher Revolution," 119–26
  see also modernization
mandarins, 1–2, 8, 12–3, 16, 25, 42, 51,
  53, 61–4, 80, 116, 122, 125, 168–
  71, 173–81, 202
  abolish permanent secretaries, 142,
    171
  "analytic cripples," 13, 76–8
  "Britain's Ruling Class," 62
  minister/mandarin monopoly, 53, 56
  thinker-doers, 122–3
Members of Parliament, 16, 44, 47–8,
  61, 169, 172, 202
Middleton, Peter, 122–3
minimal legislatures, 41–2, 148
ministers, 2, 7–8, 16–17, 25, 42, 46, 50,

59–61, 64, 116, 125, 153, 163, 168,
  170–1, 177, 202
  junior, 16, 42, 50, 60, 64, 73, 153,
    168, 171, 174
  as managers, 172–3
  ministers/mandarin monopoly, 56
ministries, 16–17, 142
  controlling the civil service, 175–8
  department management strategy,
    183–5
  managing the civil service, 175–83
  responsibility for managing, 172–5
  special advisers, 168, 172–4
Ministry of Defense, 56–7
Mitterand, Francois, 54
modern welfare state, 1, 8, 22, 24, 37,
  40, 58, 66
modernization, 3, 7–8, 12–13, 15, 22,
  25, 51, 65, 144–5, 148, 152, 156–7,
  186, 189, 198, 201
  see also British central government
Monnerville, Gaston, 188
Morrison, Herbert, 91, 108, 110–13

Nairne, Patrick, 56
National Academy of Public
  Administration, 169–70
National Audit Office, 41, 43, 45, 47,
  147, 154–5
nationalized industries, 31–2, 34, 194,
  196
New Deal, 2, 186
Newcastle, 36
Nixon, Richard, 51, 99, 157
North Sea oil, 11, 17, 34, 55, 105
Number 10 Downing Street, 41, 73, 75–
  7, 96, 126, 158–60, 195

Office of Economic Opportunity
  analytic office, 67, 81, 161, 164
  war on Poverty, 86, 128
Official Secrets Act of 1911, 55–7
openness, 8, 166–7
  see also secrecy
Organization of Petroleum Exporting
  Countries, 3, 22–3
organizational mastery, 21, 26, 136–7,
  191, 198
organization-man, 21, 90–8, 136, 156,
  169, 191, 201
outsiders, 16, 65, 85, 128, 153, 168,
  173–4, 178